CW01183308

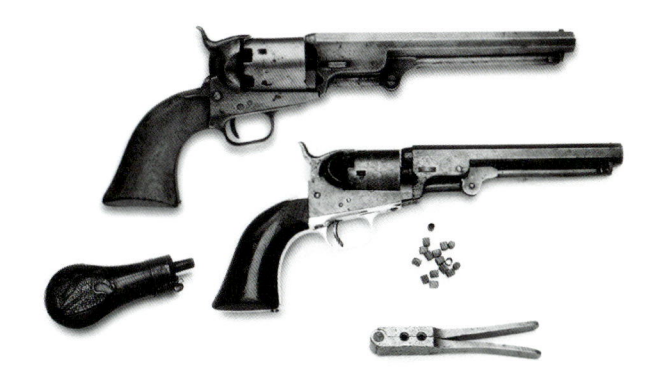

BAIL UP!

MUR
Of Police, ne
£20
REW
For Capture of offe
others, increased
offe

THE FOUR OFFEND

By Ord

BAIL UP!

A Pictorial History of
Australia's Most Notorious Bushrangers

— GEOFF HOCKING —

BAIL UP!

The Five Mile Press Pty Ltd
22 Summit Road Noble Park
Victoria 3174 Australia
Phone: +61 3 9790 5000
Fax: +61 3 9790 6888
Email: publishing@fivemile.com.au
First published 2002

Text © Geoff Hocking
All rights reserved
Designed by Geoff Hocking
Edited by Sarah Russell

Printed in Hong Kong

NATIONAL LIBRARY OF AUSTRALIA
CATALOGING-IN-PUBLICATION DATA

Hocking, Geoff.

Bail up! a pictorial history of Australia's
most notorious bushrangers.

Includes index.
ISBN 1 86503 913 6

1. Bushrangers - Australia - Anecdotes.
2. Bushrangers - Australia - Pictorial works. I. Title.

364.15520994

LEFT:
Theatre Poster – Robbery Under Arms: A Romantic Play, Depicting the Wild and Heroic Days of the Colonies ...
Theatre Royal, Hobart Tasmania, 1896
(J.W.B. Murphy Collection, State Library of Tasmania)

OPPOSITE:
Capture of Bushrangers
Engraving by Samuel Calvert, published *Illustrated Australian News for Home Readers,* 2 January 1871
(La Trobe Picture Collection, State Library of Victoria)

FRONT COVER, FROM LEFT:
Morgan the Bushranger (see page 97)
Ned Kelly, the Bushranger
(La Trobe Picture Collection, State Library of Victoria)
Portrait of a Man in the Dock (Martin Cash)
(see page 53)
Ben Hall (see page 102)

BACKGROUND:
Hold-up of the Gold Escort (A Bush Hold-up)
(see page 79)

TITLE PAGE:
The Way Her Majesty's Mails & The Public Protectors Are Served in New South Wales
Hand-coloured lithograph from *Sketches of Australian Life and Scenery,* after a drawing by S.T. Gill, c. 1860
(Rex Nan Kivell Collection NK2820. National Library of Australia)

Contents

Bound for Botany Bay - 7
Let the Crime Fit the Punishment - 12
Brutality of the Beaten - 15
The Chinese Option - 20
Exclusives versus Emancipists - 21

The Bolters - 23
Trouble at 'Home' - 24
An Unfair Game! - 28
Bolters and Brigands - 29
Gypsey and Musquito - 30
'Given Every Equality' - 38
A Taste for Human Flesh! - 39
The 'Monster' Jeffery - 41
The Brady Gang - 42

**Port Arthur and Norfolk Island –
The Last of the Convict Outlaws** - 46
The Brave But Unfortunate Irishman,
    Martin Cash - 48
'Bold' Jack Donohoe
    Last of the Convict Outlaws - 57
'The Wild Colonial Boy' - 58
The 'Billy-Can' Mutiny on Norfolk Island - 60
An End to Transportation - 62
Port Arthur Shuts Down - 63

Robbery Under Arms! - 64
The Second Generation – Scourge of the Settlers - 64
Prisoner of the 'Crown' - 65
Dark Road to the Diggings - 66
The Robbery of the Brig Nelson - 70
Daylight Robbery on St Kilda Road - 72
'Captain Melville' - 75
Robbery on the Roads - 78
The McIvor Escort - 79
The Ballarat Bank Robbery - 82
'Horse-Trading' in the High Country –
    Gentleman 'Bogong Jack' - 86

Flash Coves & Currency! - 90
John Piesley, the First Truly 'Australian'
    Bushranger - 91
The Boldest Gang of All - 92
'Mad Dan' Morgan - 97
Brave Ben Hall - 102
A Party at Canowindra - 105
The Attack on Bathurst - 106
Sticking-up the Mails - 108
The Felon's Act - 110
The Death of Hall - 111

Johnnie Gilbert - 113
John Dunn - 116
Fred Lowry: 'Tell 'em I died game' - 118
The Brothers Clarke - 120
Andrew Scott, or Was It 'Captain Moonlite'? - 123
Captain Thunderbolt - 127
The Legendary Starlight - 131

The War Against the Kellys - 133
The Kelly Gang, a Family Saga - 134
The Attack on Fitzpatrick - 136
The Unfortunate Deaths of Constables Lonigan,
    Scanlan and Kennedy - 137
Illegal Withdrawals - 141
10 December 1878, Euroa - 143
11 February 1879, Jerilderie - 143
The Murder of Sherritt - 145
The Final Showdown - 145
The Seige - 147
A Strange Apparition - 152
Taking Ned Kelly - 156
11 November 1880 - 157
The Jerilderie Letter - 162
Harry Power, the Man Who Taught Ned Kelly - 176

The Last of Their Kind - 180
Governors Hack Their Way
    into the History Books - 180

Convicts of the First Fleet - 183

Notes - 188
Bibliography - 188
Acknowledgements - 189
Index - 189

BAIL UP!

ABOVE:
Portsmouth Harbour with Prison Hulks
Oil on canvas by Louis Garneray, c.1814
Prison hulks line up across the bay at Portsmouth, England.
Due to overflowing prisons on land, the British Government appropriated
a huge flotilla of obsolete warships for a floating penal settlement.
The rotting hulks did not improve the beauty of the harbour, and the stench
that emanated from the poor wretches housed within for years on end
caused the authorties to seek a better place for its refuse.
Australia seemed just the right place, indeed.
(Rex Nan Kivell Collection, NK815. National Library of Australia)

BOUND FOR BOTANY BAY

When the First Fleet of eleven ships led by Captain Arthur Phillip R.N. sailed into Botany Bay on 20 January 1788, with a total of 717 convicts, 191 marines and nineteen officers on board, they were ready to land just the 'wrong' sort of people to build a new society on the east coast of Australia.

The convicts, of whom 180 were women, were sentenced for terms of transportation from five years to life. Although forty prisoners had perished on the nine-month journey from Portsmouth, the First Fleet arrived with two more on board than had departed, some forty-two babies having been born into captivity on the journey.

The average length of sentence was seven years, but few were ever to return home to old England. The British Government had done its best to clean out the hulks of old warships left rotting by its ports; the ships had been used as floating prisons for some years as the mainland prisons were overflowing. English society had created an underclass of desperate and disenfranchised common folk whose fall into criminality was often the result of industrialisation, the disappearance of common lands and the subsequent decline of pastoral occupations.

Most were transported for seemingly minor crimes, but those transported were often habitual offenders. There was often so little opportunity in the crowded cities and towns for those without trade or training, brawn or birthright that descent into petty crime was endemic. Sentences of five years or more were handed down for 'stealing a handkerchief', 'a loaf of bread' or 'a bolt of cloth'.

Young women fallen on hard times into prostitution were packed up, thrown below deck and cast off for the unknowable 'Great South Land', with little hope of redemption in those fetid, crowded floating cells.

The convicts came from all the big cities and towns — London, Manchester, Gloucester, Bristol, Durham, Exeter, Shrewsbury, Reading. Only a few had any experience in matters rural — just the wrong mix of characters needed to build the new Australian nation.

But, of course, that was not the original intention. The British were keen to lay claim to the island continent ahead of the French and the Dutch, who had long cast their eyes on the coast of *Terra Australis*. The British had little idea what lay within, and they knew little, if anything at all,

---

ABOVE:
The Pioneer
Hand-coloured mezzotint by Henry Macbeth-Raeburn, pub. 1836
Captain Arthur Phillip R.N. successfully guided the First Fleet of eleven ships, carrying almost 1000 convicts, troops and officers on a nine-month journey from Portsmouth to arrive at Botany Bay on 20 January 1788.
(National Library of Australia Collection)

BAIL UP!

Transportation celebrated in song, 'Botany Bay', traditional, 1790

This song from 1790, written two years after the First Fleet transported almost 1000 to the colony of New South Wales, describes the characters who were the genesis of the Australian nation.

Of course, not all were whores, pimps and bastards; there were hundreds who had just stood on the wrong of the law, or were convicted of political crimes, such as the Scottish martyr, lawyer Thomas Muir, who was transported into exile, arriving in Sydney in 1794. His crime was to be found handing out copies of Tom Paine's *Rights of Man*. He was charged with sedition and sentenced to fourteen years simply for believing in democracy.

There were also hundreds of patriotic 'sons of Erin' who were transported for their part in the uprising of 1798. Before the end of transportation in 1840, more than 50 000 Irish 'rebels' were exiled to Australia. Their hatred of the British came with them. Their mistrust of British authority, the vehement independence of their Catholic faith and the strong sense of connection to their own mythology never left them.

In many ways the 'independence' of the Irish led inexorably to the showdown at Glenrowan a century later when one of their own defiantly strode, clanking, into folklore.

Let us drink a good health to our schemers above,
Who at length have contriv'd from this land to remove
Thieves, robbers and villians, they'll send 'em away,
To become a new people at Botany Bay.

Some men say they have talents and trades to get bread,
Yet they sponge on mankind to be clothed and fed,
They'll spend all they get, and turn night to day —
Now I'd have all such sots sent to Botany Bay.

There's gay powder'd coxcombs and proud dressy fops,
Who with very small fortunes set up in great shops,
They'll run into debt with design ne'er to pay,
They should all be transported to Botany Bay…

There's nightwalking strumpets who swarm in each street,
Proclaiming their calling to each man they meet:
They become such a pest that without more delay,
Those corrupters of youth should be sent to the Bay.

There's monopolisers who add to their store,
By cruel oppression and squeezing the poor,
There's butchers and farmers get rich in that way,
But I'd have all such rogues sent to Botany Bay…

You lecherous whore-masters who practise vile arts,
To ruin young virgins and break parents' hearts,
Or from the fond husband and the wife led astray —
Let such debauched stallions be sent to the Bay.

There's whores, pimps and bastards, a large costly crew,
Maintained by the sweat of a labouring few,
They should have no commission, place, pension or pay,
Such locusts should all go to Botany Bay.

The hulks and the jails had some thousands in store,
But out of the jails are ten thousand times more,
Who live by fraud, cheating, vile tricks and foul play,
And should all be sent over to Botany Bay.

Now should any take umbrage at what I have writ,
Or find here a bonnet or cap that will fit,
To such I have this one word to say:
They are welcome to wear it in Botany Bay.

TRADITIONAL, 1790

adieu adieu my Native land.

of its indigenous peoples. Furthermore, they cared so little for any others' claims to the territory that they named Australia *terra nullius*, the 'land belonging to no one', and proceeded to abandon their unwanted on its 'empty' shores.

Arthur Phillip was not impressed by Botany Bay, so he took a long-boat and explored a much larger bay to the north, its entrance to the west. Phillip sailed into Port Jackson (Sydney Harbour) and into what he described as 'the finest harbour in the world, in which a thousand ships of the line may ride in the most perfect security'.

On his return to Botany Bay, Phillip discovered two French ships lying out to sea, unable to enter due to unfavourable winds. The following day he rushed back to 'his' harbour in his ship, the *Supply*. The British, through their emissary Captain Arthur Phillip R. N., were the first to raise a national flag, the 'Queen Anne' flag, at Sydney Cove on 26 January 1788. The British were also the first to build their prisons on the shores of this, the prettiest bay in the world.

At once, the prisoners were set to work building the means of their own imprisonment. They

---

ABOVE:
Adieu, Adieu my Native Land
Hand-coloured lithograph, pub. date unknown.
This lithograph by an unknown artist depicts a party in chains, five forlorn convicts being ferried out to the ship waiting to transport them to Botany Bay.
(Allport Library and Museum of Fine Arts, State Library of Tasmania)

BAIL UP!

Bound for Botany Bay

This is the best known of all the convict laments. However, it was not a song written at the time of transportation but much later, in the 1850s, by the 'bard of the goldfields', Charles Thatcher.

Farewell to old England for ever,
Farewell to my rum culls as well;
Farewell to the well-known Old Bailee,
Where I used to cut such a swell.

Singing too-ral li-ooral li-ad-dity
Singing too-ral li-ooral li-ay;
Singing too-ral li-ooral li-ad-dity
And we're bound for Botany Bay.

There's the captain as is our commander,
There's the bo'sun and all the ship's crew,
There's the first and second-class passengers,
Knows what we poor convicts go through.

'Taint leavin' old England we cares about,
'Taint cos we mispels what we knows,
But becos all we light-fingered gentry
Hops around with a log on our toes.

For seven long years I'll be staying there,
For seven long years and a day,
For meeting a cove in an area
And taking his ticker away.

Oh, had I the wings of a turtle-dove!
I'd soar on my pinions so high,
Slap bang to the arms of my Polly love,
And in her sweet presence I'd die.

Now, all my young Dookies and Duchesses,
Take warning from what I've to say,
Mind all is your own as you touchesses,
Or you'll find us in Botany Bay.

Charles Thatcher, c. 1851

attempted to create gardens and to clear and sow but so few had any experience of agriculture that for the first years almost all efforts failed. The First Fleet, almost starved by the failure of its own endeavours, waited anxiously for supply ships from the mother country to replenish its seriously depleted stores.

Not all of those transported were hardened criminals; there were many who were transported for political reasons. There were agitators, machine-breakers, political activists and union-organisers, plus honest men who were simply trying to find a better way up through the oppressive class-ridden system that underwrote Imperial Britain in the eighteenth and nineteenth centuries. Others were poachers and petty thieves whose crimes were born out of desperation and

ABOVE:
Portrait of a Convict (Unknown)
Watercolour by Peter Gordon Fraser, c.1810
The convicts were nicknamed 'canaries'. The origin of the nickname is obvious. The first thing the runaway would steal was clothing to ensure that identification was difficult while taking 'a vacation in the bush'.
(Allport Library and Museum of Fine Arts Collection. State Library of Tasmania)

poverty rather than criminal intent. However, many were turned hard by the terms of their imprisonment, the ritualised beatings and the pain of their banishment.

The bush surrounding the settlements was unexplored, and few settlers ventured far at all. There were rumours that the native blacks had killed and eaten some of the white settlers, and confrontation between black and white was common. This, however, did not deter the brutalised convict who was desperate to cast off his chains.

The work was arduous, the gaolers brutal, the environment harsh and unforgiving and the native blacks were not friendly to the invading white man. Cast out so far away from home, where the rule of the military was the law, the lash and the noose ever-present, is it any wonder that there were many who bolted for the bush?

There were few who knew where they were at all. They heard stories from the guards of the Dutch and English settlements in Hong Kong, Singapore and Batavia, and gave no thought to how they would get there. They simply took to the bush, believing they could survive on native foods and animals until they walked their way back to civilisation. There is no way of knowing how many perished in this vain attempt, but it is known that there were some who met an unfortunate end, cannibalised by their starving companions. Some joined up with indigenous tribes and stayed with them for a time, while most took to 'bushranging', stealing from free settlers and farmers, remaining at large until they were eventually captured or killed.

When a man at large grew weary of his isolation, grew tired of the hunger and the constant fear of capture, or worse, he could give himself up to the nearest police station, receive a mandatory fifty lashes and be back in the system to serve the rest of his time. Any further attempt at escape would earn him twelve months on a chain gang.

While the prize of freedom seemed so easily obtained, the price of capture was harsh indeed.

ABOVE:
Convicts Breaking Stones, NSW
Watercolour by Augustus Earle, c. 1826
This view from the summit of Mount York, looking towards Bathurst Plains, shows a group of convicts breaking stones for road paving. Few of those put to work had any real experience of labouring or any real expertise for the task to which they were applied. Their sweat was all that mattered; the overseer cared little if they were worked to death as a consequence.

It was to escape such hardship that many 'bolters' took their liberty in the hope that they could make their way back 'home'. Few knew how far they had come, and for most it was either death in the bush or the noose that finally set them free.
(Rex Nan Kivell Collection NK12/23. National Library of Australia)

BAIL UP!

Let the Crime Fit the Punishment

The conditions in the colonies' prisons for most unfortunate enough to be incarcerated within were a veritable hell on earth.

Tasmanian Governor George Arthur believed that the terms of a convict's imprisonment and punishment should be as fearsome and odious as possible. Although no convict ever escaped from his last penal settlement (Norfolk Island), a large number did gain their freedom from Macquarie Harbour, Maria Island and from work gangs. Eventually, Port Arthur replaced both Macquarie Harbour and Maria Island as the last confinement of the worst convicts, and the worst of these were placed in his 'Model Prison' in the solitary and 'dumb' cells.

The prisoners were forbidden to have any contact with one another. Their faces were covered at exercise, and even when at church they were separated from one another by wooden panels. The individual pews had no seating and directly faced the pulpit, which stood in the centre of the chapel. A prisoner could not even use the hour spent at worship to have a cosy nap, no matter how tiresome the preacher may become.

Arguments raged back and forth between emancipists in Britain and settlers in the colonies. There were those who sought reform of the transportation system and those who sought change in the way prisoners were classified. On the one hand were the common thieves, pickpockets, prostitutes and politicals, and on the other were the 'gentlemen' convicts, the swindlers and the forgers, the debtors and deceivers who, because of their education and social status back home, were in great demand in the colonies as clerks by both private businessmen and government offices alike.

There were also those who felt that such educated convicts should not endure the same severe punishments dealt out to the ordinary classes. They were, after all, too valuable to the management and operations of business in the growing colonies.

There were others who were afeared that, if such educated convicts were allowed to develop their 'extraordinary resources', it would be impossible in turn to preserve the colonies for the Crown.

In England, Bathurst expressed his opinion that:
if such convicts were turned loose on the community…to become merchants, tradesmen, clerks, editor…and small farmers, thus occupying… situations in Society, where, instead of being influential examples of morality and good character to the labouring classes…they find themselves actually belonging to the aristocracy of the country…filling minor municipal positions, and out of a feeling of revenge towards the Mother Country, exciting trouble by every sort of factious and republican resistance to authority. [1]

ABOVE:
'Gentleman Convict' James Hardy Vaux, 'The Convict Poet'
Vaux, thrice married, thrice convicted and thrice transported, had the pleasure of seeing his own play *Van Diemen's Land* performed in London in 1830 with the entire British cabinet in the audience.

Vaux was sentenced to death in 1808 but escaped the noose on a technicality. A spell in the condemned cell with a prisoner about to hang affected him greatly but didn't deter him from his criminal activities. He gained a ticket-of-leave in Sydney in 1831.

SOLITARY CONFINEMENT.

THE EXERCISE YARD.

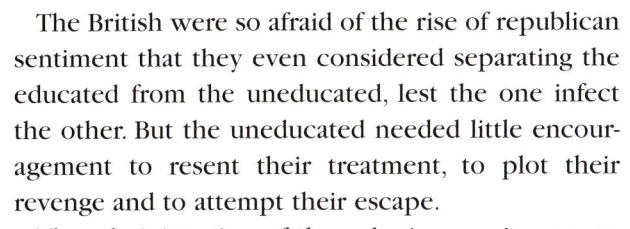

The British were so afraid of the rise of republican sentiment that they even considered separating the educated from the uneducated, lest the one infect the other. But the uneducated needed little encouragement to resent their treatment, to plot their revenge and to attempt their escape.

The administration of the colonies was in a mess. New settlers complained of the poor quality of convict servants assigned to their keep. There were complaints that the best and most skilful of the prisoners were always assigned to those who enjoyed the governor's favour.

Although there were plenty of free settlers who were constantly at loggerheads with the colonial governers, most did attempt, if rather begrudgingly, to comply with the conditions of assignment — to make their servant's term 'one of laborious employment, tempered with every consideration of humanity, and with every corrective principle of reformation'. This was despite the fact that very few of those

ABOVE:
Solitary Confinement and *The Exercise Yard*
Wood engravings from the *Australasian Sketcher*,
published 4 October 1873
(Private Collection)

Escape to China

A dishevelled band of disappointed absconders straggled, under guard, back into the settlement at Rose Hill, Sydney, on 10 November 1791.

It was only a week before that twenty-one male convicts and one pregnant female convict escaped into the bush with their clothes, tools, bedding and a week's provisions. They were setting out for China, which they believed was no more than one hundred miles to the north and separated only by a river.

They ran into some convict settlers who reported their whereabouts to the troops. They set off immediately to effect their capture. After a gruelling and fruitless march through the bush, the troops eventually returned empty-handed.

Before long the remnants of the group straggled back into Rose Hill, forced to return by hunger and fear of the Aborigines who had already speared four of their number. Three others had perished in the bush. They complained that overwork and harsh treatment had compelled them to escape on their failed 'China expedition'.

BAIL UP!

Major Johnston with Quarter Master Laycock One Serjeant and Twenty five Privates of ye New S Wales Corps defeats Two Hundred Sixty six Armed Rebels 5th March 1804.

The Castle Hill Riot

A desperate attempt at mass escape from the prison farm settlement at Castle Hill was foiled after the insurgents were routed by troopers who, with bayonets fixed, prepared to charge.

The troubles started as far back as 1796 when the then governor, John Hunter, complained of the large number of Irish convicts in the colony. The population of United Irish (transported for Seditious Practices in Ireland) had risen to more than 600 with the arrival, in 1801, of 135 'desperate and diabolical characters from Cork'. Hunter complained that the 'turbulent and worthless characters called Irish defenders' were threatening to resist all orders given them by their English tormentors.

Up until this point there were many absconders who had simply ran away. Many had became outlaws, causing a public nuisance but not seriously threatening the security of the colony at large.

The attempt on Sunday, 4 March 1804 was the first instance when the convicts planned an organised attack upon authority. They planned to seize power at Castle Hill, march on to the Hawksbury and enlist the convicts there, and with a combined strength of 1100 men march onto Parramatta and establish a 'Liberty Pole' outside Government House. Then they planned to march into Sydney, seize ships in the harbour and make their escape.

Such an undertaking as this involved the commitment of hundreds of men, and in the prison environment the jailors were not without their spies. When, on Saturday, 3 March, Governor Phillip Gidley King learned that the Irish were to rise the following day he strengthened the guard on Castle Hill.

The convicts waited until the end of the day. With the watchword 'St Peter' calling them from their bunks around 8 p.m. 200 convicts silently assembled. A bell was rung, and they surged throughout the camp searching for arms. A house was set on fire, and the chief flogger Robert Duggan was dragged from under his bed and given a brutal taste of his own medicine.

It was midnight before the news of the break-out reached Sydney. Troops under the command of Lieutenant-Colonel William Paterson and 150 armed men from HMS *Calcutta* were called out. Major George Johnston, second-in-command of the NSW Corps, took another fifty-six men to Parramatta, where at dawn they faced 400 rebels massed at Rouse Hill.

After several unsuccessful attempts at negotiation, including the entreaty of a Catholic priest, James Dixon, who had been transported in 1800 as a political offender, Johnston and a trooper strode forward to meet with the rebel leader, stonemason and former soldier Phillip Cunningham.

Cunningham and another, William Johnson, took the challenge, and with swords drawn they both stepped forward to meet Major Johnston. Johnston asked of Cunningham what it was that he desired, and Cunningham demanded: 'Death or liberty'.

Johnston replied by placing his pistol to Cunningham's head and ordering him to surrender. Johnston then called on his men to open fire on the rebels, and a short but one-sided battle ensued. The rebels turned and ran when the troopers advanced with bayonets fixed.

Cunningham was brought in and hanged without trial the following day.

The events at Castle Hill had repercussions that rang throughout the settlement. Governor King believed that there were many who were sympathetic to the revolutionary and anti-English cause.

Celebrated Irish freedom fighter, 'General' Joseph Holt, now a gentleman transportee, was taken from his farm and dispatched to Norfolk Island. King's view was that 'some artful, designing wretches, above the common class of people, are deeply implicated [in the rebellion]'.

It was not only the Irish who met the Governor's displeasure. A French vigneron working in the settlement was also banished from the colony. King wrote that 'among several who are suspected of contriving the tumult is the Frenchman. His conduct has compelled me to send him out of the colony'.

In the affray fifteen convicts had been shot dead, nine were later hanged and many more flogged.

The punishment for daring to rise against the English was ever-diligence. It was such incidents as the 'riot at Castle Hill' that entered the folklore and remained for the next fifty years as both salutary lessons, and seditious incitement, for the ever 'rebellious' Irish.

sent down to the colonies' prisons had any skills worth their keep.

A proficient pick-pocket was useless behind the plough, and most of those transported had little inclination to labour anyway:

It was complained…that the quality, no less than the quantity, of the convicts assigned as agricultural labourers was poor and inappropriate – doddering octegenarians; weak, half-imbecile boys; Cockney barbers; professional thieves whose hardest labour, hitherto, had been lifting purses and breaking locks – men who could not, or would not, work, and took every opportunity to destroy the tools and other property of masters who tried to make them do so. [2]

Brutality of the Beaten

For those fortunate enough to have been assigned to settlers or officers who treated them well there was little need to rebel, just to work without resistance or resentment and to bide their time.

In 1801, in an attempt to encourage decent behaviour, the Governor of New South Wales, Phillip Gidley King, extended the pass system for well-behaved convicts and began the issue of 'tickets-of-leave'. Convicts who held such tickets were exempted from government labour, taken off government stores and able to work for themselves — within prescribed districts.

While the system could be seen as one way of demonstrating the governor's faith in the reformed convict, it also lessened demand on government resources.

There were scores of convicts granted ticket-of-leave who soon made their way in the colony. There were also scores of convict lasses who married, both within and outside the convict class, and whose offspring were to be the first 'truly' free Australians.

Those who continued to harbour resentment of their captors, whose political beliefs refused to allow them to acquiesce with their English overlords, who

OPPOSITE:
Convict Uprising at Castle Hill, 1804
Watercolour, artist unknown
The caption reads: *Major Johnston with Quarter Master Laycock One Sergeant and Twenty five Privates of New S Wales Corps defeats Two Hundred and Sixty six Armed Rebels 5 March 1804.*
(Rex Nan Kivell Collection NK10162, National Library of Australia)

BAIL UP!

A GOVERNMENT JAIL GANG.
Sydney N.S.Wales.

Rebel Convicts Flogged

Convicts implicated in the Irish plot were brutally flogged at Parramatta. One man, Paddy Galvin, received 300 lashes. The first one hundred were across his back. The beating was so severe that his backbone was clearly visible between his shoulder blades. The second one hundred were across his buttocks which were then 'in such a jelly that the doctor ordered [the final 100] to be flogged on the calves'. 'Gentleman' farmer Joseph Holt witnessed some of the beatings and wrote in 1838:

> The way they floged them was theire arms pulled Round a large tree and their breasts squezed against the tree so the men had no power to cringe or stir.
>
> There was two flogers, Richard Rice and John Jonson, the Hangman from Sidney. Rice was a left handed man and Johnson was Right handed so they stood at each side and I never saw two trashers in a barn moove there stroakes more handeyer than those two man killers did ... tho' I was two perches from them, the flesh and skin blew in my face as they shooke off the cats.

Holt was banished to Norfolk Island after the riot.

refused to work or looked constantly to escape, their treatment remained harsh, often brutal in the extreme.

A number of the Castle Hill rebels were sent to the disbanded Newcastle Penal Settlement. Once seen as too far from Sydney for proper supervision, the settlement was re-opened as a place of secondary punishment. The prisoners were to work in the coal mines, which had given the settlement the original name of Coal River. It was not long before escapes from Newcastle were reported.

In 1805 a group, including three women, bolted from the prison, heading for Sydney. Before long they were attacked by Aborigines who stripped them of their clothing and all the food they had stored away for the journey. It is believed that some of them were able to stay with the tribes for a little while, in recognition for kindness shown to a native at Newcastle,

ABOVE:
A Government Jail Gang, Sydney, N.S. Wales
Lithograph by J. Cross (London). Printed by C. Hullmandel, 10 August 1830, from a drawing by Augustus Earle.
(National Library of Australia Collection)

but in the end only two dishevelled and very hungry men ever made it back to Sydney. It is believed that the women had perished.

The prisoners working on the road gangs suffered most of all:

> Many a time I have been yoked like a bullock with twenty or thirty others to drag along timber. About eight hundred died in six-months at a place called Toongabbie, or Constitution-Hill.
>
> I knew a man so weak, he was thrown into the grave, when he said, "Don't cover me up. I'm not dead; for God's sake don;'t cover me up!" The overseer answered, "Damn your eyes, you'll die tonight, and we shall have the trouble to come back again! . . .
>
> They used to have a large hole for the dead; once a day men were sent down to collect the corpses of the prisoners, and throw them in without any ceremony or service. The native dogs used to come down at night and fight and howl in packs, gnawing at the poor dead bodies.

This letter from Joseph Smith,* an old settler who was transported aged fourteen, continues with tales of beatings, men flogged more than 800 times and men hanged on the spot for stealing a few biscuits. He described the intolerable tasks that killed men too weak to survive:

> We used to be taken in large parties to raise a tree [carry it]; when the body of the tree was raised, Old Jones would call some of the men away – then more; the men were bent double – they could not bear it – they fell – the tree on one or two, killed on the spot.

Smith was granted his freedom after his seven years were over, and by the time of his writing, some

---

ABOVE:
Hard labour and flogging
Governor Arthur believed in strict control; punishment was meant to deter the miscreant from offending a second time: 'The English "Sunday Herald" called on the "People of England" ... to note that ... in the 19th century, under the administration of Colonel Arthur, ... Greenwood [a bolter from a chain gang], for slightly wounding an officer and absconding, got 1000 lashes!'

*Joseph Smith's letter was in the possession of Caroline Chisholm, the philanthropist of the goldfields who did much to ameloriate the suffering of colonial girls during the 1850s. Chisholm had the letter re-printed in Samuel Sidney's *The Three Colonies of Australia* in London in 1852.

BAIL UP!

fifty-six years later, the events seemed as powerful and terrible in his memory as the time of his witness.

It is not surprising that these stories did not disappear; the tales of torture and of horror, the beatings and floggings remained to charge the 'rebel sons' who came just over half-a-century later with the nefarious duty of retribution. From Castle Hill to the uprising at the Eureka diggings and the marauding and murderous Kellys, the fearsome patriotism of the Irish National was not to be denied.

However, sedition was not the sole property of the Irish or the imprisoned. In 1808, John Macarthur, one of the founding fathers of the colony of New South Wales, was charged by Governor William Bligh with sedition after they had engaged in a public wrangle over the ownership of a vessel that had left Australia carrying an absconder. Bligh demanded that Macarthur forfeit a bond of £800 for his complicity in the affair, and Macarthur refused, declaring that he had already abandoned ownership of the vessel, the schooner *Parramatta*. Following a heated session in the Sydney Criminal Court, in which the Governor was isolated in his attempt to control Macarthur, Bligh issued an escape warrant against him.

The following day Bligh was arrested by none other than Major George Johnston, the hero of the Castle Hill riot. The fact that Johnston had survived a court martial attempt a few years earlier when he

ABOVE:
Convict Stockade at Cox's River Crossing near Hartley (N.S.W.)
Watercolour, artist unknown, c.1831
This watercolour and pencil drawing is dated from the time of occupation of the stockade on the Great Western Road, which had been established to house convicts who were constructing the road across the Blue Mountains to Bathurst.
(State Library of New South Wales)

Below:
Flogging prisoners, Tasmania
Pencil drawing by James Reid Scott, c. 1850
(Petherick Collection, National Library of Australia)

was charged with supplying one of his sergeants with liquor as part of his pay may well have left him with no love for the colonial administrators — and Bligh was not the most respected of all the governors who passed through Sydney.

Following the arrest of Governor Bligh on the night of 26 January 1808, which was the twentieth anniversary of the landing of the First Fleet, the streets of Sydney were filled with drunken revellers:

> Liquor was liberally, and indeed profusely, served to the soldiers; bonfires blazed in all parts of the town; and those scenes of riot, tumult, and insubordination that are ever incident to the subversion of legitimate government and authority ensued.

Johnston was eventually sent back to England were he faced trial by court martial on 9 October 1809. In 1813 he returned to Australia, stripped of his commission, and took up the colonial life of the grazier. The NSW Corps, notorious for grog trading and money lending, were recalled to England.

It appears that there was more than one level of the law for the subjects of the British Crown. The well connected could continue into a prosperous future, having lost a little face, while the poor lost everything — liberty, opportunity and, more often than not, their lives.

Of course, Australia was marked for glory, for its people had been chosen by the finest judges in England.

BAIL UP!

Sydney, from Woolloomooloo Hill
Coloured engraving by John Carmichael, 1829
This engraving shows convicts at hard labour breaking stones.
One has already adopted the classic Australian working pose of
leaning against his shovel.
(Mitchell Library Collection. State Library of New South Wales)

The Chinese Option

Although escape to China was believed possible by most convicts, few ever made it far from the settlements at all. It is believed that there were more than fifty bleached skeletons within a day's walk from Botany Bay. The runaways died in the bush of starvation, or simply wandered lost until death or misadventure overtook them, while scores wandered back into the settlements 'so squalid and lean [that] the very crows would have declined their carcasses'.[3]

But the conditions under which they were forced to live meant that many still made their attempt at escape. In 1803, fifteen Irish convicts made a dash to 'China' from their incarceration at Castle Hill. They were at large for only four days before they were captured. In that time they had 'committed every possible enormity except murder'. One had blown away half of a constable's face with his musket, but was excused the murder charge as the constable lived. They were all sentenced to death, but Governor King relented and hanged only two.

King then fixed the sentence for bolting at 500 lashes, plus double chains for the remainder of the sentence.

At another time, sixty convicts from the work gangs at Liverpool planned to head for the bush, intending to survive by attacking the farming stations at Cambden. The guards came upon their plan, but wishing to avoid a bloody confrontation with such a large body of desperate men thought it best to let them get away. They armed twelve of their most trusted convict servants and then prepared for their capture. On discovering that the troops were armed and ready to go after them, the convicts abandoned their bid for freedom.

'At Windsor, and in the adjoining districts, the offense termed bushranging, or absconding in the woods, and living on plunder and the robbing of orchards, are most prevalent,' wrote J.T. Bigge to the Commission of Enquiry into the state of the colony of New South Wales in 1822. Bigge also added that, as the colony had been so far restricted to a rather small area bounded by the sea in the east and the Blue Mountains in the west, there had been little opportunity for the convicts to escape. Although there had been those absconders from various work parties, he believed there was no systematic attempt by desperate convicts to defy the Government of New South Wales. Bigge added that this was in contrast to the activities of the desperados of Van Diemen's Land.

Exclusives versus Emancipists

As far back as 1825, there were disputes over the direction in which the new colonial society was developing. There were many who espoused the creation of a democratic society in which all citizens, whatever their background or method of arrival in the colony, were free and in possession of equal rights.

This attitude was in direct conflict with that of the British Government, which was ever fearful of democracy. The British had lost the American colonies to free-thinking democrats, and they had also seen the French revolutionists bring 'equality, liberty and fraternity' to the common 'citizine', while hundreds of the privileged classes were forced to embrace Madame Guillotine.

This attitude was also in direct conflict with that of the colonial governments. They favoured the 'exclusives' – English-born, educated, free men and women who believed their position, title or rank made them 'more' equal than all others. There was a direct conflict between 'currency'* and 'sterling'* as society liked to brand the classes. 'Currency' were native-born, the first true Australians, while 'sterling' were the sons and daughters of English privilege.

It is not realistic to say that all currency were the children of convicts and that all were destined for a life of hardship excluded from the wealth and glory of the new Australia. There were as many descendants of convicts who rose to prominence in the colonies as there were the children of the free settlers who had also staked their claim on colonial prosperity, just as there were many from both sides who remained outside the law or among the labouring classes.

William Wentworth, whose name is writ large in the history books, was the son of a convict lass, Catherine Crowley, transported for stealing cloth, who fell pregnant to surgeon D'Arcy Wentworth[+] on their voyage to Botany Bay. This convict stain stayed with Wentworth all his life, but he was also able to

---

* The term 'currency' comes from local slang. It applies to banknotes and coins that only had value in the colonies, in other words, worthless beyond Australia's shores. This was quite unlike the highly valued 'sterling', which was accepted everywhere.

[+] Born in Armagh, Northern Ireland in 1762, D'Arcy Wentworth also fell foul of the law in England but remained without conviction. He was acquitted of highway robbery, having been before the bench four times. At his last trial he passed the comment that he was going to Botany Bay anyway, whether freed or in chains; once acquitted he still felt pressed to leave. He had taken a position as surgeon's assistant on Norfolk Island. He died in 1827.

BAIL UP!

LEFT:
'Convictos en la Nueva Holanda' —
Convicts in New Holland
Wash drawing by Felipa Bauza, 1793
(Mitchell Library Collection, State Library of New South Wales)

use his past as a means of promoting his interests. There were certainly far more currency in the population than there were sterling, and Wentworth persisted in his desire to create a new nobility, derisively nicknamed the 'Bunyip Aristocracy', in which he believed Australia should become a free colony, like America with its own government, a prison no more but a land able to compete with America in its attraction of the English migrant.

Wentworth was an emancipist who called himself an 'Australasian' and was the first native-born Australian to publicly acknowledge his birthright as 'a native of New South Wales'.

The British Parliament had little interest in Wentworth's ideas; they still saw the colonies as a place where the privileged could prosper on the backs of an enslaved work force, but the times were changing for them.

The penal system and colonial administration must have seemed incomprehensible to the hapless convict. In a letter to her aunt in Blackburn, Lancashire, in 1792, convict lass Mary Haydock* wrote:

> They tell me I am here for life, which the Governor told me I was but for 7 years wich Grives me very much to think of it but I will watch every oppertunity to get away in too or 3 years. [4]

At the end of her sad letter she concludes:

> Mr Scot Took 2 Ginnues of me and said he would get me My Libberty with my sister has been very ungrat . . . To me so I must never see you again. [5]

The fact was that in years preceding the gold rushes of the middle of the nineteenth century the currency lads and lasses were under-represented among the criminal classes.

In the years between 1833 and 1838, of all the 827 men brought before the New South Wales Supreme Court, over half were convicts under sentence, twenty-nine per cent were Emancipists, six per cent free emigrants and only four per cent were Australian born. Of those native sons none had committed grand larceny or murder and never one convicted of rape, but over half were up for cattle or horse stealing, a crime that Australians thought of as seriously as poaching in old England. The term 'cattle-duffing' was used instead of stealing, and in their usual understated manner the Australians managed to isolate their actions from crimes they considered to be real.

The young sought to distance themselves from the activities that had brought their parents to the Australian island prison. They were, by and large, keen to make an honest and 'stain-free' life for themselves under the Southern Cross.

For the next 150 years almost all Australians washed away at the convict stain; it has been only since the bicentennial year of 1988 that many Australians have looked back, not with shame, but with pride and acceptance of their convict forebears. In a curious twist it is today often a mark of pride if grandfather or grandmother once wore the government brand.

---

*Mary Haydock, who was convicted at thirteen for horse-stealing, was assigned as nursemaid in the household of Major Francis Grose. Two years later she married settler Thomas Reiby. Obviously she had found her 'oppertunity' — wed and free within 'too years'.

Thomas died from the effects of sunstroke in 1811. He had been the first free settler to establish trade in New South Wales and left to Mary and their seven children an extensive business empire, involving commodities, shipping and sealing.

When Mary died on 30 May 1855 she had achieved both affluence and respectability, not bad for the convicted horse-thief from Lancashire.

THE BOLTERS

The system of bushranging, sheepstealing, and the most daring acts of burglary was increasing upon the defenceless settlers.

REPORT FROM VAN DIEMEN'S LAND, C.1820

Honest settlers who had been encouraged to seek a new start in the colonies set sail expecting to find a well-ordered society where the rule of law would keep their investments safe, an unending supply of unpaid servants could help their investments grow, and they could safely assume a position of wealth, power and privilege in the new world.

What many were to discover was an island prison, racked with political intrigue, mistrust and argument. Few of the early colonial governors were the smartest men available for the job; a commission to take charge of a prison settlement on the other side of the world where there was almost no society, no culture, no contact, nothing but impenetrable scrub, impassable mountain ranges, unrecognisable and

ABOVE:
'Convicts' Letter Writing at Cockatoo Island N.S.W. 'Canary Birds'.
Ink and watercolour sketch by Phillipe de Vigors, 1849
The nickname given to the convicts – 'Canary Birds' – is suggested by the colour of their prison garb. It would not have been difficult to spot these fellows in the street; no wonder they took for the bush.
(Mitchell Library Collection. State Library of New South Wales)

BAIL UP!

'Black' Caesar

John Caesar has the 'honour' of being recorded in history as the first Australian bushranger.

This giant West Indian negro, who had been a petty thief and pickpocket in England, arrived in chains with the First Fleet. It was not long before 'Black' Caesar sought his freedom; in 1790 he stole a musket and absconded into the bush where he was joined by six or seven others.

The former slave was soon recaptured. He was fortunate that Governor Arthur Phillip declined to execute him as Phillip felt some sympathy towards him. Caesar escaped once again, and again avoided hanging as the colony was grateful for his shooting of the fearsome Aborigine Pemulwuy who had been terrorising the colony.

Ceaser continued to abscond until, in 1796, Governor Hunter was forced to put a price of five gallons of rum on his head. While at large Caesar and his mates survived by hunting and fishing, but they were also helped out by sympathetic settlers and convicts, given food, and obviously powder and shot as the General Order from the Governor implies:

> The many robberies which have lately been committed render it necessary that some steps should be taken to put a stop to a practice so destructive of the happiness and comfort of the industrious.
>
> And it is well known that a fellow known as Black Caesar has absented himself some time past from his work, and has carried with him a musquet [sic], notice is hereby given that whosoever shall secure this man Black Caesar and bring him in with his arms shall receive as a reward five gallons of spirits.
>
> The Governor thinks it further necessary to inform those settlers or people employed in shooting, who may have been occasionally supplied with powder and shot, that if it shall be discovered hereafter that they have so abus'd the confidence placed in them as to supply those common plunderers with any part of their ammunition, steps will be taken immediately for their punishment, as they will be considered accomplices in the robberies committed by those whom they have so supplied.

Not long after this proclamation, Caesar lay dead, shot by a settler named Wimbow on the evening of 15 February 1796.

Ironically, he was killed at a place called Liberty Plains near Sydney.

inedible flora, hazardous coastline, hostile natives, blazing heat, mosquitoes and unrelenting soils, was not, for most, a step up the ladder of British society.

So many of the colonial governors fought long and hard battles with the settlers who saw little need to continue to acquiesce to the norms of aristocratic petulance in the governance of their affairs. So many openly disagreed with the governors, a 'crime' that could have had them transported if they were still at home, and so many were keen to take control of their own affairs that colonial society seemed a hotbed of sedition.

Men and women lauded today as the visionary founders of the great Australian nation were often in fear of the governor's displeasure as they fought to establish the free society enjoyed by today's Australian nation.

Not all were necessarily philanthropic; most were self-serving capitalists who saw opportunities to start anew in a country that was like a clean slate.

Among the free settlers were those who had no love for the British Crown — the Scots and the Irish had come to the colonies in large numbers, both free and bound in chains. They sought every opportunity to make their way without interference from the representatives of the Crown.

Trouble at 'Home'

In 1820, following a long period of economic stagnation, depression and rising prices, workers in Scotland rose up against their masters. Three of the leaders, convicted of treason, were hanged and beheaded before a stunned crowd. Scores of others were transported to the colonies.

In 1830 workers rampaged across southern England, smashing industrial machinery which they claimed was destroying their livelihood. Nineteen of these workers were hanged and 481 transported for daring to attempt to protect their way of life.

Of the most celebrated were the Tolpuddle Martyrs, who were sentenced in 1834 to seven years

RIGHT:
Hardware of imprisonment and punishment
(Queen Victoria Museum and Art Gallery Collection, Launceston)

— THE BOLTERS —

BAIL UP!

transportation for protesting against deplorable working conditions and attempting to establish a farm labourers union. They aimed to gain a wages rise of ten shillings a week but instead found themselves in court, charged under a little used statute for 'having administered unlawful oaths', convicted and transported for sedition. George Loveless, who, because of illness, did not immediately leave for the colonies with the others, explained in his written statement to the courts that: 'we were uniting to preserve ourselves, our wives and our children from utter degradation and starvation. We have injured no man's reputation, character, person or property'.

In fact there was such a public outcry and constant pressure put on Parliament over the treatment of these six honest and hard-working farm labourers that a pardon was granted to all on 10 March 1836.

Conditions in the colonies for the convict were far worse than even for the dispossessed labourers of Britain. One young fellow wrote home to his parents describing the events that followed the killing of an overseer by a group of convicts he had been working with:

We have to work from 14 to 18 hours a day, sometimes up to our knees in cold water, 'til we are ready to sink with fatigue.

[After four refused to work] the inhuman driver struck one, John Smith, with a heavy thong, which caused the gang to rise and dreadfully beat the drivers, by which one of them died the same day.

The soldiers were immediately sent for, and 47 of us immediately taken into custody.

Nine were sentenced to die, and 18 were sentenced to go to the mercury mines to work underground.

Above:
Skirmish between Bushrangers and Constables, Illawarra
Watercolour by Augustus Earle, c. 1820

(Rex Nan Kivell Collection NK12/49, National Library of Australia)

On Saturday, July 2, at 7 a.m., we were all paraded in front of the scaffold. The nine unfortunate men came on with a firm step, the chaplain taking leave of them. The executioner commenced tying them up to the beam, by which they hang 16 at a time.

He concludes his melancholy note by stating:

The nine men seemed to cry out with one voice, "We die happy".

It is no wonder that convicts who bolted for the bush were often helped by the settlers or farmers who were sympathetic to their plight. Among the farmers were many ex-convicts who had served their term and been granted a ticket-of-leave. They too had suffered the lash, or dispossession at the hands of the English. They too had been denied their own birthright, a place in their own country, transported into a future cast away from their families, away from their own culture and kind.

Many of these ex-convicts were better educated than their tormentors, and once freed were better off. There were even some troopers who committed minor crimes so that they too would be imprisoned, assigned to farms or an office in the towns and live better lives than they did under military command.

There were also those settlers who sought to use the criminal habits of their servants to achieve their own ends, and often this was to demonstrate their displeasure with the governor and the failure of the system to act fairly and without favour.

Escape from Botany Bay

On 29 March 1791 eight men, one women and two children escaped the settlement at Botany Bay by stealing the governor's personal six-oared cutter.

First fleeters, convicts William and Mary Bryant, led the escape, much to the annoyance of the governor. William was a Cornish fisherman transported for resisting arrest by excise officers (smuggling) and Mary for robbery. She gave birth to one of the children while on the voyage out aboard the *Charlotte*.

Investigations later showed that their escape had been many months in the planning. Bryant, who had been in charge of the colony's fishing fleet, had been secretly storing away food for some time. He had received one hundred lashes for selling some of his catch on the sly and it seems that this indignity tipped the balance. He became desperate to get away.

The escapees sailed silently through Sydney Heads that night, unseen by the lookout, and turned north, heading towards New Guinea. In what was recognised as a miracle of navigation they made their way up the coast, through the dangerous coral reefs to Cape York and headed west across the Arafura Sea.

The cutter reached the Dutch settlement of Koepang in Timor on 5 June, thus becoming the first vessel to navigate the east coast since Captain James Cook in 1770. The group on board passed themselves off as survivors of the wreck of a ship off the Australian coast, and were received by the Dutch governor who fed and clothed them and extended his hospitality until such time as they were able to join a ship heading through to England.

For some unknown reason William Bryant spilled the beans, telling the governor the whole story. They were all immediately put behind bars. Eventually, the group were taken on board a Dutch East Indiaman and taken to Batavia. It was here that the first tragedy struck poor Mary Bryant. Both William and his son Emmanuel perished, just before Christmas 1791.

The remaining escapees were then transported back to the Cape and then on to the man-o'-war the *Gorgon*, which was heading back to England with a marine detachment on board.

Watkin Tench of the Royal Marines, also on board the *Gorgon*, had also been on the First Fleet and remembered both Mary and William. He knew them to be a decent pair 'distinguished by their good behaviour'. He later recorded that on hearing Mary's story he had been saddened by her plight. But she was yet to suffer a further blow. On 7 May her young daughter Charlotte died and was buried at sea. When Mary arrived back in England she was again alone. Incarcerated once more in Newgate she had nothing to look forward to, except imprisonment, irons and another trip to Botany Bay.

The 'heroic' case of the convict seafarers became a *cause celebré*, with James Boswell leading the charge to have Mary freed. In May 1793 she was pardoned, and Boswell settled an annuity of £10 on her. She retired into obscurity in Cornwall, in the south of England.

BAIL UP!

An Unfair Game!

The case of Irish settler William Bryan and the 'Wild Cattle' was one that caused considerable public interest both in the colony and in Great Britain.

Bryan was a wealthy gentleman who, over a financial hiccup, had some difficulties with Governor George Arthur upon arrival in Van Diemen's Land. He did, however, succeed in gaining the maximum grant of 11 000 acres near Westerbury, on which he ran extensive herds. He also had interests in the Pennyroyal Creek flourmill, a 'steam vessel' project, mercantile investments and the sale of meat and hides.

Bryan saw little need to comply with assiduity to the laws of England, being so far away from its physical influence. He was eventually caught dealing, illicitly, in 'Wild Cattle'. His herdsman faced the magistrate and was sentenced to death for cattle-stealing. There were many who felt that 'the master and not the servant' should have been standing in the dock, but wealth and position still stood for something even in the colonies. He did, however, suffer the withdrawal of his twenty-two servants and was ostracised by local society.

But Bryan, who had himself been appointed a 'Gentleman' Magistrate, had also been accused of acting very strangely indeed for a man in his position. He was accused of engaging in improper transactions with convicts', 'harbouring an absconder' who he used as an agent to scour the country buying up cattle and allowing the 'bolter' to profit from his part in the venture. He had allowed his herdsman to build up his own small herd, of unknown origin, and bought the meat from them. He induced his servants to bring unbranded cattle onto his property. He put his own brand on any cattle that he impounded.

Not only was Bryan a 'cattle-duffer' himself, but he had broken the law by allowing his servants to buy and sell. He had introduced into the Stringey Bark Forest and the Penny Royal swamps a new class of settler comprised of convicts and absconders, including one who had been a notorious cattle thief from New South Wales.

The 'Gentleman' Magistrate had used his position to behave just like any other common criminal, only it was not he who was brought before the bench. His nephew Robert, whom he had instructed to get rid of any evidence that may tie a noose around their necks, was sentenced to death for cattle-stealing, a sentence later commuted to life.

The governor had very strict rules concerning the behaviour of assigned convicts, and Bryan seemed to have tested almost all of them. No doubt the absconders among them were pretty happy with their lot, but the governor didn't want convicts just taking their leave as they saw fit and pretending to make their way up in polite society. The law was after all still the law, and punishment must prevail.

Arthur believed that it was the duty of the master to apply himself to the task of 'unpaid overseer in

Convicts 'Bolt' for China

There were many among the convict population who held the firm belief that if they escaped from the settlement all they had to do was head west and they would eventually reach China. Obviously, there were few among them who even understood the most rudimentary geography; considering that it had been only a few years since Captain James Cook had mapped the coastline of Australia, that is not at all surprising.

In Sydney Cove on 31 January 1792 the 'muster' at the end of the day showed that forty-four men and nine women were unable to be accounted for. Their names are not recorded nor is the fate which befell them; most would have become lost in 'the perfect maze made by nature that was the foothills of the Blue Mountains', and some would have staggered back into the settlement, starving and exhausted by their sojourn in the bush.

Convicts also held the belief that somewhere 'out there' was a settlement where the inhabitants were civil and peaceful and no hard labour was demanded — that sounded like heaven, and few were destined for that place.

THE AUSTRALIAN BUSHMAN

carrying out the design of the State in the punishment of transportation'. He also believed that it was an opportunity for convicts to learn by their hard labour those skills that could contribute to the commonwealth of the colony and for the reformed convict to eventually earn his, or her, freedom.

This, of course, worked for the many who were not destroyed by his system. There were, however, plenty whose knotted backs bore the scars of their misdemeanours and they looked for any way out.

Bolters and Brigands

A large number of those who were declared to be bushrangers were convicts who had been 'at large' while in the service of their masters. In the very earliest days of the settlement in Van Diemen's Land, due to the failure of supply ships to arrive when expected, the settlement was faced with starvation.

ABOVE:
The Australian Bushman
Lithograph by George Hamilton, 'Australian bush life', c.1848–1856
The freewheeling spirit of adventure and Australian mateship was forged in the vastness of the Australian bush, where a man could be the master of his own destiny, whatever means had brought him to the colonies.
(Mitchell Library, State Library of New South Wales)

The 'Notorious' Whitehead

John Whitehead was a convict 'at large' when he was shot by a party of soldiers in October 1814.

He had arrived in Van Diemen's Land on the ship *Minerva* on 16 May 1801. He had been sentenced to a term of seven years transportation for stealing 'two pairs of breeches'.

Unlike the gentlemen of the bush who displayed great courtesy when robbing the coaches on the goldfields fifty years later, many of the Tasmanian bushrangers earned a justifiable reputation for unspeakable brutality.

Whitehead was no exception. Angered by the knowledge that the half-wit 'Looney' Hopkins had become police informant, Whitehead had a pair of mocassins made from bullock-hide into which were placed a quantity of large red ants (bull-ants). The 'boots' were fitted to Hopkins's feet. Hopkins died in agony.

It was in October 1814 when soldiers finally caught up with Whitehead. On that fateful day he begged his compatriot Michael Howe to cut off his head so that he could not be identified. It appears that Howe acceded to this request as the *Hobart Town Gazette* reported in 1817: 'a human head has been found near New Norfolk wrapped up in a handkerchief… we may therefore presume it is the remains of the misled culprit [Whitehead].'

BAIL UP!

In 1805, the authorities ordered the release of several prisoners, gave them arms and sent them into the bush to hunt kangaroos and other wild animals.

Even after the supply ships had arrived and the 'liberated' convicts ordered to return to their 'hard labours', the response was not all that encouraging. Many had learned how to survive in the bush and joined with others of their own kind, and some made a nuisance of themselves around Hobart Town.

It was in the *Hobart Town Gazette* dated 10 September 1810 that Lieutenant Governor Davey first referred to 'a gang of bushrangers'. He offered rewards and indulgences to convicts who could assist with the capture of any of the gang of brigands led by the convict John Whitehead.

Twice transported, Whitehead had been publicly flogged in 1800 during the period of his first incarceration. Considering the apparent ordinary nature of his first conviction — stealing two pairs of breeches — it stretches the imagination to conceive of the point at which the common thief becomes a notorious outlaw capable of the worst of all debasement.

Whitehead gathered to his side a huge band of some sixty to eighty men, and they terrorised local farmers and settlers until, on 14 May 1813, a proclamation called the 'bolters' to surrender. Those who ignored this demand were 'outlawed'. Beyond that point they had nothing to lose but their lives.

Gypsey and Musquito

Gypsey was a most unusual candidate for the role of bushranger. A free-born and unfettered Englishman he may well have been a high-spirited young lad. He had ventured to Van Diemen's Land of his own accord, although obviously at the insistence of his parents who must have been pleased to see the back of him for a while. It was not uncommon for well-to-do families to send their 'adventurous' offspring to the colonies for a bit of education at the university of hard knocks and harsh reality.

ABOVE:
Settlement, Port Arthur
Watercolour painting by John Skinner Prout, c. 1845
Governor George Arthur much preferred 'the savage, uninviting, natural qualities' of Tasman's Peninsula and King's Island to the beautiful scenery and mild climate of Norfolk.
  He thought that Port Arthur was best fitted to provide 'the very last degree of misery consistent with humanity'.
(National Library of Australia Collection)

— THE BOLTERS —

'Constant, active, unremitting employment of every Individual Convict in very hard labour'— even if it only consisted 'in opening cavities and filling them up again ... continued rigid, unrelaxing discipline', so that, 'the whole class of Convicts would absolutely dread the very idea of being sent there'. — GEORGE ARTHUR

BAIL UP!
AUSTRALASIAN SKETCHER

No. 75.—Vol. VI.   MELBOURNE, SATURDAY, DECEMBER 21, 1878.   WITH LARGE COLOURED SUPPLEMENT   PRICE 6d.

OUTLAWS IN CAMP.

Michael Howe, 'the Worst and Last'

On 19 October 1812, the *Indefatigable* was the first ship to set sail directly from England to Van Diemen's Land. On board was a young man who was to become known as 'the worst and last' of the bushrangers – Michael Howe. He had already served one term of imprisonment without apparent incident, but it seemed that he was not intent on doing his second term quite so easily.

Howe was a troublesome prisoner who escaped after repeated floggings and other punishments and joined Whitehead's gang *(see page 29)*. He took charge after Whitehead was killed. He had been a footpad in England, and this experience had obviously served him well as leader of the pack.

Howe organised a raid on a native encampment with the purpose of providing wives for himself and the rest of the gang. The natives, naturally, resisted, but Howe persisted, and many were shot. Because of this act he was later held responsible for many attacks of retribution against white settlers in Van Diemen's Land.

It seems, however, that some of the black women were happy to stick with the white men, and Howe's 'wife', Black Mary, is said to have assisted him on most of his escapades. Her knowledge of the bush enabled him to escape from many an attempt at his capture.

Howe was the self-styled 'Lieutenant-Governor of the Woods' who took the unusual step of communicating with the governor in an attempt to secure his freedom. In a letter 'From the Bush-rangers to the Hon. T. Davey. Lieutenant-Governor of Van Diemen's Land' he protested that he had never committed murder and had only used violence when it was necessary to avoid capture.

The letter was carried to the governor by an American, Richard Westlick, who returned with this message from Davey: '[he] did not wish to take the life of any man, but merely to preserve order. If Howe or any of his comrades would surrender, no charges should be made against them for their acts while 'in the bush'.

Howe later wrote to Sorell who had succeeded Davey, addressing Sorell: 'From the Governor of the Ranges to the Governor of the Town'. Howe offered to give himself up as an informer on all his old colleagues in exchange for a free pardon. Sorell dispatched Captain Nairne of the 46th Regiment to meet with Howe and bring him in safely to Hobart Town.

For a while Howe was able to move freely about Hobart where he was quite a celebrity until he became aware of the rumour abroad that the governor, on hearing of some of the crimes attributed to Howe, was about to deny him his pardon.

Howe immediately took off again for the bush. He was declared an outlaw and £100 was offered for his capture.

It was not long after that George Watts and William Drew, two ticket-of-leave men, came across Howe sleeping in the bush. They captured and tied him up. When the three were eight miles from Hobart Town, Howe slipped his bonds and stabbed Watts with a knife he had hidden. Then he seized Watts's gun, turned and killed Drew. Watts escaped through the bush to a nearby farmhouse and gave the alarm, but he died later from loss of blood.

Although Howe was now isolated from other bushrangers, he continued his reign of terror. He had many skirmishes with the troopers sent out to find him, but he always managed to get away, until in October 1818 a kangaroo hunter named Warburton led two soldiers, 'Big Bill' Pugh and Thomas Worrall, to Howe's camp, in dense bush, near the Shannon River. They jumped Howe, but he was too quick for them and fired a few shots, and then made a dash for the bush. He slipped down a steep bank, allowing Worrall to catch up to him. Howe stood still for a moment, then challenged Worrall: 'Black beard against grey beard for a million'. He fired, but missed again. Worrall took aim and hit his mark. Howe staggered and was just about to steady himself when Pugh ran forward and bashed his skull in with the butt of his rifle. Howe slumped to the ground, and Pugh, taking no chances, 'battered his brains out'.

Howe's body was buried where it had fallen, and the severed head of 'the worst and last' was carried into Hobart where it was exposed in a public place as a lesson to all. Unfortunately, as history has shown, he was neither the worst nor the last!

OPPOSITE:
Outlaws in Camp
Engraving from *The Australasian Sketcher*, 21 December 1878
Although drawn years after the end of the 'glory days' of bushranging, this engraving captures the constant fear and desperation that stayed with the outlawed. These men had nothing at all to lose; in fact, upon capture, many said that they were glad that 'at last, it was all over'. The next step was usually to the gallows.

BAIL UP!

Gypsey married soon after he had arrived in Van Diemen's Land, but after the death of his young wife *(see page 37)* he joined with a band of other adventurers and they roamed the highways and byways, getting up to mischief as they went. Before long the band were outlawed and Gypsey had become a bushranger.

Gypsey's band also ran with the black bandits known as Musquito, Black Jack and Black Tom. Together they formed a large and formidable force and terrorised the farmers in the hills around Hobart. After the attacks by Michael Howe and his gang on the native camps and the theft of their women by the whites the Aborigines took retribution on the white settlers at large.

Settler William Thornley recalled in his diaries the kind of attack by the bushrangers and the natives that struck fear into the hearts of the whites. Thorley and a rescue party were chasing the trail of Gypsey's gang who had taken their neighbour, Moss,* hostage when they came upon a hut burned by natives:

Amidst the ruins of a stock-keeper's hut, recently burned down, we beheld a form which we recognised as human from the outline of the body. One arm was totally consumed and the other was shrivelled up. The body was literally roasted and charred . . . we endeavoured to trace the features of the disfigured head. It was a shapeless mass of calcined bone. The clothes which might have served to identify it were, of course, utterly destroyed.

. . . [we] dispatched two horsemen to make circuits of the ruins, and one of these hailed us from a distance to join him. We proceeded towards the spot where he was standing and presently came on two

---

*Some time later Thornley was surprised when he met Gypsey on the road quite by chance. Gypsey begged a favour of Thornley, knowing that his time was nearly up. He asked him if he would look out for his daughter once he was gone.

Thornley asked the bushranger why he had captured Moss. He replied that he 'was obliged to save his life. Some of my men would have knocked him on the head, if I had not prevented them . . .'

ABOVE:
Capture of Bushrangers at Night by Gold Police
Watercolour by George Lacy, c. 1852
Not long before Matthew Brady was about to meet the hangman, he is quoted as saying: 'A bushranger's life is wretched and miserable. There is constant fear of capture and the least noise in the bush is startling. There is no peace day and night.'
(Rex Nan Kivell Collection, R4113. National Library of Australia)

dead bodies, evidently stock-keepers from their clothes and appearance. They were quite dead and cold. Their wounds at once informed us that they had been killed by the natives. On laying bare their clothes, we found their bodies pierced by innumerable small holes caused by the long thin spears used by the natives in their encounters. The heads were battered to a jelly-like mass, from the frequent blows of the waddies ...

Around this time a native of the Australian mainland by the name of Musquito, a tall and powerful man, had been committing many atrocities in Van Diemen's Land ... It was known that he was at the head of a mob of about thirty natives, but we had no idea that he was in this part of the island. However this looked like some of his work.[1]

Thornley and his group went after the murderers. He had an experienced gun-dog who, sensing an unusual presence, stiffened and, standing up, began pawing at his forelegs. The dog looked into the bush and Thornley went carefully to investigate. To his horror he spied a native standing stock-still within the trunk of a blackened and hollowed tree. The men began to be fearful that other natives were about and that soon they would have a shower of spears raining down upon them. But no movement was to be seen. Shouldering his fowling-piece, Thornley advanced upon the tree.

One of the group with Thornley asked if he should fire, but another said they should take him alive. No such luck as they had come across a native's grave. On inspecting the body, they discovered the mark of a musket-ball that had gone straight through the heart and passed out the back. While they were standing looking at the dead man, a long thin spear passed through the air, thudding into the bark of the tree.

One of the men who had been left aside as a sentinel came riding in with a spear sticking out of the left side of his back, and pieces of spear sticking out of the flanks of the horse.

This watercolour by goldfields artist George Lacy, although done at a later time when the hard men were active again preying on the innocent and the unwary, certainly expresses the sentiment conveyed by Brady. Even the yapping mongrel shown in this drawing was not enough to waken the desperadoes from their slumber, in time to escape.

Musquito

Musquito was a Port Jackson native who had spent many years working alongside 'civilised' society. He had been transported to Tasmania for the murder of a black gin (possibly his wife) in 1823.

He had been employed on a cattle station in New South Wales, and was therefore given the task of stock-keeper. He later worked as a black-tracker for the police and was used against the bushrangers, his expertise bringing many to justice and the hangman's knot.

After the capture of 'the worst and last' of the bushrangers Michael Howe, Musquito's services were no longer required. Musquito was dismissed without reward. This proud black who had risked his life so many times in the pursuit of the outlaws was no longer afforded police protection.

Musquito was despised by many of Hobart Town's police-hating population and suffered persection from fellow convicts for his efforts against their own class. He appealed to the police for protection, but this was denied, and in the end he absconded and became a bushranger.

Musquito's attacks on settlers were so well planned and executed that few believed a black man capable of such cunning. He had joined up with the Oyster Bay tribe who had also suffered at the hands of soldiers and sealers during the first years of the colony. With Musquito as their leader, they took retribution on the white 'invaders' and terrorised the population around Hobart for about two years until he was finally captured in August 1824.

Musquito was brought in by Tegg, another local Aborigine who had come across Musquito alone, unarmed and resting by a campfire. Tegg fired three shots, and although badly wounded Musquito fought back violently with sticks and stones. Finally, exhausted by his wounds, Musquito surrendered.

When the sentence of death was passed on him, Musquito replied: 'Hanging no bloody good for blackfellow.' He was asked, 'Why not as good for blackfellow as for whitefellow?', to which he replied, 'Oh, very good for whitefellow, he used to it.'

Musquito was hanged in Hobart in February 1825, alongside 'Black Jack' and 'Black Tom', two other members of the Oyster Bay tribe.

BAIL UP!

*This was Thornley's first description of 'the Gypsey'. Written some years after the event and in hindsight, his description may have somewhat glorified the bushranger.

It is known that 'Gypsey' was the son of a well-to-do English family, and it is therefore likely that his stature and confident, physical presence was quite unlike the common criminal with whom he was travelling. Most convicts transported were short, stocky, unused to physical labour, and therefore not well developed and not at all fine of feature.

Thornley, and his wife, had also taken some care of Georgianna, Gypsey's daughter. It is most likely that Thornley had made him appear as robust and noble as possible, for her sake.

Another young man sitting on his horse had his hat knocked off by a spear, and then a shower of spears rained down on them all, hitting a few but doing little damage. One of the party exclaimed:

> It's no use to stand here to serve as targets for these black rascals. Let us make a rush into the bush and come to close quarters. [2]

They realised that they would need to split up and move around the natives to drive them into the open to be able to engage with them. The natives' spears fell short of Thornley's party and they took some comfort knowing their fowling-pieces could cover a fair piece of ground.

The group was chasing after the blacks when just ahead of them thirty armed men stood up from beneath a bank and fired into them. One of Thornley's party dropped to his knees. It appeared that Musquito's mob was travelling with a bushranging gang and the rescue party were now hopelessly outnumbered. However, they decided to persist and chased the bushrangers for another day and night until they came upon them unexpectedly. A warning shot had ripped through their party, and rushing forward to take cover they scrambled up a green knoll and ran smack into the bushrangers, lined up waiting for them. A battle raged between them, and before long several bushrangers lay dead. Thornley's party had escaped serious injury, a magistrate travelling with Thornley had his hat blown off for the second time by a musket ball, and one man had his arm ripped open. The two men on horseback charged in to the blacks with their swords flailing before them. 'Every cut told on the naked bodies of the natives', who were as afraid of the horses as they seemed of the swordsmen. They rushed, terrified, into the bush.

> There was one man among the bushrangers whom we could not help noticing and admiring. He was one of the finest men I ever saw. Tall, broad-shouldered, and muscular, his whole form denoted a great strength, combined with great activity. He stood a little in advance of his party, as a cool as a cucumber and quite regardless of the shots that flew about him.* [3]

Having rid themselves of the blacks, the group turned their full attention to the bushrangers, and before long several of them had been shot and fallen. However, Thornley's party had suffered injurious losses too.

The next day, Thornley and his group set out again in their disastrous attempt to rescue their neighbour. Taking the magistrate's horse, Thornley followed his dog who again indicated to him that something was up. He stumbled upon a group of troopers who presented themselves lined up with their bayonets at the ready.

Owing to Thornley's rough appearance, after days at battle in the bush and riding the magistrate's horse, the sergeant mistook Thornley for a bushranger and immediately placed him under arrest. Poor old Thornley, embattled, burned, bitten,[+] beaten and bruised, was now bound.

Thornley's arrest, release and journey home is a long and amusing story. The troops marched back to where he had left his companions, thinking, as they did of Thornley, that they too were bandits, but on recognising the magistrate they realised their mistake. On hearing that the man they had arrested was the settler Thornley, the sergeant said:

> Thornley? I have a letter for that gentleman. Sorry to be the bearer of ill news, sir, but your house and farm have been burned down.

It was not long after this meeting that Thornley became separated from his companions and decided to set off for what was left of his home, but it was not long before he was, again, set upon by another mob of natives who, as well as spears, began throwing boomerangs at him. Thornley had never seen a boomerang before, but he was soon made to feel its power as one struck him on the leg, making it almost impossible for him to walk. He fought back valiantly, not knowing that it was Musquito and his band who had beset him this time.

[+]Thornley was almost burned alive when he clambered up and into the hollow of an old gumtree to try to get away from the hostile natives who had fallen upon him.

As he settled into the darkened trunk he was unpleasantly surprised to discover that he was standing on a possum. The animal clawed at his legs until half of his trowsers [sic] were torn to strips and his calves were bleeding from the long claws of the angry marsupial. Just as he was coming to terms with this attack, he smelled smoke. A female native carrying a fire-stick had lit a fire at the base of the tree in an attempt to smoke him out.

Thornley was facing a dilemma: either he could die of asphyxiation or jump and be speared to death. He did neither. He clambered out along a branch, and just when he thought his time had come he blacked out and fell to the ground. He came to, water splashing his face, surrounded by his companions who, seeing the smoke, had rushed to his rescue and frightened the natives away.

Thornley seemed to have a time of it. He travelled into Hobart to be a witness at the trial of the bushrangers, but had no heart for it after spending a few moments chatting amicably with a man, just before he found out his new acquaintance was about to be hanged. Heading home, he was close to New Norfolk when he came upon a group of troopers standing around a body lying still on the ground. He took one look at the cadaver and immediately recognised the dead man:

'Do you know who this man was?' I said to the corporal.

'No. Do you?'

'Yes. He was known as the "Gypsey". He was the leader of the bushrangers. What happened to him?'

'Oh, we came upon him while he was skinning a sheep and he fired on us, so we let him have it with all our barrels.'*

Thornley insisted that the papers found on the body of the Gypsey be left unopened and that they be delivered to the magistrate. The corporal found a bundle of one pound notes in Gypsey's kangaroo-hide jacket, which was hanging from a nearby tree. He offered to split the find with Thornley, who again insisted that they be taken with the papers to the magistrate.

Gypsey had made a friend of Musquito and the natives of the Oyster Bay tribe, and it was Musquito who vowed to avenge his death. As Musquito was captured in August 1854, he was unable to carry out this threat.

Musquito went to his death on the gallows alongside Black Jack and Black Tom the following year. Black Jack had been caught attempting to stow away on a ship. He was smoked out of the hold. The sailors told Thornley who just happened to be on the scene of this event as well that it was much easier to smoke someone out of a ship than it was to search it.

Thornley knew only too well the power of smoke, having expected to meet his maker earlier than he would have wished, when the natives had done the same thing to him only a few weeks before.

---

*In another account written for a London newspaper, Thornley recalled that Gypsey was killed while he was engaged in conversation with him. Gypsey had just said to him, 'the chances are that I must be taken at last, and that if I do not perish miserably in the bush I shall be betrayed, and shot or hanged'. With that they were surprised by a group of soldiers who forced Gypsey to the edge of a cliff, where he and one of his captors, engaged in bitter struggle, rolled over to their deaths.

Georgianna Shirley at Gypsey's Grave

Gypsey's real name was George Shirley. He was the son of a wealthy English family. His parents packed him up, gave him a couple of hundred pounds to see him on his way and sent him out to Van Diemen's Land. There he met and married a girl who, sadly, died giving birth to their only child, Georgianna.

Shirley was so distressed at the death of his young bride that he took off and joined a bushranging band. He must have been a rascal at home for his parents to pack him off to the other side of the world, and so it may be no surprise that Shirley took the adventurous path away from his grief.

Before he ran away, he did take the unusual step of placing his daughter in the care of a woman at a place called The Red House, in Molle Street, Hobart Town.

William Thornley was a corn agent from England who had also ventured to Van Diemen's Land. He wrote a memoir of his adventures which was published in England in the 1840s. In his recollections he described a meeting with the bushranger known as 'Gypsey', and his subsequent meeting with Gypsey's daughter, when he escorted Georgianna to visit her father's grave, not more than a mile from his own house.

One of Thornley's workmen, who was an accomplished stonemason, had carved a neat headstone on which were inscribed the words 'George Shirley, Father of Georgianna'. When they reached the grave, to their surprise, they discovered that they were not the first to visit Gypsey's last resting place. On the mound was set a rough-hewn stone bearing the crudely carved words: 'GYPSEY MY FRIEND'. It appeared that Musquito had honoured his ally before he, himself, was taken.

After his death it was found that Shirley had willed half the money found on him to be given to the woman who had cared for Georgianna, and half to a magistrate or his agent to manage her affairs until she was able to be sent to England to the care of his family. It was always Musquito who had brought the money on Gypsey's behalf to the Red House for her keep.

After they had placed the stone on Gypsey's grave, Thornley's wife placed her arm around seven-year-old Georgianna Shirley and said comfortingly: 'Your father was a good man. The white people did not understand him, but the natives did and they loved him as a friend'.

BAIL UP!

'Given Every Equality'

While there was a toughening in the attitude towards those who had simply taken their own leave of their labours, there were conscious efforts to assimilate those who had served their time and were making a fresh start at life in the colonies. In June 1813 Governor Lachlan Macquarie appealed for more liberal attitudes to the emancipation of former convicts. He spoke out against the resistance of some citizens who refused to recognise the rights of convicts to be 'given every equality'.

It was not the first time that Macquarie had spoken in favour of the convicts. He had an altercation with Reverend Samuel Marsden only a few months earlier when Marsden had refused to take an appointment by the governor to a board on which two of the others members were ex-convicts. On the other hand, Macquarie warned that there were too many convicts applying for indulgences. His seemingly accommodating public position had encouraged hundreds of 'time-wasting' petitions for royal clemency.

It made sense to represent the cause of ex-convicts in their quest for full equality. There were too many of them abroad now in both the city and the bush who had little love of the system and were not averse to assisting the bushrangers as they took pot-shots at the government. Bringing these 'new settlers' into the fold of 'respectable' society may have done much to isolate the bandits, but the ways of British rule do have a habit of falling foul of its own prejudices. Too many honest citizens had also fallen foul of the troopers' indiscretion.

Martial law was declared in Hobart Town on 25 April 1815 in an attempt to drive the bandits from the hills around the town: 'Any person now caught committing acts of murder, robbery, rape or other capital offenses will be the subject of a speedy court-martial and summary execution'.

Other earlier attempts to bring the bushrangers' activities to an end had met with failure. Two amnesties encouraged only a few to surrender, and a reward of £50 for informants was not at all encouraging to terrorised settlers. News of the treatment dished out to 'Looney' Hopkins by Whitehead and Howe would have travelled fast, and it can be seen why most preferred to mind their own business. Meanwhile, the gangs continued to roam at will.

Michael Howe's headless body might still lie in its shallow grave by the Shannon, but 'the worst and last' were yet to come. There were several convicts whose escapades chilled the blood of all decent folk and terrified the convict alike.

ABOVE:
South-west View of Macquarie Harbour
Pen and ink and watercolour drawing by Thomas Lempriere, c. 1827
How could so much misery emanate from such a pretty harbour? It was from here that Pearce and his doomed mates absconded in September 1822. Only two came back, Pearce and Brown. As Brown died soon after, only Pearce survived, but not to tell his gruesome tale.
(Petherick Collection. National Library of Australia)

A Taste for Human Flesh!

Lieutenant-Governor George Arthur wrote in a despatch to the Colonial Secretary in 1822 that since the destruction of Howe and his gang bushranging had been 'totally suppressed in Van Diemen's land during the past three years'.

However, on 20 September 1822, eight men, whose names would bring terror to all who learned of their deeds, made their escape from the recently established settlement at Macquarie Harbour. One of the only survivors of this party was Alexander Pearce who was to become one of the most notorious of all the Tasmanian 'bolters'.

The eight went to a nearby mine where they liberated fellow-convict Bob Greenhill who was known to be a good navigator. Stealing a boat, they doused all the signal fires on the shore and smashed the miners' chests with an axe, taking all their provisions.

Once, about a quarter of a mile offshore, they saw the fires flare up again. Fearing that a boat would be sent after them, they headed back in, landing just a little further up the coast. Knowing that it would be useless to proceed in open water, they smashed up the small craft. The party took to the hills right opposite the settlement. They feared that they would be spotted from the opposite shore, so they lay low until evening when they climbed to the top of a hill, lit a small fire and camped.

The eight men marched on all of the following day. One of the party, James Brown, was unable to keep up and was almost left behind. Although he was the only one left alive at the time of the capture of Pearce, he died later in hospital.

The party marched on for the next eight days until they were weakened by hunger and exposure. Bill Cornelius made the unfortunately prescient remark that 'I'm so hungry I could eat a piece of man'. Bob Greenhill replied that he had seen it done before and that it tasted just like pork. John Mathers objected. Although they were hungry, he said it was still murder and that they may not be able to eat it anyway. Greenhill replied that he would be the first to eat, but they should all be in it as they would all be equal in the crime in the end.

RIGHT:
Alexander Pearce, 'the cannibal'
Pearce was hanged before a huge crowd at Hobart Town on 5 August 1824. After he was taken from the gallows, his body was dismembered in accordance with the terms of his sentence. Such was the horrific nature of his crimes that in retribution his sentence, itself, was horrible.

(Mitchell Library Collection, State Library of New South Wales)

BAIL UP!

The group decided that Alexander Dalton should be the first one to be sacrificed: he had offered to be a flogger and for that he deserved to die.

They built their camp for the night, and at around three in the morning Greenhill belted Dalton over the head with an axe, killing him instantly. They dragged him away from the campfire, Mathew Travers cut his throat and bled him and with Greenhill's assistance the pair dismembered Dalton's body. They cut out his heart and liver, put them into the frying pan and ate 'heartily' even before the organs were fully warmed. No other man felt able to feast that night, but come morning they all took their share of the fresh meat.

The group headed off again into the bush with Cornelius and Brown going ahead to blaze the trail. Cornelius was never seen again.

After four more days, crossing swollen rivers and battling the seemingly endless tangled scrub, the group lay weak and hungry on a hillside overlooking the Gordon River. They decided on their next meal. Poor Thomas Bodenham who, up to this point, knew nothing of his companion's culinary activities was the next to go. Greenhill cracked his head open with the axe and Travers cut his throat. The remaining band dined on heart and liver that night.

Greenhill took Bodenham's shoes and wore them; there was, after all, no need to waste good footwear.

After camping for a day during which they dried the meat cut from Bodenham's corpse, the group moved on again. After two days they camped again and boiled a piece of meat for their meal, but it made Mathers so sick that he began to vomit. Greenhill strode up and banged him on the forehead with the axe. The blow did not kill him, and Mathers, who was stronger than Greenhill, fought back, taking the axe from him, throwing it to Pearce and exhorting Pearce to have a go at Greenhill and not to let him be murdered.

Mathers took to the bush but was caught by Greenhill and Travers who pulled him to the ground.

The pair allowed Mathers half an hour to make his peace with 'the Lord', and when his time was up, Mathers simply handed the prayer-book to Pearce and Greenhill finished him.

The next to die was Mathew Travers, who was unfortunately stung by an insect, which caused his foot to swell. A couple of days later his foot went black and he was unable to go any further. He lay down, deciding that he would prefer to die in peace, free at last, under the open sky. Pearce and Greenhill marched on. But Greenhill couldn't leave him alone; he turned back, and at around two in the afternoon found Travers asleep. Greenhill lifted his axe and struck the dreadful blow. According to his pattern he cut his throat, bled him and carved up the meat.

The men dined on Travers, but then Pearce became concerned that Greenhill, who always kept the axe beneath him when he slept, may be preparing to have him for the next meal. Pearce watched him carefully for the next two days until, just before dawn, Greenhill dozed off to sleep and Pearce pounced. He stole the axe from beneath Greenhill, took one mighty blow and sent him into the afterlife. Pearce took 'a thigh and one arm and travelled on for four more days until the last was eaten'.

In a fit of self-disgust, Pearce then decided to hang himself with his belt, but he decided against this idea. He continued on until he came upon a native's campfire around which there were pieces of kangaroo and opossum. He ate as much as he could and carried the rest away. He walked until he was in sight of Table Mountain where he stumbled upon a flock of sheep. Ever hungry, he caught a lamb, and as he was in the middle of this repast he was surprised by the returning shepherd who threatened to report him to his master. Naturally enough, Pearce threatened to shoot the shepherd.

Eventually, Pearce joined up with two other escapees, Davis and Cheetham, and together they had a jolly time, marauding the farms of the district and stealing their sheep until they were captured. Nobody knew what had transpired in the Tasmanian wilderness, and Pearce, who denied that he had taken any part in the raids by the Davis and Cheetham gang and was only responsible for the care of the 'selected sheep', was only charged with sheep-stealing and sent back to Macquarie Harbour as a bolter.

Pearce escaped again from Macquarie. This time he enticed a young Thomas Cox to bolt with him, but he had no intention of a long journey. He was hungry again for human flesh. His campfire could be seen on the other side of the harbour, and after only a few days of freedom Pearce was captured by Lieutenant Cuthbertson who had responded to what he thought was a signal fire of someone in distress.

When Cuthbertson landed, he found Pearce dressed in Cox's clothing, having killed him and already feasted on his remains. He showed Cuthbertson where the body of Cox lay – only the bones and innards remained, all the flesh having already been consumed by Pearce.

Pearce was taken to Hobart for trial. His revelations were sensational. He admitted to the horrified courtroom that he had developed such a craving for human flesh that he had persuaded Cox to escape with him for the sole purpose of cannibalism. He offered the court his opinion that 'man's flesh was delicious; far better than fish or pork'.

Pearce was hanged in Hobart Town, before a huge crowd, on 5 August 1824.

The 'Monster' Jeffery

Thomas, or Mark, Jeffery, Jeffries or Jefferies arrived in Tasmania, from Sydney, aboard the brig *Harvies* on 22 April 1822. While most suggest that Mark Jeffery was the monster baby-killer others suggest that his name was Thomas. Jeffery's record (shipping indenture) does, however, announce his arrival in Van Diemen's Land in the following way:

> Indents of one Male Convict (arrived) from Sydney New South Wales per Brig Harvies, Jameson Master, at Port Dalrymple 22nd, April 1822 –

Thomas Jeffery – Ship came in from England – Prince Regent – Tried, July 29th 1819, Where, Nottingham – Sentence, Life – Trade or Calling, Painter.

Up until this point Jeffery had been a useful prisoner, a flogger and executioner, who was rewarded for his efforts with employment as a watch-house guard. On the scaffold four years later he confessed that his weakness for drink was the cause of all his misdeeds, and it wasn't long before the grog caused him to abuse his position of trust. First, he had been caught drunk and next caught taking a female prisoner out of the watch-house. Although he was only fined for each offence he didn't stop there. He was flogged, fifty lashes for absconding, and then sent to Macquarie Harbour for twelve months for threatening a constable with a knife. From there it all seemed to go downhill for Jeffery.

In 1825, in company with two other convicts, Hopkins and Russell, Jeffery escaped from Macquarie. He had stolen some food, a gun and some ammunition from the soldiers, and for the next few days the and the others scrambled through the bush.

ABOVE:
Thomas, or Mark, Jeffery, Jeffries or Jefferies – the 'monster'
Pencil drawing by Thomas Bock, c. 1825
The child-killer and brutal murderer Jeffery was hanged at Hobart Town on the same scaffold as the much-loved Mathew Brady, who went to his death protesting that he had to share his last breath with the one man he despised the most.
(State Library of New South Wales Collection)

BAIL UP!

When their food ran out and they were unable to find any game, they entered into a pact, tossing up to see who would be sacrificed to save the others. Russell lost and Jeffery summarily dispatched him. The two lived on Russell's flesh for the next five days until they came upon an isolated sheep station. They threw what remained of Russell away, killed a couple of sheep and settled down to clean and cook them. Discovered by the shepherd, they advised him not to interfere as they only wanted to have 'a good feed'.

From this time on Jeffery was committed to the outlaw life, and had no desire to return to captivity. He seemed also to have little regard for his fellow man at all. When he held up the homestead of a Mr Tibbs, he demanded that Tibbs, his wife and their stockman go into the bush with him. The stockman refused and was immediately shot dead.

Tibbs and his wife were forced to march out across an open paddock, and then into the bush. Mrs Tibbs, who was clutching her five-month-old baby to her breast, complained that she could not keep up the pace. Jeffery snatched the child from her, dashed its brains out against a tree and asked if she could go faster now. Tibbs turned and rushed at him but he too was shot and the bushranger walked on, leaving Mrs Tibbs alone with her dead.

In another of his callous escapades Jeffery stuck up and robbed a fellow at Georgetown who was forced to carry his knapsack for him. After they had walked along the road for a while, without warning or reason, Jeffery shot him in the back and killed him.

It was the bounty hunter John Batman, later the founder of the city of Melbourne, who tracked Jeffery down and brought him to justice. Batman had been engaged by the authorities to track and capture bushrangers and was also responsible for the capture of Mathew Brady with whom Jeffery had ridden until he was kicked out of the gang for molesting women. He was the man that Brady despised most – a baby killer and callous murderer – everything that Brady professed not to be. It took a struggle with his gang to prevent Brady from attempting an attack on the Launceston lockup, freeing the prisoners and hauling Jeffery from his condemned cell and flogging him to death.

When Jeffery was being delivered from Launceston to Hobart prison the public throng almost pulled him from the cart and would have lynched him on the spot if they had succeeded. He was convicted and sentenced to be hanged on 4 May 1826. He stood on the scaffold in 'good company'… the bushrangers Bryant, Perry and Thompson, and Mathew Brady.

Brady protested bitterly at having to be hanged alongside 'the Monster' Jeffery, but his protest fell on deaf ears, and the trapdoor swung open.

The Brady Gang

> Having mounted the scaffold with trembling step, and at the conclusion of the final prayer, which closed with the word *death*, – the executioner withdrew the bolt – the platform fell, and the miserable men dropped to eternity.
> – THE HOBART TOWN GAZETTE 6 May 1826

So ended the career of Mathew Brady and his band of outlaws, which had begun twenty-two months earlier when another group of convicts broke away from Macquarie Harbour in a stolen longboat and headed for the Derwent with Mathew Brady as their leader.

Brady had been born in Manchester, England in 1799, the son of Irish parents. A good-looking young man, he was able to read and write and was a good horseman. He had forged his master's signature to pay off a debt, and for that he was sentenced to seven years transportation. He arrived in Botany Bay aboard the *Julianna* on 11 April 1820. Not a model prisoner, Brady was accused of insubordination and was transferred to Van Diemen's Land in the middle of the busiest time for bushranging.

Obviously, Brady did not take at all well to prison life, where he seemed to be in constant trouble – twenty-five lashes for neglect of duty, punished for

It has caused Matthew Brady much concern that such a person known as George Arthur is at Large.
Twenty gallons of rum will be given to any person that can deliver his person to me. — MATTHEW BRADY

plotting to escape from the colony, twenty-five lashes for not going to the barracks with his gang at the regular hour, fifty lashes for going on board the ship *Castle Forbes* with the intent to escape, fifty lashes for remaining absent for three days. In all, by the time he did get away, he had received a total of 350 lashes for his repeated attempts at escape.

The repetitive beatings may well have urged Brady to make one more desperate bid for freedom. Brady and fourteen others absconded from Macquarie Harbour, landing near Hobart Town on 9 June 1824.

The gang began to raid settlers' homesteads and farmhouses and soon gathered more 'plundering sons' to their side. Among the gang were Patrick Bryant, John Burns, James Crawford, Patrick Connolly, John Downes, John Griffiths, George Lacy, James McCabe, Charles Rider, Jeremiah Ryan, John Thompson and Isaac Walker.

The pattern of murder and robbery was only distinguished from crimes committed by other gangs by the courtesy with which Brady treated womenfolk. He ruled his gang with an iron fist and almost military rigour: while they were allowed to steal anything they needed and were permitted to kill

ABOVE:
James McCabe, Mathew Brady and Patrick Bryant
Pencil drawing by Thomas Bock, c. 1825
Brady had gained such notoriety that when was hanged on 6 May 1826 alongside, to his disgust, the 'monster' Jeffery, women in the crowd wept at his passing. Although he had terrorised the farms around Hobart for twenty-two months, he had never harmed a woman or shot at an unarmed person.
(Mitchell Library Collection, State Library of New South Wales)

Brady's Sour Joke

Even though Brady had strict rules about the behaviour of his men, he did do some stupid things himself.

He enjoyed forcing the servants of the homesteads that he raided to take a few glasses of the master's liquor, which meant that they would then be too drunk to recall who he was or which way he and his gang went.

While this may have been a hilarious and useful ruse, on one instance Brady picked the wrong unfortunate man.

On one occasion he instructed the assigned servant of the farmhouse he was robbing to join his band. The man refused. Brady walked to the sideboard in the house, took a glass, filled it with rum, then offered it to the defiant servant asking if he would drink. The servant replied that he didn't touch strong liquor. Brady put his gun to the man's head and exclaimed: 'Well, you will this time'. The terrified man took the glass and emptied it down his throat. Brady was consumed with laughter as the man staggered away.

The next morning the servant was found in the bush lying some distance from the house – still drunk. His employer rushed to try to arouse him. He opened his eyes and cried out for a drink of water, then rolled over and died.

When Brady learned of the servant's death, he felt real sorrow for his victim, as he had only wanted to play a joke on the man but had killed him instead!

BAIL UP!

Above:
Convicts Plundering Settlers' Homesteads
Engraving from *The Picturesque Atlas of Australasia*, ed. by Andrew Garran M.A., LL.D., pub. Sydney and Melbourne, 1888
(Private Collection)

traitors, they were instructed to treat women with courtesy and honour and never to injure a defenceless person. When one of his men attacked a woman he was thrashed by Brady, had his weapons taken and was kicked out of the gang.

Governor Arthur, so angered by the deeds committed by the gang, the public sympathy Brady was enjoying and the apparent pleasure some folk in the colony took as he continued to make a mockery of Arthur's efforts at his re-capture, issued a proclamation on 27 August 1824 that offered £25 for the head of any member of the Brady gang. By this time, the gang was believed to number more than one hundred. In addition, a conditional pardon was offered for the man who caught the leader himself. Cheekily, Brady replied with a notice pinned to the door of the Royal Oak Inn in which he offered twenty gallons of rum to the person who was able to deliver George Arthur to him.

The Brady gang was brought undone by a convict spy who had been allowed to escape from a chain-gang, scampering into the bush with broken chains on his legs. This betrayer, Cowan, joined up with Brady and fought alongside his gang, looting houses and attacking farms. It was the devious Cowan who completely hoodwinked his bushranging friend. He betrayed Brady to Lieutenant Williams commanding the 40th Regiment who were scouring the bush in search of the bandits.

The 40th fell upon the camp, and in the mighty battle that ensued several of the gang were shot dead. Others lay wounded and were captured; also wounded Brady escaped into the bush with several others, but they were hounded to ground by John Batman and his black trackers.

Exhausted by his wounds Brady was almost unable to continue with his escape when Batman came upon him. Brady pointed his gun at Batman, and asked if his attacker was a military officer. Batman replied that he was not a soldier, but John Batman, and told Brady that if he shouldered the gun he would be shot. Batman then told Brady that he was finished and the bushranger agreed. He acknowledged that his time had come, and yielded to the bounty hunter. Brady then admitted to Batman that he would never have given himself up to a soldier.

Much to Brady's disgust he was forced to travel down to Hobart in the same cart as the 'monster'. Brady despised Jeffery so much that he even refused to sit on the same side of the cart.

Brady was tried in Hobart Town before a packed courthouse. He had become such a charismatic and popular 'folk hero' that, when the sentence of death was passed, several women in the court wept so loudly that the judge had to stop proceedings and wait until order was restored. While awaiting execution, his cell was filled with flowers, and baskets of fruit were sent by well-wishers, along with confectionery to sweeten his darkest hour.

And as that hour surely came it was remarked that 'he died more like a patient martyr than a felon murderer'. The remnants of the Brady gang, including Hopkins, Jeffery's partner in the most hideous crime of them all, dropped to eternity the following day.

However, the government could not expunge Brady's name from public memory – his exploits are commemorated by Brady's Lookout, a 1300-metre peak that allows a view of the Tamar River in both directions.

Cowan was pardoned for his part in the capture, receiving several hundred pounds and a ticket back to 'old Blighty' for his services.

John Batman

John Batman had been in Tasmania during the great roundup of Aborigines of 1824. His was one of the more successful of the Roving Capture-Parties, but Lieutenant Governor Arthur believed that even though he 'proceeded not with a sword but with an olive branch' he also had 'much slaughter to his discredit'.[4]

Batman was born in Parramatta, a true native of New South Wales. It was a time of great adventure and he decided to go to Van Diemen's Land and earn his keep bringing bandits to justice. At that time even free-born 'currency' lads were unable to travel out of the colony without express permission and the placement of a notice in the *Government Gazette*, so it came to pass that the following notice appeared as required: 'Mr John Batman, leaving this colony by an early oportunity, all claims to be presented November 17th, 1821'.

On arrival he was granted a parcel of land, but his natural abilities as a bushmen were soon evident to all. Tall and strong with dark, curly hair and a proud, yet jovial and gentlemanly demeanour, Batman soon became popular with all classes.

He became a bounty hunter for the governor, and his bush skills and excellent horsemanship led him to capture the most feared bushrangers of them all. His capture of the notorious Brady led the governor to offer to him anything he desired – within his official powers, of course.

Brady asked not for land nor for money, nor a position of power and influence but for a pardon. A pardon for 'a fair and youthful dame, an outcast and outlaw, who had escaped from [her] overseers'.[5] He had come upon the young lass in the woods. She was 'too interesting a bushranger to be readily delivered by him to the public authorities', and she had 'captured' his heart. Batman was granted his wish: his 'maid of the mountains' was pardoned and soon became his wife.

Batman later joined exploring parties across Bass Strait on behalf of the Port Phillip Association which wanted to expand their business interests in the unknown southern territories of New South Wales. He sailed from Launceston on 12 May 1835 with seven Sydney blacks whom he took to translate the negotiations for land he hoped to conclude with the chiefs of the Port Phillip tribes.

On his return to Launceston Batman was able to announce that he had secured 600 000 acres around Port Phillip Bay for the total cost of forty pairs of blankets, forty-two tomahawks, 130 knives, sixty-two pairs of scissors, thirty mirrors, 250 handkerchiefs, 150 pounds of flour, four flannel jackets, four suits of clothes and eighteen shirts – and an annual payment of the same.

BAIL UP!

PORT ARTHUR
— AND —
NORFOLK ISLAND
— The Last of The Convict Outlaws —

*Etablissement penitentiare de Port Arthur,
Terre de Van-Diemen*

Engraving by N. Rémond from *Campagne de Circumnavigation de la Fregate L'Artemise pendant les Annies*, published Paris, 1854

The pententiary at Port Arthur had chosen one of the prettiest harbours on the island around which to build its house of horrors.

(Rex Nan Kivell Collection NK10,363, National Library of Australia)

Come all you gallant poachers that ramble from care,
That walk out of a moonlight night with your dog,
   your gun and snare,
Where the lofty hare and pheasant you have at your
   command,
Not thinking that your last career is on
   Van Diemen's Land.

— Traditional

BAIL UP!

The 'Brave But Unfortunate Irishman', Martin Cash

Martin Cash is the only famous Australian bushranger to have died peacefully – in his own bed aged sixty-nine.

He was born in 1810 in the town of Enniscorthy, County Wexford, Ireland. His father was an extravagant, indolent and often dissipated 'gentleman' who had inherited his fortune and did his best to drink it all away. Luckily for Cash and his brother their mother had her own fortune. She was devoted to her boys and would not deny them anything. The boys did, however, inherit much of their father's love of the horse-track, the gaming room and the public bar.

His father took no interest at all in Martin's upbringing, and the young man was already running wild before he was even sixteen years old.

At sixteen he enlisted in the 8th Hussars, but found that military discipline was not to his liking so he implored his mother to seek his discharge. Once free from the rigours of army life, he soon fell back into his old habits, and before long he took up with a young lass who, with her mother and sister, made straw bonnets for a living. Cash started to divert some of his mother's fortune to his mistress, until one of his drinking companions advised him that a rival named Jessop was seen visiting with his lass and that he had been a constant visitor to her house.

Cash went straight home, took down and loaded his gun with shot, then marched back to the house of his mistress, his loaded gun cradled in the crook of his arm. There he spied Jessop with his arm around her waist. Cash stepped back a step or two, took aim and fired through a window, lodging a musket ball in Jessop's shoulder.

Cash was arrested and sent to trial. Although his mother and her wealthy and influential relatives petitioned the court to secure his release, it was to no avail. Martin Cash was sentenced to be transported for seven years.

Shortly after arriving at Cork gaol, where he was held awaiting transportation, he learned of his mother's death. Cash was ashamed to realise that his behaviour had probably hastened her demise. He also learned that his father had been shot in a duel on the same night that he had punctured Jessop. The Cash family was coming to an unhappy end.

Accompanied by another 170 convicted Irishmen, Cash embarked on the *Marquis of Huntley* and arrived at Botany Bay in January 1828. He was only eighteen years old.

Cash must have done his best to keep out of trouble. He did his time and earned his freedom, and was granted a ticket-of-leave and settled down working as a farm-hand in the Hunter Valley of New South ales. But it seemed that bad luck was chasing Martin Cash. One day he was innocently branding some cattle for a friend when two men rode up and watched him at work for a while. After they had ridden on, his friend told him that the beasts were stolen and that Martin would soon be in trouble if they were reported. Cash recalled the two men who had watched so intently. Knowing that a life sentence to Norfolk Island was the punishment for cattle-stealing, he left for Van Diemen's Land with his partner Bessie Clifford, whom he had persuaded to leave her husband and run away with him.

The pair arrived in Hobart Town in 1837, and Cash looked for work as a labourer, but after twelve months his troubles had begun again. He was falsely accused of theft twice; the first case was dismissed

Flogged for an Accident

Carpenter George Douse was shaping a beam to be fitted into a windmill under construction when he accidentally let the end fall from his grasp. It hit the ground and the end damaged.

The overseer known as 'Musha Pug' took Douse to the office and charged him with neglect, although poor old Douse insisted that it had been an accident.

The 'monster of Norfolk Island' Muster–master John Price sentenced the carpenter to 100 lashes, just to let the other prisoners know that while he was on the island (VDL) he would continue the pursuit of their punishment as relentlessly as ever he had done on Norfolk.

ADAPTED FROM THE MEMOIRS OF MARTIN CASH, AS DICTATED TO FELLOW-PRISONER JAMES LESTER BURKE

OPPOSITE:
Martin Cash, the Only Bushranger to Die in His Own Bed
Cash was probably one of the most unfortunate of all the Irishmen beset by English petulance and obstinancy. His nemesis was the 'monster of Norfolk Island', John Price, who did his best to see that Cash paid dearly for every infringement of the prison rules he may have broken – whether or not he was innocent. Price died with a blow to the back of the skull at Gellibrand Quarry in 1857.
(Allport Library and Museum of Fine Arts Collection, State Library of Tasmania)

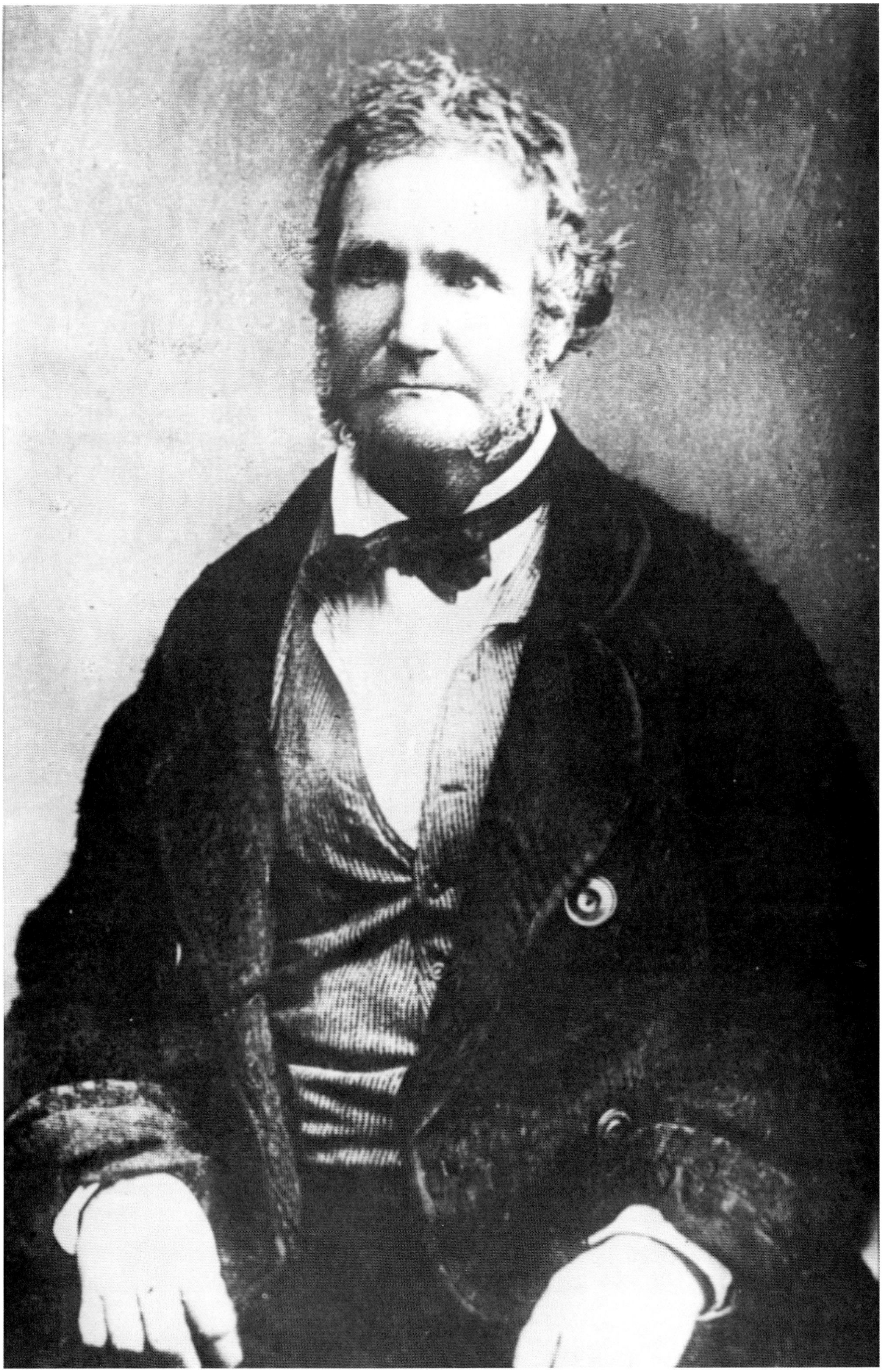

BAIL UP!

but the second time he had beaten the arresting officer so badly that, from then on, he was a marked man. He was convicted and sentenced to serve another seven years at one of the island's settlements.

Cash spent only two days on the job before he escaped, making his way back to where he had left Bessie. When he was re-captured he received an additional nine months to his sentence and a further nine months on the road gang. While he was waiting to be sent away, he again took his liberty; this time he found his Bessie and made his way to Hobart, planning to leave Van Diemen's Land for Melbourne.

Death on 'the Stretcher'

The prisoner Alexander Campbell was sentenced to thirty days solitary confinement 'for giving insolence to his overseer'.

He was visited in his darkened cell by Mr Price, and being a violent-tempered man Campbell abused Price and threatened him. After his thirty days were up he was again brought for trial, sentenced to another thirty days and thrust back into the cell.

Once more, he was visited by Price, and seemingly unable to hold his tongue abused and threatened Price yet again.

Campbell was placed inside a new item of torture and restraint that was being introduced – 'the stretcher'. It was an iron frame about six feet long and two and half feet wide with hoops of iron winding around its length about twelve inches apart. The prisoner was placed in the frame with his head sticking out the top, and the frame was laid horizontal with the prisoners head having no means of support.

Campbell was placed in this cage and left in the dark for the next twelve hours. His continued insolence caused him to suffer this treatment regularly.

One morning the turnkey opened the solitary cell to find the Campbell dead inside the cage.

Martin Cash wrote in his memoirs that Campbell had not been out of solitary for more than twelve days in the six months since he was first locked away by Price. Cash was convinced that Price was the one and only cause of Campbell's *murder*.

ADAPTED FROM THE MEMOIRS OF MARTIN CASH, AS DICTATED TO FELLOW-PRISONER JAMES LESTER BURKE

But, as luck would have it, the pair was recognised in the street while they were waiting for a ship. Cash was again imprisoned. He was brought before the presiding magistrate, the much-despised John Price.

Price excused Cash's good behaviour as just his 'cleverness'. 'But you will not best me, Martin,' said the judge as he added two more years to his sentence and another four at Port Arthur.

By this time Cash must have felt as though he would never be freed, but it was while at Port Arthur that he made his boldest bid for freedom. Along with robbers, Lawrence Kavanagh and George Jones, he braved the waters of Eaglehawk Neck,* avoiding the dogs and the guards who had been put on special alert as the prisoners' absence was discovered immediately after they had started to run.

By the time the group reached the Neck their clothes had been torn to shreds by having to crawl the last mile on hands and knees through the scrub. The Neck was swarming with guards and the dogs chained every few yards were howling for blood. The three absconders took to the water and with some difficulty swam to the other side of the inlet, balancing their clothes on top of their heads. When they clambered up the opposite bank, they were stark naked, their clothes and boots having been carried away by the waters of the Neck. Cash remembered that they they fell about laughing at the state they were in when they had finally reached the safety of the wooded shore – three wet white naked desperados, at last free as birds without any idea what to do next.

The robbers followed Cash until they came upon a hut he had noted on his last escape attempt, and they bailed up the hut-keeper, tying him to the post in the middle as they helped themselves to clothing and enough food to last them a few weeks.

It was the next day when Kavanagh asked of Cash what was to be done. Jones replied: 'Take up arms and stand no repairs'. They all agreed and from this point on they were outlawed – bushrangers all.

Cash later recalled an instance not long after he had arrived in Van Diemen's Land, where he saw a

---

*Eaglehawk Neck is a small isthmus running between the Tasman Peninsula and Forestier Peninsula on the mainland. Port Arthur was on the Tasman Peninsula and the only exit was along this narrow land-bridge.

A row of ferocious hounds were chained, one every few yards, all along the strip of land and guards prevented any attempt at escape.

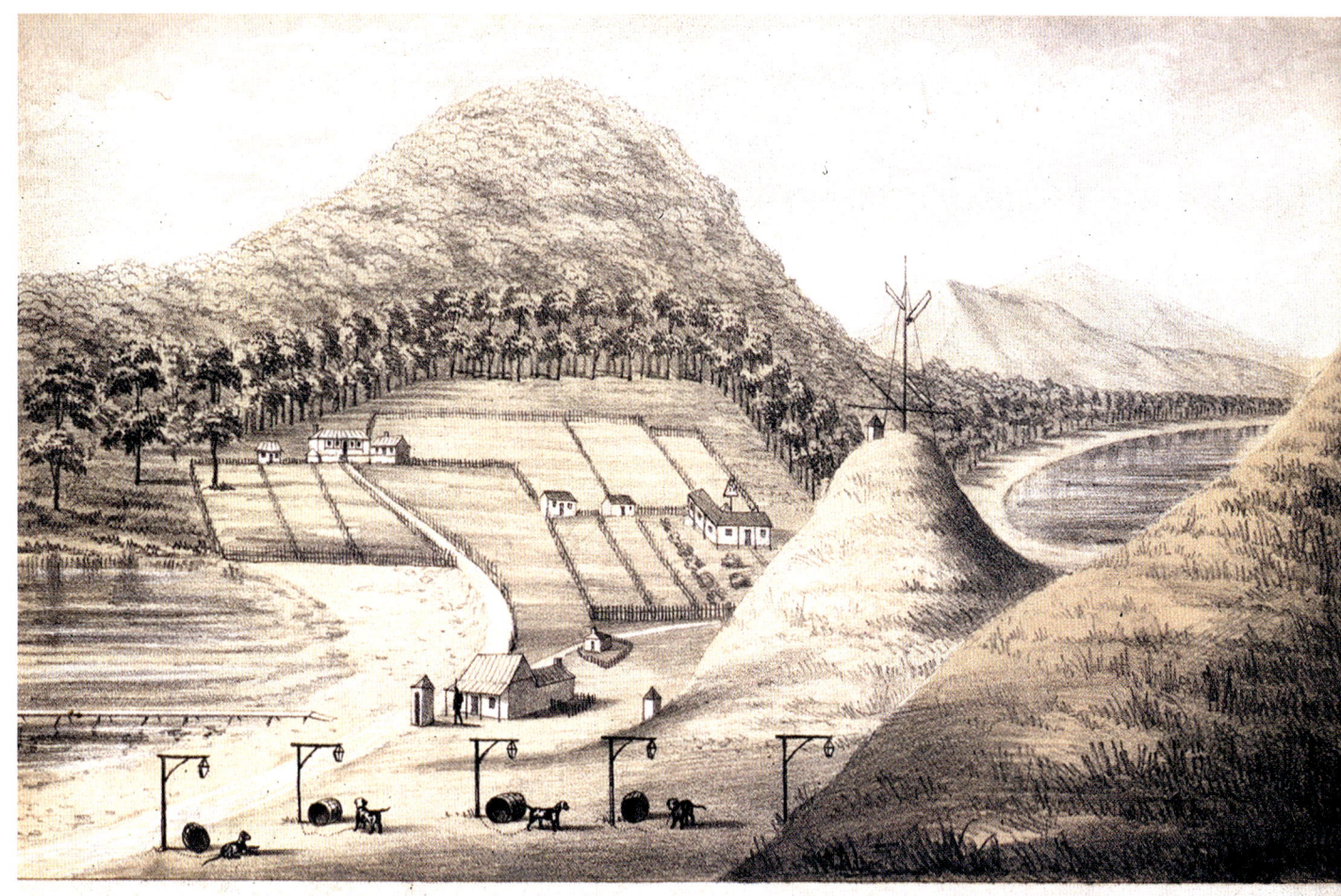

cart conveying along the road a coffin. Upon enquiring he was informed that the body within was that of a recently hanged, convicted robber and murderer McCoy, who was being transported to the scene of his crimes. It was a condition of his sentence that his body be further desecrated by hanging in a gibbett until it had decomposed.

McCoy was duly hanged upon the gibbett post about one mile from Perth on a bend of the Launceston road.

The body became such an offence to the local inhabitants that they petitioned the authorities for its removal. They complained first of the disgusting stench and second of the fat black flies that, after feeding on the rotting McCoy, flew into their houses and lit upon their provisions – and to their horror onto their persons.

There was no doubt that the authorities' intention was to impress upon the labouring classes that the law had little respect for those who dared to transcend. That the actions of the capricious and obdurate law-makers and law-enforcers did much to force the miscreant to seek his revenge on the society that continued so to abuse was of little interest – the law

ABOVE:
North View of Eagle Hawk Neck, which joins Tasman's Peninsular to the main land of Van Dieman's Land
Lithograph by Charles Hutchins, c.1840
Below the illustration are written the words: 'There is, at this place, a chain of dogs, which are so savage, that should any convict escape from the penal settlement at Port Arthur, it is impossible for them to pass into the colony.'
(Allport Library and Museum of Fine Arts Collection. State Library of Tasmania)

BAIL UP!

REWARD!
FIFTY SOVEREIGNS, and a Conditional Pardon.

WHEREAS the three Convicts (Runaways from Port Arthur) MARTIN CASH, GEORGE JONES, and LAWRENCE KAVENAGH, whose descriptions are as under, stand charged with having committed divers Capital Felonies, and are now illegally at large: This is to give Notice, that I am authorised by His Excellency the Lieutenant-Governor to offer a Reward of Fifty Sovereigns to any person or persons who shall apprehend or cause to be apprehended and lodged in safe custody either of the said Felons; and should this service be performed by a Convict, then, in addition to such pecuniary Reward, a CONDITIONAL PARDON.

19th January, 1843.

M. FORSTER,
Chief Police Magistrate.

DESCRIPTION OF THE ABOVE-NAMED CONVICTS.

Martin Cash, per Francis Freeling, tried at Launceston Q.S., 24th March 1840, 7 years, labourer, 6 feet, age 33, native place Wexford, complexion very ruddy, head small and round, hair curly and carroty, whiskers red small, forehead low, eyebrows red, eyes blue small, nose small, mouth large, chin small. Remarks remarkably long feet, a very swift runner.

Lawrence Kavenagh, per Marian Watson, tried at Sydney, 12th April 1842, life, stonemason, 5 feet 10½, age 30, complexion pale, head long large, hair brown to grey, whiskers brown, visage long, forehead high, eyebrows brown, eyes light grey, nose long and sharp, mouth and chin medium size, native place Wicklow. Remarks A. D. above elbow joint left arm, 2 scars on palm of left hand, lost little finger on right hand.

George Jones, per Marian Watson, tried at Sydney, 14th April 1842, life, labourer, 5 feet 7, age 27, complexion ruddy fair, freckled, head long, hair brown, whiskers brown, visage long, forehead perpendicular, eyebrows brown, eyes blue, nose medium, mouth medium, chin pointed, native place Westminster. Remarks H. W. anchor on right arm, breast hairy.

JAMES BARNARD, GOVERNMENT PRINTER HOBART TOWN

Lawrence Kavanagh

Kavanagh was a hard man from Waterford, County Wicklow Ireland. He was transported for life after his conviction on 24 August 1828 for a house robbery in Dublin. He arrived at Botany Bay aboard the *Ferguson* the following year.

Following the aborted attempt by Martin Cash to seek out his 'wife' Bessie, Kavanagh was seriously wounded when he accidently shot himself in the arm, falling on stony ground. The ball entered his arm at the elbow, ran along the bone and exited at the wrist, rendering his arm quite useless. This put an end to his bushranging career. After several days of agony and becoming increasingly weakened, Kavanagh gave himself up to Mr Clark at Cluny.

Kavanagh was sent to the notoriously tough prison on Norfolk Island. Even though there was no possibility at all of escape from Norfolk Island. He tried to get away and received 150 lashes for his efforts. After the failed Fourth of July Rebellion in which 'Jacky Jacky' Westwood killed four men over the confiscation of the prisoners' billy-cans, Kavanagh was implicated by the false report of 'Dog Kelly', an Irish prisoner, from whose cap he had snatched a shamrock on St Patrick's Day, accusing him 'that he was a disgrace to his country (unfit) to wear the national emblem'.

Kavanagh was hanged with twelve other 'rebels' at the insistence of John Price.

was the law and those who disobeyed were without its protection – outside the law.

Kavanagh, Cash and Jones soon behaved just like any other of the marauding gangs in Van Diemen's Land at that time, committing the same repertoire of hold-ups, shootings, robberies, fights and brawls. They decided to hold up the Woolpack Inn about ten miles out of New Norfolk, but a convict shepherd they met along the way warned that they would find a party of constables stationed there. The trio had only recently acquired some stolen weapons, and they decided to persist with their plan to attack the Inn. They felt it would be a good idea to test themselves and their weapons against the constables, while they believed that the shepherd would broadcast their intentions anyway and they wanted the district to be aware of their bushranging prowess.

They raided the Inn only to discover the son of the owner behaving in a sarcastic and cocky manner. Cash assumed that he was being overly brave becaue he knew that the constables were not far away. Cash then saw some figures coming towards the inn from

ABOVE:
Reward Poster – Fifty Sovereigns and a Conditional Pardon
A reward was issued for the apprehension of the escaped convicts Martin Cash, George Jones and Lawrence Kavanagh on 19 January 1843. There were so many convicts, ex-convicts and ticket-of-leave abroad in the colony who also shared no love for the authorities that no one would even consider 'dobbing in' one of their own kind.
(La Trobe Picture Collection, State Library of Victoria)

a hut 100 yards away. One called out to him to 'Stand', and he did. Cash stood still while he could draw a bead on the man, and fired. The constable hit the dirt. Cash discoverd later that his ball had ripped through the constable's side, tearing two ribs away from his backbone. A flurry of musket balls sang through the air as the troopers and Cash fired at each other. Cash called to his mates but heard no reply; affeared that they may have been killed already, he rushed inside the Inn to discover them cowering in two corners of the bar. The cocky young lad was hidden in an angle of the chimney, having forgotten the bravery he was displaying before the bullets began to fly. Picking up a three-gallon barrel of rum, he decided it was time to make his getaway.

Back on the road Cash heard a sound behind him. Thinking he was being tracked by the constables he turned and challenged. Kavanagh and Jones stepped from the shadows; neither had been wounded and the three once again took to the hills.

Making for the Dromedary they were again short of supplies so they robbed the hut of Mr Crawthorn at the foot of the Mount. As well as food and other

ABOVE:
Portrait of a Man in the Dock (Martin Cash)
Watercolour by Charles H.T. Constantini, c. 1843
The original of this painting bears the inscription *'Martin Cash in the dock at Hobart'* on its back. This sketch of Cash represents his court appearance after he was wrongly accused and attacked the arresting officer. He stood in the dock the next day bearing the wounds of the beating he received in return.
(Allport Library and Museum of Fine Arts Collection. State Library of Tasmania)

The Bushrangers Act *1830*

Following is an abbreviation of the Act that was imposed on the colony in 1830 in an attempt to bring to justice the marauding gangs of Van Diemen's Land.

1 ~ It was lawful for anyone who suspected another of robbery, house-breaking or of being a transported felon unlawfully at large to, without warrant, apprehend, or cause to be apprehended, that person and taken to a Justice for examination.

2 ~ Every such person brought before a Justice was obliged to prove their innocence of the charges for which they were apprehended. It was the onus of the person charged to prove their right to be free. If not satisfied the Justice could, at his discretion, have that person removed to Sydney for examination.

3 ~ Anyone found on the roads with firearms or other instruments of a violent nature would be taken before a Justice and again had to prove that the weapons were not intended for any unlawful activity.

4 ~ If anyone even thought that anyone else had firearms or instruments of a violent nature hidden or concealed about their person, that any suspicious person should be searched and if any weapon or instrument was found to be taken before the Justice and . . .

5 ~ If anyone had any creditable information about any other person a Justice should provide a general search warrant and any goods, chattels, weapons etc. be seized by a constable and any persons to be brought before a Justice and . . .

6 ~ Any person tried and sentenced, to be executed within two days of the trial – except if that day were a Sunday, then the next Monday would be the fateful day.

7 ~ Anyone found to have aforesaid weapons, and not able to prove that they were not intended for illegal use, were to be sentenced for a 'high misdeanour' to three years imprisonment.

A lot of innocent 'felons' were taken into custody and wasted much time and energy just trying to avoid the noose. No doubt there were many who didn't succeed.

BAIL UP!

supplies Jones appropriated a silk dress intended for Mrs Cash when they met again.

Cash took the dress to the house of an old acquaintence at Cob's Hill on the northern side of the Mount. From here a message was sent to Bessie, and she joined them there shortly after. By the time Bessie arrived, Cash, Kavanagh and Jones had constructed a fortress on the top of the mount with a commanding view in all directions. The fortress consisted of three huge logs formed together in a triangle, and within this were placed saplings and brush to afford protection from the winds. Although it had no roof it was comfortable enough for the trio who expected little more from their outlaw life in the bush.

After a few days Cash learned that there was a contingent of the 51st King's Own light Infantry out looking for them, and not wanting to put Bessie in any danger they escorted her back to the town. It seems that she was watched all the way by the police, who, on her arrival, arrested her and took her into custody.

Cash was furious at this affront to his beloved Bessie, and attacked the farm of a Mr Kerr. Once everyone in the house had settled down, Cash put them at ease by his assurance that he never harmed women and they should not be insulted. Then he sat down and Jones wrote the following letter to the governor:

> Messrs. Cash & Co. beg to notify his excellency Sir John Franklin and his satellites that a very respectable person named Mrs Cash is now falsely imprisoned in Hobart Town, and if the said Mrs. Cash is not released forthwith, and properly renumerated, we will in the first instance, visit Government House, and beginning with Sir John,

Cash for a Cabbage

It was back in Wexford, when the young Martin was paying court to the lass who was at the cause of all his troubles, that he acquired a skill that was to bring him some good fortune, and some bad.

Years later Cash recalled that he had plaited a cabbage-tree hat for himself while he was out with cattle and earned his first shillings making the same hats for the other drovers. But it was years later when the same skill earned him six days in solitary.

Cash was working in charge of the plaiter's shop when a constable came in hoping that he would repair the brim of a hat he had earlier made for him. Cash obliged, the quick repair job taking only a few minutes. But, as Cash's luck would have it, he was reported and sentenced for neglecting his 'proper' duties.

ABOVE:
Philips Island from the north-west extremity to the overseer's hut, Macquarie Harbour
Ink wash drawing by Thomas Lempriere, c. 1828
Imprisoned, Cash served much of his time clearing land, digging fields and weeding crops. He first landed in trouble for not clearing enough in one day. As he had been helping the mistress around the house during that day he felt wrongly accused, a feeling not unknown to 'the unfortunate Martin Cash'.
(Allport Library and Museum of Fine Arts Collection. State Library of Tasmania)

A VIEW of QUEENBOROUGH on Norfolk-Island

administer a wholesome lesson in the shape of a sound flogging: after which we will pay the same currency to all his followers.

Given this day, at the residence of Mr. Kerr, of Dunrobin.

Signed Cash Kavanagh Jones

Following the delivery of this letter Cash was lured into Hobart in the search for his Bessie whom he had been told was spreading her favours a little too widely. He was again recognised in the street, where he heard someone cry out: 'Look, it's Cash, blow his brains out', whereupon he turned about, fired his pistol and ran. He had severely wounded a constable who died later ... '[he had] discharged a leaden bullet, which did strike, prostrate and wound the left breast of the said Peter Winstanley, of which he died on the 31st August'.

ABOVE:
A view of Queenborough on Norfolk Island
Watercolour drawing by John Eyre, 1804
Martin Cash served his last sentence on Norfolk Island. Maybe it was the isolation of Norfolk, but by this time it seemed that he had had enough. He was a model prisoner; his death sentence, which had been commuted to life, was shortened to ten years and he was then released.
(W. L. Crowther Library Collection, State Library of Tasmania)

George Jones

Jones was a Londoner who was transported to Botany Bay in 1830 for highway robbery.

Jones was the only member of Cash & Co to escape capture until later. He teamed up with escaped convicts John Liddell and James Dalton, and together they carried out raids on farms and houses, operating out of Cash's old hide-out on the Mount. They even held up a hawker's cart and left the man, McCall, tied to a tree after relieving him of everything they wanted from his cart.

The police captured Liddell and Dalton, then they laid a trap for Jones, nabbing the remainder of his gang inside a hut where they sometimes held up on the Dromedary. One of the gang was shot as he tried to crawl away on his hands and knees. Jones was blinded by a faceful of buckshot as he rushed from the hut, and the only one left, Platt, was taken uninjured.

Liddell and Dalton were both sentenced to be hanged. When the death sentence was passed, the judge added that he could not recommend either for mercy. Liddell's retort was: 'I don't want mercy from you or any one else. I've been eleven years at Port Arthur and I don't want to go there again. I'd rather die than live'. Dalton's answer was: 'I don't care a .... what you do'.

BAIL UP!

The hapless Martin Cash was caught again, tried again and sentenced, yet again, to death for the constable's murder. His sentence was commuted, and Cash was able to look forward to life on Norfolk Island. By this time he had probably had just about enough. On Norfolk he became a model prisoner and was only to serve ten years before he was released.

Cash took no part in the Fourth of July Rebellion, and it was a remark by his old friend Lawrence Kavanagh that stung him right to the heart. As they were passing each other one day, Cash in charge of tools for the masons who were building a new blacksmith's shop, Kavanagh on his way to the courthouse after his part in the outbreak *(see page 60)*, Kavanagh remarked, 'Martin, they have got you', implying that he had become 'a tool in the hands of government officers'. As Cash himself recalled: 'His observation … in the presence of prisoners had a most injurious tendency'.

While on Norfolk Island, Cash married Mary Bennett, the convict servant of the Island's Medical Officer, and it was with Mary that he returned to Van Diemen's Land. The transportation of convicts was drawing to an end and Norfolk Island was closing down, the island being given over to the descendants of the *Bounty* mutineers who were at that time still on Pitcairn Island. The prisoners remaining on Norfolk were to be transferred to Tasmania.

On 31 July 1854, the trusted Martin Cash was made a constable, and only two months later, on 19 September, he was at long last granted his ticket-of-leave.

On his return to Tasmania Cash took an appointment as overseer of the gardeners in the Government Domain and settled down to family life with Mary. A son, also called Martin, was born the following year. This wild colonial boy now had his own 'father's only hope', their own 'pride and joy'. But tragedy and sorrow were never far behind Martin Cash, as young Martin died from the effects of rheumatic fever in 1871. The 'hard-old man' of the bush was left broken-hearted.

It is said that because of his son's untimely death Cash became an alcoholic; it is true that he died after falling ill at the Lord Rodney Hotel, but Martin Cash died in his sleep, in his own bed, on 26 August 1878. He passed away in the farmhouse he had built for himself and Mary Bennett, his convict bride, on 160 acres of land at Glenorchy, Tasmania. His tomb stands in the Cornellian Bay Cemetery, Hobart, and the headstone reads: 'to the Memory of that brave but unfortunate Irishman Martin Cash'.

RIGHT:
Martin Cash's Grave at Cornellian Bay Cemetery, Hobart
(Photographs by Anna Gregory)

'Bold' Jack Donohoe, Last of the Convict Outlaws

John Donohoe was transported to Botany Bay, arriving aboard the ship *Ann and Amelia* on 2 January 1825. On arrival he was assigned to a settler at Parramatta, but he managed to get into trouble before long, and spent some time on a chain gang until he was re-assigned to a Parramatta surgeon, Major West.

Donohoe soon took up with two other Irish convicts, and this small band began a robbing career, stopping the bullock drays on the Windsor Road. This was easy as bullocks move along slowly – the bandits didn't even need a horse. They were, however, apprehended and sentenced to be hanged. Donohoe's mates, Kilroy and Smith, took the drop but he managed to break free between the court and the cells.

Donohoe brought together a band of Irish and English absconders who ranged across the Liverpool, Parramatta and Windsor districts. Among his band were William 'Darky' Underwood, Jack Walmsley and Bill Webber. Together, they stripped coaches and travellers, stole horses and annoyed the governor so much that he issued a reward of a 'pardon and passage' that for Donohoe, thankfully, was never claimed. They robbed in true 'Robin Hood' style, taking from the well-to-do, fencing their booty through the scores of poor settlers who welcomed the opportunity to benefit from Donohoe's daring deeds.

They robbed the farmhouse of Charles Sturt, the well-known explorer. When Donohoe recognised Sturt, he apologised, directing his mates to 'stand back boys — we don't rob him'. They even had the temerity to stick up Reverend Samuel Marsden, a man few would ever dare insult. They roamed as far as Bathurst in the east, down to Yass in the south and as far north as the Hunter River. As the newspapers of the day reported on 14 December 1827:

There has been an outbreak of bushranging on the road between Sydney and Windsor. Several vehicles have been stopped and the passengers stripped of all valuables.

Donohoe and his men, curiously noted as 'remarkably clean' bushmen, preferred to dress in raffish style, 'Bold Jack' himself fitted out in 'black hat, superfine blue cloth coatlined with silk . . . plaited shirt . . . [and] laced boots'. He acted as if he could go wherever he pleased, and there were plenty of convicted men and women, and newspaper editors, in the colony who enjoyed the fools he made of the governor and his ineffectual troopers. He even rode into Sydney one day and partook of a couple of bottles of ginger beer – just as bold as brass!

The same newspapers were able to report on 1 September 1830:

With the shooting down of 'Bold Jack' Donohoe, the most notorious of the bushrangers currently operating in New South Wales has been brought to account. Donohoe, 'a native of Dublin, 23 years of age, five feet four inches in height, brown freckled complexion, flaxen hair, blue eyes and has a scar under the left nostril', was shot in a police ambush in the Bringelly scrub near Campbell-town, bringing to an end two and a half years of pillage and murder.

Donohoe had been betrayed by Jack Walmsley, who led the troopers to his capture to save his own neck. They came upon the gang in bush near Campbelltown; when he realised there was no escape for him this time, 'Bold Jack' waved his hat, then threw it in the air shouting, 'Come on you 'effing' buggers, we're ready, if there's a dozen of you . . .'

Donohoe was felled by a pistol ball through the forehead, shot from the carbine of trooper John Muggleston.

No one today remembers Muggleston, whose keen eye and steady hand brought an end to the reign of the most-feared and best-loved of the convict bushrangers but even over a century-and-a-half later

BAIL UP!

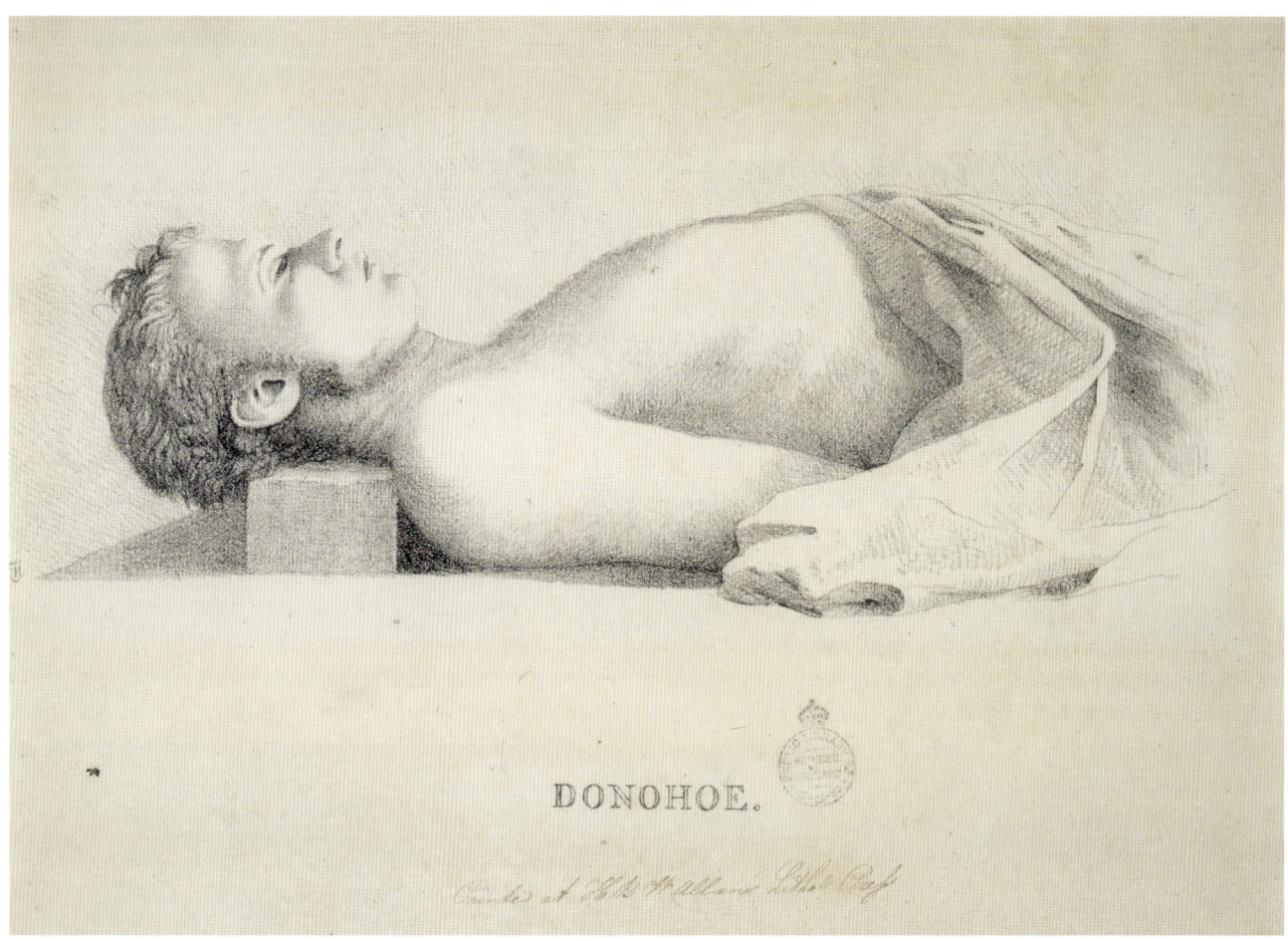

the ballad of 'The Wild Colonial Boy' still stirs the rebel heart.

Within days of Donohoe's demise an enterprising Sydney shopkeeper had produced a line of clay pipes sporting an effigy of 'Bold Jack' complete with the tiny bullet hole in its forehead.

'The Wild Colonial Boy'

Dublin-born John Donohoe has the honour of having several ballads penned to commemorate his exploits on the roads of New South Wales.

There are even several versions of the most famous bushranging ballad of them all – 'The Wild Colonial Boy'.

At times Jack Donohoe becomes *Donahue* or *Donahoo;* at others the name has been changed to *Jack Doolan*, or *Jim Doolan*, and even to *John Dowling*, but in all cases the ballad remains a lusty tribute to the blue-eyed, flaxen-haired young Irishman, who terrorised the highways and endeared himself to ex-convicts and sympathetic settlers alike.

Many saw him as a 'son of Erin' who had taken on the authorities and made a mockery of them. The ballad 'The Wild Colonial Boy' became Australia's first unofficial anthem, and has been sung over and over again by generations of Australians with rebellion in their hearts. The song was often rendered to the tune of 'The Wearin' of the Green'; it is therefore easy to see why the authorities were resentful of the empathies it aroused among the seditious Irish.

Greatly enjoyed by colonial sympathisers, the song was eventually banned for its seditious sentiment. However, it would not die and with the name changed to Doolan and the title changed from its original 'Bold John Donohoe' to 'The Wild Colonial Boy' the authorities simply gave up.

It is known that 'The Wild Colonial Boy' was sung heartily in Jones's Glenrowan Hotel the night before Ned Kelly was taken in 1880.

ABOVE:
'The wild colonial boy', John Donohoe
Pencil drawing by Thomas Mitchell
Beneath this post-mortem portrait of 'the wild colonial boy', Thomas Mitchell, who was acting as Governor Darling's Surveyor-General at the time, quoted this passage from Byron:
   No matter; I have bared my brow.
   Fair in Death's face – before – and now.
(Mitchell Library Collection, State Library of New South Wales)

Sedition, Celebrated in Song

Bold Jack Donahoe

In Dublin Town I was brought up, in that city of great fame.
My decent friends and parents they will tell you the same.
It was for the sake of five hundred pounds I was sent across the main,
For seven long years, in New South wales, to wear a convict's chain.

I'd scarce been there twelve months or more upon the Australian shore,
When I took to the highway, as I'd oft-times done before.
There was me and Jacky Underwood, and Webber and Webster too,
These were the true associates of bold Jack Donahue.

Now, Donahoe was taken, all for a notorious crime,
And sentenced to be hanged upon the gallows-tree so high.
But when they came to Sydney gaol, he left them in a stew,
And when they came to call the roll, they missed bold Donahoe.

As Donah0e made his escape, to the bush he went straight-away.
The squatters they were all afraid to travel night or day –
For every week in the newspapers there was published something new
Concerning this dauntless hero, the bold Jack Donahoe.

As Donahoe was cruising, one summer's afternoon,
Little was his notion his death was near so soon,
When a sergeant of the horse police discharged his car-a-bine,
And called aloud on Donahoe to fight or to resign.

'Resign to you – you cowardly dogs, a thing n'er will do,
For I'll fight this night with all my might,' cried bold Jack Donohoe,
'I'd rather roam these hills and dales like a wolf or kangaroo,
Than work one hour for Government,' cried bold Jack Donohoe.

He fought six rounds with the horse police until the fatal ball,
Which pierced his heart and made him start, caused Donahoe to fall.
And as he closed his mournful eyes, he bade this world *Adieu*,
Saying, 'Convicts all, both large and small, say prayers for Donahoe'.

RIGHT:
This version of the unofficial anthem of Australia of the nineteenth century was so changed that the real events were hardly recognised in the lyrics. Rendering this boisterous tune would not land the singer in gaol, as was the case just following the time of Donohoe's reign.

The Wild Colonial Boy

There was a Wild Colonial Boy,
Jack Doolan was his name.
Of poor but honest parents
He was born in Castlemaine,
He was his father's only hope,
His mother's pride and joy
And dearly did his parents love
Their Wild Colonial Boy.

Chorus
So come away, me hearties,
We'll roam the mountains high,
Together we will plunder,
And together we will die.
We'll scour along the valleys,
And we'll gallop o'er the plains,
And scorn to live in slavery,
Bound down by iron chains.

At the age of sixteen years
He left his native home,
And to Australia's sunny shore
A bushranger did roam.
They put him in the iron gang
In the government employ,
But never an iron on earth could hold
The Wild Colonial Boy.

In sixty-one this daring youth
Commenced his wild career,
With a heart that knew no danger
and no foeman did he fear.
He stuck up the Beechworth mail coach,
And robbed Judge MacEvoy
Who, trembling cold, gave up his gold
To the Wild Colonial Boy.

One day as Jack was riding
The mountainside along,
A-listening to the little birds,
Their happy laughing song,
Three mounted troopers came along,
Kelly, Davis and Fitzroy,
With a warrant for the capture of
The Wild Colonial Boy.

'Surrender now! Jack Doolan,
For you see it's three to one;
Surrender in the Queen's own name,
You are a highwayman'.
Jack drew a pistol from his belt,
And waved it like a toy,
'I'll fight, but not surrender,' cried
The Wild Colonial Boy.

He fired at trooper Kelly,
And brought him to the ground,
And in return from Davis
Received a mortal wound,
All shattered through the jaws he lay
Still firing at Fitzroy,
And that's the way they captured him,
The Wild Colonial Boy.

BAIL UP!

The 'Billy-Can' Mutiny on Norfolk Island

Every prisoner on Norfolk Island had for his tea-making a personal billy-can (tin kettle) made for him as an item of barter by the prisoner mechanics on the settlement. Each man considered his billy-can to be his personal property, the billy not being a part of government issue. At night the prisoners generally left their billy-cans on the mess tables when they went to bed.

On the night of 1 July 1846, the constables were ordered to confiscate all the unauthorised vessels and lock them up in the stores – for 'security'. The following morning a 'strong party' of prisoners broke open the store and retrieved their billies, pots and kettles.

Among the party who broke into the store was Martin Cash's old bushranging accomplice Lawrence Kavanagh. Having taken possession of their prized tin-pots the raiding party left for breakfast, having disturbed nothing else, and not wanting to give the Commandant any cause for retribution. However, they underestimated the English passion for revenge for a law not obeyed. And they also underestimated the brutality and hatred with which their fellow inmates were consumed.

One of their fellows was William Westwood (Jacky Jacky) who had been sent to Norfolk in 1846 following a short but 'glorious' career bushranging in New South Wales. The twenty-six-year-old had been in prison since he was sixteen and was heard that day to bellow: 'I'm going to the gallows: I'll bear this oppression no longer'. With that he attacked.

A small party of about twenty men burst into the cookhouse, and Westwood attacked the overseer with a cudgel, killing him with one stroke. They turned back through the timber yard, passing through a covered archway leading to the mechanic's shop. Westwood came upon a guard and bashed his brains out against the brick wall as he sat at his watch.

Westwood's blood was up, and the now-fevered party headed for the lime-kilns where several constables were stationed. Westwood had picked up an axe on the way, and bursting into their billet killed one instantly, then he turned to find another who still in bed foolishly called out: 'I seen who done that!' Westwood swung and sent him into the afterlife as well.

ABOVE:
The penal settlement at Norfolk Island
Norfolk Island was originally settled by the British because of the long straight pine trees found in abundance. The British were ever fearful of losing access to supplies of timbers from the Baltic and sought to find ready replacement.
  Unfortunately, Norfolk pines are short fibred and are prone to splintering and will snap without warning when put under pressure. This rendered them totally unsuitable for the long spars needed for shipping. So the ever-resourceful British turned the beautiful island into a prison.
(La Trobe Library Collection, State Library of Victoria)

BELOW:
Norfolk Island — the convict system
Hand-coloured wood engraving, pub. London 1847

This engraving is taken from a London illustrated newspaper of the time. What pleasant reading it must have been, to learn of the penal settlements in the colonies over 'elevenses'.

(National Library of Australia Collection)

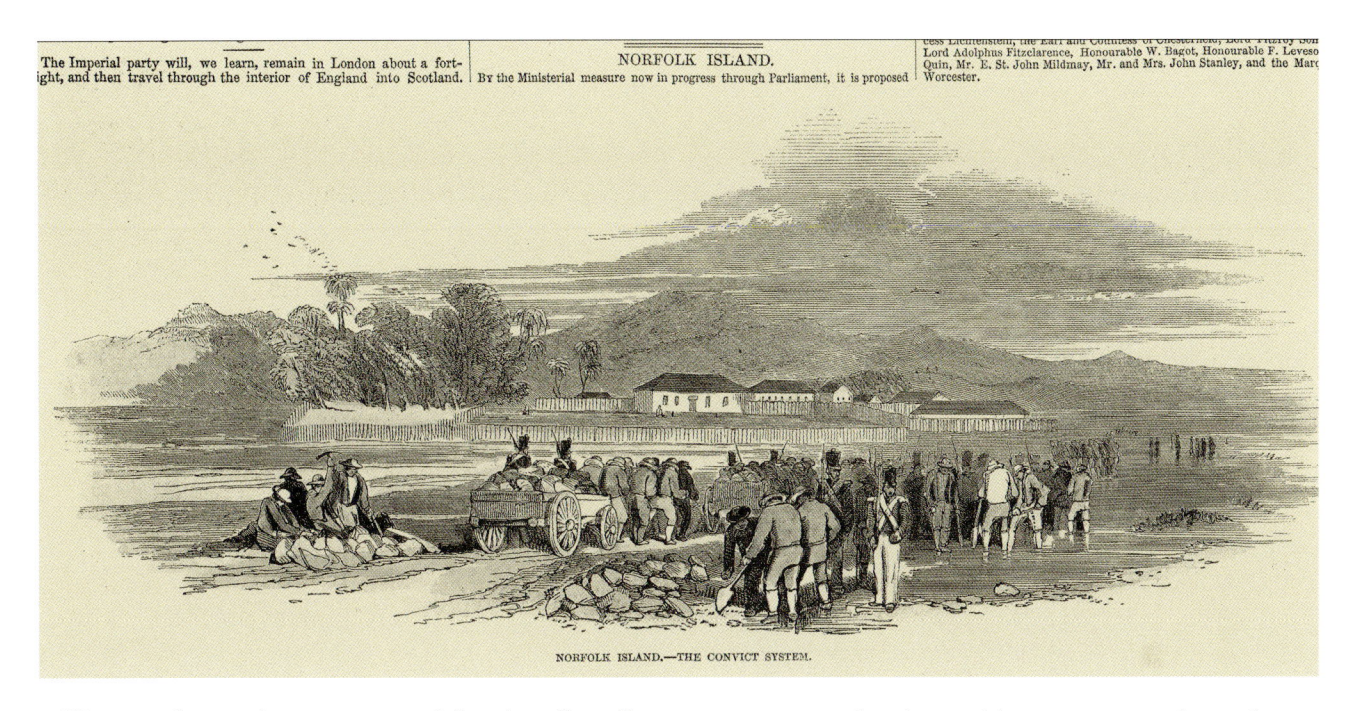

Westwood must have gone mad: he then literally hacked this man to pieces.

Almost all of the prisoners on Norfolk Island joined in the riot. One thousand and six hundred prisoners of the 1800 took their revenge on the overseers and the floggers who made their daily lives a constant and terrible horror.

Martin Cash stayed at his breakfast; he had no desire to add to his already long life in prison.

The riot was brought down by the garrison who, with bayonets fixed, prepared to attack. Fearing death by cold steel the prisoners fled back to their bunks. Westwood and his raiders were captured and placed under guard to await their fate.

Although it was only Westwood who had killed, the rest of the men not even knowing what he planned to do, they were all sentenced to hang.

Kavanagh asked to see Martin Cash before he took the scaffold. He asked Cash's forgiveness for remarks he had made and added that if only he had listened to Cash's advice he wouldn't be where he was that day. Although he said that he was innocent of the crimes for which he was to die, he agreed that 'his conduct in other respects was highly reprehensible'.

Westwood welcomed his moment at the end:
I welcome death as a friend; the world, or what I have seen of it, has no allurements for me... Out of the bitter cup of misery I have drunk from my sixteenth year — ten long years — and the sweetest draught is that which takes away the misery of living death.

'Jacky Jacky' Westwood, Lawrence Kavanagh and ten others were hanged on 13 October 1846. They were tossed into a pit outside the Norfolk Island cemetery. 'Mr Price would not permit them to be buried in consecrated ground.'[1]

RIGHT:
Murderers' mound, burial ground, Norfolk Island
Photograph, c.1860
The bodies of murderous men were not permitted to be laid to rest in consecrated ground. They were simply placed in a common grave outside the cemetery gates.

(Queen Victoria Museum and Art Gallery, Launceston Collection)

BAIL UP!

An End to Transportation

At the time of the demise of 'The Wild Colonial Boy', there were also moves afoot to lobby the British Parliament in an attempt to put an end to transportation. The free settlers were concerned that, with the almost never-ending supply of convicts dumped on Australia's shores, they would never see their society develop into one of culture, enterprise and independent status. They felt the convict stain was being allowed to run too deep. They were also interested in the federation of the separate colonies into one Commonwealth, but these ideas were abhorrent to the British Parliament. After all Australia was a very useful prison; what need was there for its inhabitants to be able to take control of their own destiny? That smacked a little too much of dreaded American-style republicanism.

A conference held in Melbourne in 1851 formed the Australasian Anti-Transportation League whose aim was to put an end to transportation. The league warned the British Parliament that unless the policy of transportation ceased British settlers would quit the colonies. They advised that if the young people of Australia could not travel without feeling:

> … they were born in a degraded section of the globe, we are at a loss to imagine what advantages conferred by sovereignty of Britain can compensate for the stigma of its brand.

ABOVE:
The Australasian Anti-Transportation League Flag (1851)
This silk flag was created fifty years before the federation of the separate Australian colonies into one Commonwealth. How prescient was the design with its blue background emblazoned with a bright southern cross — the new symbol of the national rebel heart.
(Queen Victoria Museum and Art Gallery Launceston Collection)

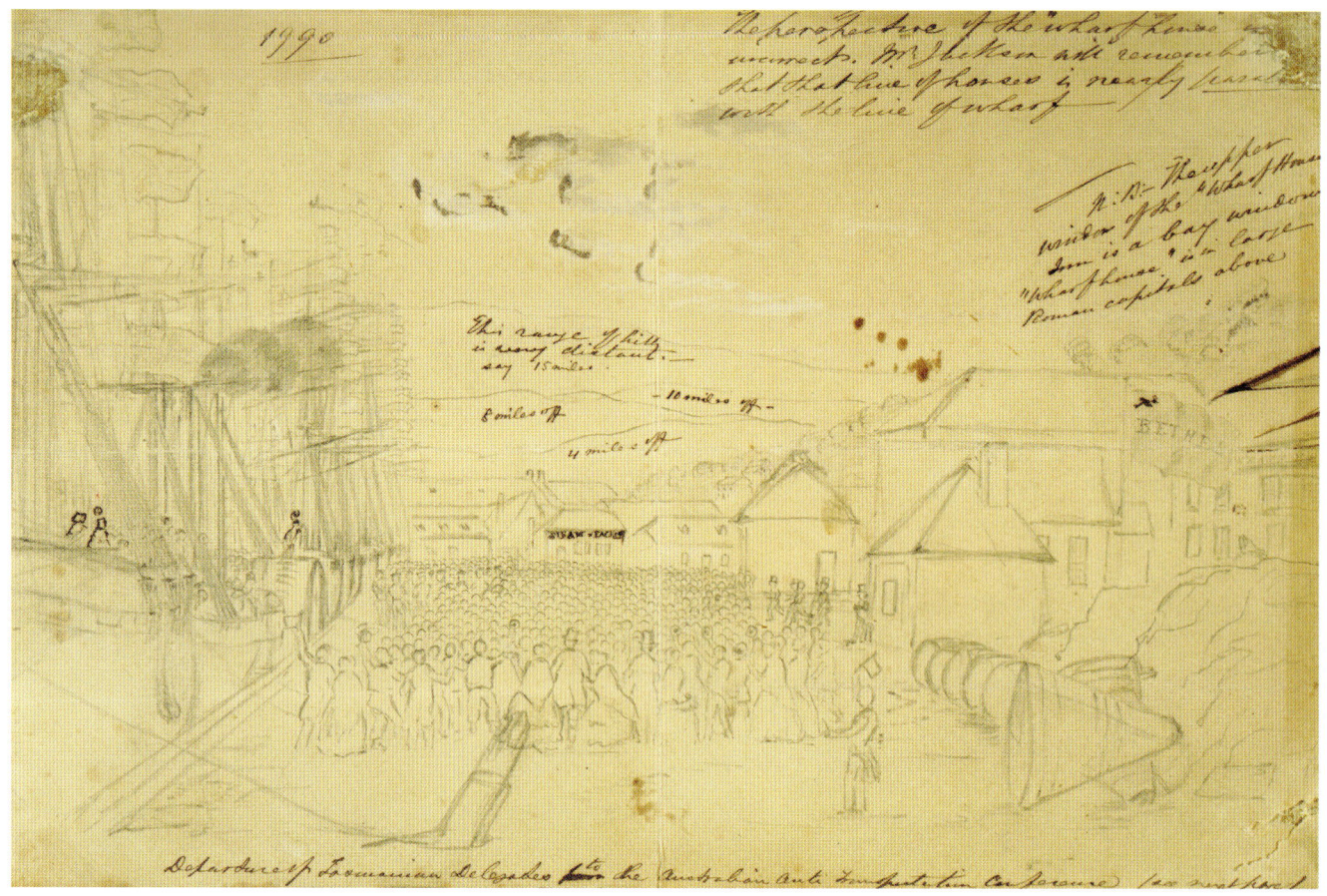

TOP:
Departure of Tasmanian delegates to the Australian Anti-Transportation Conference in Melbourne (1851)
Pencil drawing, artist unknown, 1851
The settled population of Van Diemen's Land was keen to stop the constant flow of convicts to the island. They wanted to build a better society without any more felons marked by the convict stain.
(Rex Nan Kivell Collection NK6870, National Library of Australia)

London, December 29th 1853:– The revocation of the order-in-council making Van Diemen's Land a penal colony has effectively terminated transportation to the Australian colonies.

Sustained pressure from the colonies for self-government, the opening up of Mitchell's 'Australia Felix' that followed the Victorian gold rushes, the separation of Victoria from the colony of New South Wales, which created an independent colony born without convict chains, and the increasing cost of maintaining such a huge and unwieldy prison system led the British Government to accede to the will of the 'new Australians'.

In acknowledging the inevitability of self-determination for the Australian colonies flung so far away from the corridors of 'real' power, the Home Secretary, Lord Palmerston, remarked with a degree of sceptical cynicism:

> We had conceded to those colonies the principle and right of self-government, and that cession being made, we must submit to its consequence.[2]

The *St Vincent* was the last ship to bring convicts to Van Diemen's Land, arriving on 26 May 1853. Convicts were still welcomed in Western Australia, but even that colony came into line with the east when it too received its last 'human cargo' on 10 January 1868. The convict ship the *Hougoumont* docked at Freemantle, discharging 229 convicts including the Irish revolutionary John Boyle O'Reilly and sixty-two other Fenians.

After eighty years of transportation, Britain had shipped to Australia's sunny shores 160 500 of its unwanted citizens of whom 24 700 were women.

It was not long before Caroline Chisholm, the Catholic philanthropist wife of an Indian Army Captain, was filling ships in England with young women to redress this obvious imbalance.

Port Arthur Shuts Down

After three-quarters of a century of suffering and degradation, the penal settlement at Port Arthur closed for business on 17 September 1877. Although the last convict ship had arrived in 1853, it took more than a decade for the remaining prisoners to serve out their terms and be free to leave. Many of those incarcerated at that time were serving time for crimes committed in Australia.

Marcus Clarke, whose epic novel *For The Term of His Natural Life* was published in 1874 and serialised in the *Australian Journal* in 1870, visited Port Arthur a few years before it was closed. The author observed:

> I saw Port Arthur for the first time beneath a leaden and sullen sky; and ... I felt that there was a grim propriety in the melancholy of nature ...
>
> For half a century the law allowed the vagabonds and criminals of England to be subjected to a lingering torment; futile for good and horribly powerful for evil; and it is with feelings of the most profound delight that we view the probable abolition of the last memorial of an error fraught with so much misery.[3]

Clarke had visited the settlement when it was still 'home' to 300 convicts, thirteen convict invalids, eight convict lunatics, 166 paupers and eighty-six lunatics. Clarke was at last able to observe what he had imagined in his monumental work that laid bare the horrors and desperation of the life of the convicted.

RIGHT:
Port Arthur from the Commandant's Gate
Photograph by Stephen Spurling, c. 1906–1930
The gates remain open at Port Arthur; no longer are prisoners tormented by their captivity in this prison at the end of the world. The settlement ceased to exist in 1877.

(Spurling Collection, National Library of Australia)

BAIL UP!
ROBBERY U

The Second Generation – The Scourge of the Settlers

With the demise of 'The Wild Colonial Boy', the governors of the eastern colonies were satisfied that they had put an end at last to the era of bushranging. The marauding bands of desperate runaways had all been rounded up, imprisoned or executed.

They had no such luck.

While there may have been a few years of relative peace in the colonies, the end to transportation, the release and emancipation of the convict classes, the emigration of free workers into the rural and emerging manufacturing economy and the arrival of ship-loads of young women eager to settle into the adventure of colonial life saw a dramatic shift in the colonial power base.

The common man was feeling his strength and demanding his place under the sun. No longer were the working classes prepared to sit back and let the squatters and the politicians (quite often the same people) have it all. The people demanded a fair go, and they weren't going to get it without a long and bitter struggle.

The discovery of gold in 1851 made revolutionary changes to the opportunities available to all who cared to work at it, and the world was soon turned 'topsy-turvy'.

Above:
Bushrangers at work
Wood engraving by Samuel Calvert
Pub. *The Illustrated Melbourne Post*, 2 August 1862
The roads were seemingly safe for a few years after the demise of 'The Wild Colonial Boy', but there were still plenty of 'wild boys' ready to wear the mantle. Most eventually wore the noose instead.
(State Library of Victoria Collection)

There were those who could not wait for that bonanza on a distant horizon. Many of these people were convicts or ex-convicts who had had enough of hard labour and still looked for the easy way out of their misery. Between the years since the death of Donohoe and the discovery of gold, they were the ones who took to the roads in search of 'their share'.

Prisoner of the 'Crown'

A skull had been unearthed at the junction of the Forest and Barker's Creeks in what is now known as the City of Castlemaine. It was dug up by some natives, and Captain John Hepburn, one of the first squatters to pass through the region in 1838, came upon the skull lying in the sand. Hepburn recalled:

> On the brink of a waterhole at the junction of the creeks ... I buried the skull of a prisoner of the Crown who was murdered by his mates after absconding. It was dug up by the natives twice, and the third time I buried it in the dry deposit in the waterhole.

It would appear that the skull was part of the remains of a group of escaped convicts, including George Comerford and Joseph Dignum, who, on bolting from a work party near Yass with six other absconders, made their way towards Melbourne, planning their escape to South Australia. They attacked settlers and homesteads on their way south. Unsure of their whereabouts, they headed west until they crossed through the newly discovered region that was soon to become known as the central Victorian goldfields.

Tiring of his bickering companions and wearied by constant hunger, Comerford decided to go it alone. He waited until the rest had fallen asleep and rose with an axe in hand; Dignum, who must have had the same idea, rose as well. They killed the others as they slept, and just to finish them off they threw their bodies onto the campfire.

The next day Comerford and Dignum set off together for Melbourne. They worked for a while for a squatter they had met on the way, but they had bigger fish to fry. As they left their employment unannounced the squatter had a warrant issued for their arrest. Before they could be brought to trial they broke away again, taking some muskets with them.

Comerford and Dignum went on a bushranging spree before they headed once again for South Australia. This time it was Dignum who decided that he would be better off alone, so he took a shot at Comerford. He missed, and Comerford scurried off, heading back to Melbourne. Hoping to save his own neck, he turned Queen's evidence against his old friend and the pair were eventually brought to trial. Nobody believed Comerford's story about the campfire in the Castlemaine creeks so he was taken back into the district to prove his account.

The police who escorted Comerford back to the foothills of Mt Alexander were shocked to discover that his account was true; bones, skulls and blackened clothing were still sticking out of the ashes of the long-cold fire.

On the way back to Melbourne Comerford escaped again. After snatching up the carbine of one officer who had left it standing against a tree, he turned and killed the officer as he attempted to rush at him. Once again George Comerford was at large. He returned to his old tricks, and eventually a reward of £50 was offered for his capture. A convict hutkeeper named Kangaroo Jack recognised Comerford when he came into a hut on a cattle station just out of town. As Comerford settled down in front of the fire and proceeded to light his pipe, Kangaroo Jack belted him over the head, knocking him to the floor. He was soon set upon by others in the hut, then bound and carted away once again to face the judge.

To make sure that Comerford didn't escape again, this time the judge ordered that he be taken away and hanged by the neck until dead. Dignum escaped the ultimate penalty, sentenced to only seven years for his part in the murder of seven convicts. George Comerford died on the gallows for the murder of one policeman. Who says that British justice isn't fair?

Victoria had attracted the refuse of the adjoining penal settlement of Van Diemen's Land, herded together and [they] were ready to undertake any crime.

— MCCOMBIE AUSTRALIAN SKETCHES

BAIL UP!

A HINT FOR DOWNING STREET

THE REFORMED EXILES

E.J.HARTY, LITH. 9, DAME ST DUBLIN.

Dark Roads to the Diggings

In 1851 gold was discovered near Bathurst in New South Wales. In September of the same year, gold was discovered in the central highlands of the newly separated Colony of Victoria.

Within months of these discoveries thousands of eager gold-seekers rushed into the goldfields from across colonial borders, across Bass Strait and from across the seas.

At one time there were so many ships left crewless in Port Phillip that the scene resembled a European pine forest. As ships lay offshore their sails furled on masts thrust silently into the sky.

Among the thousands of hopeful 'new chums' were the old lags, the 'vandemonians', the absconders from the chain gangs and work parties who had found their way across Bass Strait with the sealers and whalers who had, for many years, been lying-to in the safe harbours of the southern coast.

The 'vandemonians' were the most feared of all in the new colony. These men, and some women, who had been brutalised by the lash and triangle, and seen all manner of deprivation and degredation, had little time for the niceties of the civilisation that they had left behind them so long ago when they were first trundled aboard the prison ships and cast out of their homeland.

Once freed from the chains of their oppressors, the 'vandemonians' treated those they found on the roads in much the same way as they had been treated when they were held captive.

Lord Robert Cecil wrote in his journal following a trip to the central Victorian diggings that 'Mr Latrobe [the Governor] told me that no fewer than 400 were missing from Van Diemen's Land, and were doubtless at the diggings'.

Lord Cecil continues in his diary: 'These men, though bad characters, have a wholesome respect for the law from having been experimentally made

---

ABOVE:
A Hint for Downing Street, the Reformed Exiles
Lithograph by E.J Harty (Dublin), c.1850
This satirical illustration is mocking the efforts of the colonial governors in releasing convicts from their bonds. Here the 'reformed' ex-convict is readily lapsing into old ways.
(Rex Nan Kivell Collection NK1642/A, National Library of Australia)

acquainted with its terrors; and they dare not brave it openly'.[1]

It was a common practice for bushrangers to ask travellers on the road whether they were 'going up' or 'coming down'. Wayfarers were in greater danger if they answered 'coming down' as it would be assumed that they carried gold receipts, cheques or money with them – which they wouldn't keep for much longer:

> It was not an uncommon thing in those days for "road agents" to take into the bush anyone who had gold receipts or cheques, bind him to a tree and place a sentinel over him, and then despatch one of their number to Melbourne either to cash the cheque or to get possession of the gold by giving up the receipt ... [2]

So wrote gold-digger William Craig who travelled the roads to Bendigo and Ballarat in the 1850s. He also wrote:

> A little before noon we sighted a spring-cart *en route* for Melbourne, in which were seated a man and a woman who informed us they had come from Ballarat, and had been bailed up at their camp the previous night by five men ... the robbers had taken from them about five pounds' weight of gold, and what money and valuables they possessed, with the exception of an old silver watch ... [3]

Craig records that the woman had recovered her treasured keepsake from the top branch of a tall tree where one of the villains had placed it after she had 'roundly abused them'. She refused to give up her

---

ABOVE:
Bushranger on His Way Back from the Goldfields
Watercolour by William Strutt, 1851
Captain Dana's native troops were well respected by the diggers but after his early death they were disbanded. Several tried their hand at digging, but without the uniform they were just as vulnerable to discrimination as any other man.
(State Parliamentary Library Collection, Victoria)

BAIL UP!

Black Douglas

Black Douglas was a mulatto Indian who began his bushranging career around the Maryborough region. He later moved operations to the Black Forest on the road between Melbourne and Forest Creek and Bendigo.

Hundreds of diggers made their way up and down this road daily, and everyone of them was aware of the dangers that lurked within that darkened forest of close-growing tall trees and thick scrub. Tracks wound all over the forest floor, and the unwary traveller could easily lose his way, his possessions or his life.

There are many records of confrontations with Black Douglas, or there are at least countless references to him in diaries and recollections of adventures on the diggings. The name 'Black Douglas' was the most feared of all. It was the one name that all travellers were warned of before they set off for the goldfields.

He pops up time and again:

> I saw at one time sixteen ... poor fellows fastened to a log with that notorious robber, Black Douglas ...

So wrote Henry Leversha in a letter to the Castlemaine Pioneers in 1880, when describing licence defaulters chained 'to the logs' at the Castlemaine Police Camp.

A Polish migrant, Seweryn Korzelinksi, who had a shop on the Alma goldfield near Maryborough in Victoria, recalled that Black Douglas and his band of thieves had made their headquarters only three miles away. While they pretended to work at gold-digging, their main occupation was stealing from tents and shops. This was an easy sort of robbing as the tents were empty during the day and the shops at night:

> The method was to organise a fight late at night in the vicinity of the front of the shop, and when the merchant came out curious to see the fisticuffs, accomplices would cut the canvas wall at the rear and grab what they could.[4]

Korzelinski recalled the capture of Black Douglas when the diggers, fed up with the thieves, surrounded their tents one night, tied the robbers up and burnt the tents to the ground. Douglas, who was a huge and powerful man, fought hardest until he was wounded, and then able to be overpowered. He was carted to Maryborough with an escort of more than 200 miners.

Korzelinski says that he was taken to Melbourne and hanged, but there is no record today that confirms the demise of Black Douglas.

GOLD LEVIED WITHOUT LICENSE.

"They were standing against a gum-tree, with their double-barrelled rifles, with which they intended, the first opportunity, to make a hole in the *living clay* of some successful digger who might be returning to deposit his findings in Melbourne."

watch as it was a gift from a near relative, given to her before she had left the 'old country'.

Craig felt the woman had been quite forthright with the bushrangers in expressing her demands, but she said that she had been in the colonies for several years and was not ready to give in so easily. Curiously enough, the villains did leave her this prized possession – just that it was at the top of a tree – and 'she might have it if she cared to climb for it'.

There was one name that was on every digger's lips as he set off for the diggings – 'Black Douglas':

> Before we started next morning we heard of bushrangers, Black Douglas and his men were about, and as the majority of us were armed we felt particularly plucky, but as we would not know a bushranger if we saw him we suspected everybody ... I really think that if anyone had looked black at

ABOVE:
Gold levied without license
Lithograph by S.T. Gill, c. 1853

'They were standing against a gum-tree, with their double-barrelled rifles, with which they intended, the first opportunity, to make a hole in the *living clay* of some successful digger who might be returning to deposit his findings in Melbourne'.
(From The Gold-Finder in Australia *by John Sherer, pub. Clarke, Beeton & Co., 1853)*

us we would have done a bit of shooting, but if, on the other hand, a revolver had been pointed at us, I have my doubts of the pluck holding out.[5]

Everyone had to go armed as there was so much sticking up and horse stealing. Many a poor fellow had been put out of the way during those times, and never heard of any more. It was every man for himself.[6]

We unloaded, and returned to a place called the Devil's Elbow, where we camped. A man rode up, and after fastening his horse came towards my cousin. Suspicions were aroused, so he went towards his dray and got underneath. I stood by the fire and had an axe in my hand. He came towards me, asked me for a drink, at the same time pulling a bottle from his coat pocket. As his coat lifted, I saw two revolvers stuck in his belt. I declined, as I saw his object was to get us together and then he would have stuck us up …[7]

Then, later, back on the road to Bendigo …

One night as I came through the Black Forest, two men suddenly sprang out from the bushes, and sang out for me to stop. I had between £60 and £70 in my pocket. My horses were fresh and lively, and I slashed my whip around them in a moment, and if the men had not jumped out of the way, my cart would have dashed over them; thus I saved myself from being robbed …[8]

Bushrangers stick up returning diggers, tie them to trees, rob them of their gold, whether concealed in belts or boots. This plunder they spend in debauchery, and so endure the headaches that the lucky digger escapes by being fleeced.[9]

Whilst we were camped in the Black Forest . . . some highwaymen slit our tent with the intention of robbing us, but the men who were camped along with us heard the would-be depredators and immediately opened fire on them. Our visitors took to their horses and made off, firing back at us as they galloped away …[10]

There were any number of bandits who caused concern on the roads to and from all of the goldfields both in Victoria and New South Wales, and there are some familiar and famous names among them – Captain Melville, Captain Moonlight, Captain Thunderbolt – to name but the most adventurous of them all. However, there were also plenty of others whose selection of witty sobriquet was not as exciting as these three grand 'gentlemen of the highways'.

ABOVE:
Melbourne 1855, as seen from the north, near the road to Mt Alexander
Lithograph by Henry Burn, 1855
Diggers make their way north to the central Victorian goldfields as a heavy-guarded gold escort brings the booty back to the treasury. Some of the most spectacular hold-ups were on such parties.
(La Trobe Picture Collection, State Library of Victoria)

BAIL UP!

The Robbery of the Brig *Nelson*

Under cover of darkness on 2 April 1852, an unknown number of men took two boats from Mr Liardet's mooring at Sandridge Pier and, with muffled oars, rowed out to the brig *Nelson* anchored two miles down the bay. They quietly clambered aboard. The bulk of the crew had scarpered for the diggings, leaving only a few sailors and passengers aboard that night. They were asleep in their bunks when they were wakened by shouts from the upper-deck.

As each man came upon the deck to see what the fuss was all about, he was immediately grabbed and lashed to the bulwark. One of the assailants demanded that Draper, the mate in-charge, show him where the hoard of gold was hidden.

The *Nelson* had just been loaded with £25 000 worth of gold, 8000 ounces in twenty-three boxes had been ferried ashore during the day, and it seemed that nobody considered a waterborne assault as any threat to the security of this treasure.

Draper refused to comply with the demands of his attacker and received a shot in his side, and a few pokes with a sword as further encouragement. Fearing that he would be killed, he gave in and showed the 'pirates' to the strongroom.

They broke down the door and carried the twenty-three boxes out onto the deck. Locking all those aboard inside, they nailed the strongroom door back into place. The robbers lowered the gold into Liardet's boats, and then headed back for the shore. The gold was buried in the sand and recovered the next day.

TOP:
Bushrangers Waiting for the Mails in New South Wales
Watercolour by S.T. Gill, c. 1851
Two desperados behind the scrub, with rifles readied, await the arrival of the mail coach.
(La Trobe Picture Collection, State Library of Victoria)

BELOW:
The Nelson *in dry dock*
Photograph by Charles Nettleton, 1878
(National Library of Australia Collection)

The unfortunate crew and passengers were forced to stay in the strongroom until a stevedore came upon them the next morning.

A reward was offered for the capture of any of the large number of men who had taken part in the daring and most lucrative robbery. For capture and conviction £250 was offered, and a further £500 from the consignors of the gold, Jackson, Rae & Co.

Before long some familiar old felons were taken into custody – 'vandemonians' all – John James, transportee fifteen years VDL, James Morgan, transportee fifteen years VDL, James Duncan, stonemason free on arrival in the colony but took to bushranging around the Black Forest area at the beginning of the gold rushes, and Stephen Fox, transportee. There were inconsistencies in the reported account of this black night; some say there were seven or eight bandits, others estimate as many as twenty-five, while some are convinced there were only four. Whatever the number, there were also others who were added to the list and may well have faced court for a crime they did not have commit, but no doubt would have proud to have had the audacity to pull of such a big heist.

At the Geelong court on 29 June 1852 Duncan, James, Morgan and Fox were each sentenced to fifteen years on the roads, with the first three years to be spent in irons.

BAIL UP!

Daylight Robbery on St Kilda Road

The Argus, 18/10/1852
BUSHRANGERS ON THE ST. KILDA ROAD:–
On Saturday night information was given at the Police station that four mounted and armed bushrangers were committing the most daring depredations on the St. Kilda and Brighton Road. About five o'clock in the evening, Mr and Mrs Bawfree were stopped, bailed up, and robbed, and upwards of fifteen other persons were also stopped that evening by the same gang.

A watch was then kept up and down the road, and every individual who came up on foot, or horseback, or in a vehicle, for two hours and a half, was stopped, and robbed.

This daring daylight robbery certainly captured the attention of the citizens of Port Phillip. They may have been aware of the bandits in the bush, but they certainly didn't expect them in the town. While the St Kilda to Brighton Road was, at that time, still in open country, influential citizens had already begun to establish properties south of the river and surrounding the bay and they were ripe for picking.

When John Flanigan, Thomas Williams and three others bailed up, they created the sort of fuss that had the media buzzing. John Sherer wrote in his book *The Gold-Finder in Australia*, published in 1853:

ABOVE:
Study for Bushrangers on the St Kilda Road
Pencil drawing by William Strutt, 1886
Strutt's meticulous attention to detail can be seen in the many drawings he sketched before tackling the big canvas. They seem as fresh and contemporary as any works done over the next 150 years.
(National Library of Australia Collection)

On Saturday afternoon, about half-past three o'clock of a bright sunny day, two residents of Brighton – W. Keel and W. Robinson – were driving in a cart along the high road leading past the St. Kilda racecourse leading to the special survey. Two men were walking before them at a little distance. They saw two or three other men, with guns at their sides, apparently looking up into the trees for birds. On a sudden they found themselves surrounded, guns were placed at their heads, and at that of the horse; and they were ordered to dismount.

The attack was so outrageous that they thought it was a joke; but as they were addressed in the most abusive language, and told that their brains would be blown out if they delayed, they got out of the cart and submitted to be rifled …[11]

One of these men lost £23 and the other £46 before they were both ordered into a wattle scrub, tied hand to hand and forced to sit on the ground. What an indignity!

The two men that they had just passed on the road were brought in to join them, robbed, tied, bound and also on the ground. For the next hour and a half every individual on foot, horseback or vehicle

---

ABOVE:
Study for Bushrangers, 12 figures all sitting at once for proportion
Pencil drawing by William Strutt, 1886
Strutt used these sketches as the basis for a large oil painting executed when he returned to England. While living in Brighton, Victoria at the time of the robberies he observed at close hand the impact this event had on the people of the colony.
(Rex Nan Kivell Collection NK3967/1, National Library of Australia)

BAIL UP!

suffered the same indignity. There were now twenty-seven hapless citizens lined up in the wattle beside the St Kilda Road. When a Mr and Mrs Bawtree came along the road in their jaunty gig, they too were manhandled into the bush. Bawtree complained of this profanity and demanded that his wife not be subjected to a search. One of the bushrangers shouted at him with the vilest of bad language that he would have his brains blown out if he didn't move along pretty smartly. As this couple was being forced to the ground, one raider instructed another to 'put them all together, so that if you miss one, you will kill another'.[12]

A gentleman on horseback came trotting down the road. He too was called to surrender, but he was not to be taken. He dug his spurs deeply into the flanks of his mount and galloped off. Two shots were fired after him as cries of murder were heard from the bush. One of the bushrangers, apparently worse for the liquor, started to become very loud and aggressive, when one the others, angrily, advised him: 'You had better be quiet; there has been one man shot already. I should not like to shoot another.'

Diggers Attacked on the Mt Alexander Road

Flanigan and Williams were among a party of bushrangers who were active across the roads to the goldfields. At Flanigan's trial for the stick-up at Aitken's Gap, at the foot of the Great Dividing Range just north of Melbourne, his guilt was confirmed when one of the diggers he had robbed claimed the pistol found on Flanigan as his own.

Anthony Waring proved that the 'A.W.' carved on the stock of the gun was most assuredly him and not the initials of the captive John Flanigan (whose real name was Owen Gibney anyway – born Dublin, transported to Van Diemen's Land in 1842 for seven years for the crime of highway robbery).

It seems that even after a decade on the roads and several years in irons, Flanigan had not had enough of the highways. He was back in court again for playing the same old game.

Flanigan spent his next ten years inside the floating hulks in Hobson's Bay. There were no roads there for him to roam.

At sundown the bushrangers drew off the man acting as guard, and shortly afterwards the sound of horse's feet was heard galloping off through the bush apparently in the direction of South Yarra. They [the victims] then liberated themselves, and proceeded to their residences.

However, this affront to the good citizens of the Port Phillip district was not to go unanswered. A £2000 reward for information leading to the capture of the 'five armed Bushrangers' was offered on 19 October. The eager bounty hunter was about to be disappointed as the police apprehended two men in Flinders Lane just after the reward had been posted. Some policemen had approached two suspicious-looking horsemen just after midnight. When they were unable to give a satisfactory reply to the officers' questions they were summarily pulled off their saddles and taken into custody. The horsemen were none other than John Flanigan and Thomas Williams, who were responsible for a hold-up at Aitken's Gap on the Mt Alexander Road earlier that same day.

Flanigan was carrying £47, Williams £55 in notes and sovereigns, and a small nugget, obviously souvenired from the diggers they had robbed on the road to the Mt Alexander diggings. He also had a bundle of clothing and two 'chooks' trussed up ready for their dinner. Both had with them a pair of loaded pistols.

At their trial, a pistol stolen at Aitken's Gap was used in evidence against Flanigan. It bore the mark 'A.W.' on its stock, and one of the diggers robbed at Aitken's Gap was there to declare it belonged to him.

Victims of the earlier robbery at St Kilda were also called as witnesses, and they all remembered the pair who had so sorely interrupted their journey along the Brighton Road.

Flanigan and Williams were gone – both received thirty years for their jaunt south of the Yarra.

Williams later paid the ultimate price, going to his death on the gallows for his part in the brutal murder of Inspector-General John Price at the Gellibrand Quarries in March 1854.

'Captain Melville'

Frank McCallum – alias 'Captain Melville' – and William Roberts held up diggers Thomas Wearne and William Madden on the road to Ballarat on 19 December 1852. Melville was one bushranger who seemed to have a split personality. He was, on the one hand, a charmer, polite and gallant especially where the ladies were concerned; on the other hand, he could turn, in an instant, to unseeming brutality.

McCallum had been transported to Van Diemen's Land in 1838 at the age of twelve. He was one of the 'boy convicts' who were sent out to the colony at the time when there was a repeated push for an end to transportation, and 'free' labour was becoming scarce.

The government thought that boys would pose no threat to the community, so they rounded up 150 petty thieves, pickpockets, pimps and pederasts and sent them into a swirling morass of pain and loneliness. Few of these boys survived their interment; without suitable adult examples, few of these boys survived their education at the hands of the 'old masters' without returning to the only life they had once known. Prison was no reforming power: it simply served to debase the juveniles at the pleasure of the old lags.

It is a surprise that young Frank had turned out so well at all. He arrived in Port Phillip in late 1851, intending to look for gold, but like so many other 'vandemonians' he too tried to get it the easy way.

William Craig met Captain Melville when he visited Cartwright's home-station at Sailor Creek to purchase his weekly provisions. As he came towards, the property he observed a well-cared-for horse tethered to the front fence of the house. Thinking it must have been the horse of a government official, he lifted the latch and entered the kitchen where he was surprised to be staring into the barrel of a revolver:

> I found myself facing a revolver and was ordered in a peremptory way to throw up my hands ... my facial aspect, and perhaps my then somewhat

---

ABOVE:
Lake Albert Mounted Police Chasing Bushrangers, Overland from Port Phillip to South Australia
Watercolour by S.T. Gill, c.1840
(Rex Nan Kivell Collection NK2043. National Library of Australia Collection)

BAIL UP!

dilapidated 'new chum' clothing, afforded him considerable amusement, and with a loud hearty laugh he lowered the weapon and ordered me to [sit].[13]
Melville had been eating when Craig walked through the door, and after he was satisfied that Craig was no threat he continued with his meal. Craig observed that he was well dressed and ate with refinement. His language was polite and without blasphemy, but when he heard a footfall on the verandah step he swung about as quick as lightning and his revolver was once again covering another poor digger as he stepped into the room. Melville asked the digger if he had any money, and when he replied that he had only a few shillings, Melville proferred him one pound and a few shillings from his own pocket, half of what he had himself, saying, 'Well, old man. I'm Melville the outlaw – you've doubtless heard of me. I'm not flush of loose cash just now, but I'll share what I have with you.'

Craig also observed the way in which Melville treated his horse. When the horse heard his master approaching he whinnied with pleasure; Melville fondled and whispered to the beast, watered him and the horse responded, rubbing his nose against the outlaw's face and shoulders. Swinging up onto his mount, his rifle slung across his shoulders, he lightly touched the horse's flanks and disappeared into the Bullarook Forest. Craig was sorry that he heard no more of the charming Captain Melville until his name began to appear in the newspapers.

After taking £33 from Wearne and Madden, on the road to Geelong he handed back £10 as it was so close to close to Christmas he didn't want to spoil the holiday they were planning when they got there. Melville was heading that way himself. That holiday was to prove his undoing. With his mate, William Roberts, they continued down the road, sticking-up and stealing from everyone they met on their way.

It had been a long and lonely time on the road, and they began their festivities with a trip to a house of ill-fame. Roberts was ready for a drink and Melville for a bit of the other. After a while, Roberts, a little worse for liquor, couldn't stop himself from boasting to the girl he was with. He declared himself to be a bushranger – in the company of 'Captain Melville'.

The lass slipped away at the first opportunity and summoned the police. Melville tried to escape by knocking one of the policemen off his horse, but he was not successful in gaining his freedom. He was handcuffed and led away to await his fate.

Tried and convicted in February 1853, the 'Captain' was sentenced to the hulks at Williamstown. Now aged thirty Frank McCallum was again imprisoned; this time the hulk *Success* was to be his floating hell for the next thirty-two years.

McCallum wasn't at all fond of prison life. He began this sentence attacking a warder threatening to bite off his nose. For this he was flogged and spent the next twenty days in solitary confinement.

Each day the convicts were taken ashore in launches where they laboured in the construction of wharves and other buildings around the bay. Some worked breaking stones at the Gellibrand quarries. McCallum was aboard one boat when nine of the convicts seized the tow rope and attacked the guard throwing him overboard. The owner of the boat refused to leave, and he was brained by one of the other prisoners with his stone-breaking hammer. Shots were fired at them from the *Success*, killing one of the rioters. Melville and the murderous crew headed off down Hobson's Bay, making for a schooner they planned to seize to make their escape from Port Phillip.

The sentinel on the hulk had signalled to the shore, and a police launch set off, taking the bolters into custody agin. Now, heavily chained, they were cast back into their cells.

McCallum received the death penalty for this affray, but as the Crown could not show a warrant for his being removed from one boat to another he was spared on a technicality. His sentence was commuted to life imprisonment. After a glorious life on

MELVILLE'S CAVES.

the diggings, dressed in the flashest of clothes, astride a gleaming steed, the ladies at his feet, the prospect of spending the rest of his miserable days aboard a rotting hulk must have proved too much for him. It was also believed that McCallum had planned the attack on Inspector Price *(see page 87)* as part of his plans for a general revolt of convicts.

He became his own executioner, choking himself with a handkerchief in August 1857. Roberts had also been sentenced to thirty-two years, in the hulk *President*. He was released in 1864.

ABOVE:
Melville's Cave at Mt Kooyoora, Victoria
(La Trobe Picture Collection, State Library of Victoria)

Melville's Caves

Rumours have it that 'Captain Melville' had stashed his ill-gotten gains somewhere in the many caves that riddle this granite outcrop at Mt Kooyoora, near Inglewood, on the central north-eastern Victorian goldfields.

Melville would retreat into his fastness in these hills after a raid, and the police could never get near him.

As William Craig had observed, Melville had developed a unique relationship with his horse Bob and Bob was as good as any watchdog, alerting Melville of the arrival of any interlopers that may have placed his gentle master in jeopardy.

It is a pity, for Melville, that his Bob was not allowed into that brothel in Geelong on that fateful day.

BAIL UP!

BELOW:
Attacking the Mail, Bushranging, NSW
Chromolithograph printed by Hamel & Ferguson, 1864
from a drawing by S.T. Gill
(National Library of Australia Collection)

Robbery on the Roads

In July 1853 four young enterprising American gentlemen arrived in the Colony of Victoria with the intention of establishing a coaching business that would service the Victorian goldfields. The first coaches ran between Melbourne and Castlemaine, the closest diggings to Port Phillip at that time.

By 1862 they had moved the centre of their operations to Bathurst, the oldest inland settlement in Australia at the heart of the New South Wales goldfields. Before the end of the century Cobb & Co. had coaches running all over the country.

Although Cobb & Co. coaches ran across Australia for almost eighty years, ceasing its last Queensland operations in 1929, there were surprisingly few hold-ups, considering the enormous number of trips taken. But those that faced the barrel of the bandits' gun certainly made the news of their day and have their place written proudly into Australia's history books.

Cobb & Co.'s coaches were held up thirty-six times. There was a period when hold-ups were more frequent than others. In the years 1862 and 1863 coaches around Forbes and Bathurst were attacked by bushrangers on at least nine occasions.

Attacks had become so frequent that a special Commissioner was appointed to try the accused felons in Sydney in February 1863. On 10 February, three men were sentenced to be hanged on the one day, five more sentenced to fifteen years hard labour, one to ten and another to twelve.

At times the attackers did not have it all their own way. There were times when passengers fought back against their attackers. On 20 April 1868 bank manager Mr R. D. White fought back against five armed attackers who had bailed up the Gympie coach. He only escaped with his life by leaping from the coach and hiding in the bush beside the track.

On 6 January the following year the Reverend G. E. King and another brave bank manager, Mr W. E. King, also resisted an attack on the coach in which they were riding, wounding their attackers in their defence. Although the bandits still managed to abscond with £25, one was captured and sentenced to twenty years for his crime.

The McIvor Escort

On 20 July 1853 a gang of bushrangers attacked the Melbourne Gold Escort Company as it was carrying gold and mail from the McIvor (Heathcote) diggings en route to Kyneton where it was to meet up with the convoy from Bendigo.

As the dray, protected by a superintendent, a sergeant and four troopers, turned a difficult bend in the road the driver was forced to swing around a large tree that was fallen across his way. As the superintendent came closer to the tree he became suspicious and called the escort to a halt.

Two men were secreted behind the fallen trunk and immediately opened fire. The troopers were also greeted with a volley of shots that rang out from an 'Aboriginal-style shelter' that had been thrown up beside the road. The driver of the dray was killed and several officers were wounded, but not wanting to suffer the same fate as their driver, they turned tail and fled in the middle of a sustained attack. Approximately 2230 ounces of gold lay ripe for the picking.

The superintendent had dashed through the barricade and galloped off to the nearest police station where he raised the alarm. The others had headed back to McIvor.

On Monday, 23 July, a reward was posted:

£250 for the apprehension and conviction of the parties who robbed the McIvor branch of the escort … and a further sum of £250 for the recovery of the stolen property, or a proportional sum, for the recovery of part thereof.

It wasn't long at all before most of the gang was apprehended attempting to leave the colony. There were so many characters with a past spent in chains abroad in the community that any felon would have

ABOVE:
Hold-up of the Gold Escort (A Bush Hold-up)
Pen and wash drawing by William Strutt, c. 1855
(National Library of Australia)

BAIL UP!

ATTACK ON THE GOLD ESCORT BETWEEN McIVOR AND MELBOURNE.

little chance of hiding his identity among them all. Generous rewards brought speedy arrests.

Only £2501/10s. in gold notes, sovereigns and bankdrafts were recovere. Most of the booty was suspected of already having left the country. It was also believed that a large part of the Bendigo Petition of 1853 also disappeared with the gold, so thousands of miners who had signed to show their displeasure at the government gold-license fee did not have their voice heard thanks to the McIvor Road robbers.

Some of those responsible for the daring daylight raid committed suicide before they were brought to justice. Three were sent to the gallows.

The leader of the gang was a man named Gray. It is believed that he was one of a large number of ruffians believed to have been on board the *Madagascar*, which was lying in Hobson's Bay, ready for sea, at the time of the robbery.

While all of the rest of the gang had got down to Melbourne by various routes, one of two brothers, George Francis, returned to McIvor where his abscence had been noted. As he couldn't account for his whereabouts on the day of the robbery, he was placed under arrest. He confessed all, but on his way to Melbourne for trial he became so distressed that he had betrayed his mates, especially his brother, that he got hold of a razor and slit his throat from ear to ear.

One of the other hold-up merchants, George Wilson, had already paid for his ticket on the *Madagascar*, but it was his fondness for strong liquor that also saw him captured. He was safely aboard the ship when the police searched the vessel for ticket-of-leave men. Narrowly avoiding discovery he thought the coast was clear and decided to have a few drinks, but he had a few too many.

He was playing cards when he drew his revolver and threatened to shoot his playing companion. The water police were summoned from the shore, and Wilson was summarily placed under arrest and taken away. Fearing that one of his mates must have turned traitor, he too confessed everything, then instructed the officer to pull in alongside a barque making ready to sail to Mauritus. Once on deck, Wilson inquired if a George Melville (not to be confused with Frank McCallum, or Edward Melville or any of the other Melvilles who misbehaved on the roads to the goldfields) was aboard and to everyone's surprise Melville appeared. The police had been looking for him on another charge and were more than pleased to make his acquaintance finally.

William Atkins, George Wilson and George Melville paid for their assault on the gold escort – they climbed to the gallows and were hanged before a huge crowd on 3 October 1853. It took so long for George Melville to expire that the hangman had to pull down on his legs with 'considerable force before life was extinct'.

Melville's devoted young wife took George's corpse back to be displayed in the window of an oyster shop in Bourke Street, Melbourne, where it must have proved an excellent advertising gimmick. Following this incident all bodies of executed felons were buried within the walls of the prison.

The *Madagascar* sailed from Port Phillip and was never heard of again. She had on board £60 000 of gold and a large number of homeward-bound diggers who had made their fortunes on the goldfields. There were also, unfortunately, a large number of hardened felons and ticket-of-leave men whose appearance on board should have made the captain quake in his boots. It is believed that some of the men implicated in the *Nelson* robbery were also on board.

Rumours were abroad for many years, some saying that the ship headed for Patagonia where the gold was put into long-boats and, as it was ferried ashore, the ship was sunk by bandits who, after throwing all other passengers overboard, drilled holes in the hull. Others say it caught fire and all aboard perished, or it hit an iceberg or:

... as human monsters had taken passage in her who were capable of surpassing in atrocity the deeds of the Spanish main, it is not all unlikely that the ship was scuttled.[14]

Gray, the leader, was never heard of again.

OPPOSITE:
Attack on the gold escort between McIvor and Melbourne
Engraving, published in *Cassall's Picturesque Australasia*, 1889
(Private Collection)

BAIL UP!

Conveying Gold from the Diggings to Melbourne. The Government Escort. 1851.

The Ballarat Bank Robbery

Although ticket-of-leave meant that ex-convicts were free to work, and to live, making their own way in the colony, they were expected to remain within the boundaries of the district indicated on their ticket. Few did.

When the water police inspected the *Nelson* and the *Madagascar* looking for the gold thieves, they were, primarily, looking for ticket-of-leaves absconding from the colony and making their own way back to England.

There were four such fellows who had made their way to the Bank of Victoria at Ballarat on 14 October 1854. The bank on Bakery Hill, the sight of continuous agitation over the next few months, was a wood-framed building clad with galvanised iron, known locally as the 'Iron Pot'.

The four robbers, John Bolton, Henry Garrett, Henry Marriott and Thomas Quinn, were all 'graduates' of Port Arthur. Their backs bore the marks of their education, and their ankles still bore the scars of the irons that once kept them at bay.

Quinn had travelled up from Geelong to join his old companions in their quest for riches, but didn't want to be involved in the robbery if there was going to be any violence. So they agreed to do their hold-up with unloaded pistols.

The four waited outside the building until closing time and, timing their entry just right, walked into the bank at the end of a good trading day. They profferred their empty pistols at the tellers and offered to blow their brains out if any more than a whisper was raised.

The bank employees had their arms and legs 'fastened together like trussed fowls' and were forced to lie down on the floor while the bandits helped themselves to the open vault.

Without any further ado they got away with £18 000 in notes and gold, and headed for an abandoned shaft near the Gravel Pits, which was also the site of most of the agitation leading up to the events of 3 December, two months later that year.

After dividing up their ill-gotten gains, the gang split up and went their separate ways.

While this may have seemed the perfect crime – no one was hurt, no one was recognised and they all got away clean with a large sum of money – unfortunately for the gang the cash had only been delivered to the bank by escort on the morning of the robbery and a dutiful clerk had already made a record of the numbers on this fresh delivery of crisp £50, £20 and £10 notes.

Garrett, like Gray before him, cut himself off from his companions. He travelled down to Port Phillip, sailed up to Sydney and boarded a ship for England. Marriott and Quinn carried their share down to Geelong in a covered wagon where they lay low for a while in a boarding-house, while the third burglar, Bolton, lay low in Ballarat.

The 'lady' of the boarding-house was no longer enamoured of her husband. On hearing that a bank at Ballarat had just been hit and observant of the manner with which her newly arrived guests liberally splashed their cash around, she waited for her moment. Once her guests had gone out on a spree, she gave their room a once over. Finding the cache of banknotes, nuggets, gold dust and coins under the floor covers, inside the mattresses and in their swags, she saw an easy solution to her marital woes.

With her portmanteau filled with loot and a male companion at her side, she was off, also to Sydney.

TOP:
Conveying Gold from the Diggings to Melbourne, 1851
The Government Gold Escort, 1852
Watercolour by William Strutt, 1852
Gold and notes were carried up and down the roads on convoys such as these. Although heavily guarded the prize aboard was too great to be discounted by the desperate felon.

(State Parliamentary Library Collection, Victoria)

OPPOSITE:
Deep Sinking, Ballarat
Lithograph by S.T. Gill, published by J. Blundell & Co., Melbourne, 1855
The gravel pits at the Eureka diggings required a consistent effort of over six months work to get at the gold-bearing rock. This meant that a huge investment was needed, and the delay and costs were often the cause of so much agitation against the government licence fee.

(Rex Nan Kivell Collection S3954, National Library of Australia)

The Government Gold Escort, 1852. — William Strutt

When the burglars returned to their room, they discovered to their surprise that someone else had been rummaging through their 'belongings'. When they inquired of their landlady and discovered that she too was missing, they put two and two together. Wisely, Marriott decided that the best thing to do was just to shut up; after all they had been left with 'the biggest share of the cake'.

When the landlady attempted to pass a £20 note in Sydney, she was, unfortunately, in a tradesman's shop who had in his possession a list of the stolen notes, which the Ballarat bank had quickly disseminated across the colonies. Not wanting to spend the rest of her days in prison, she spilled the beans, leading to the arrest of Marriott, Quinn and Bolton, who was by this time in Adelaide readying to board a vessel, 'homeward-bound'.

By this time Garrett was already in London. Although Scotland Yard had received news of the robbery from a ship that had arrived a few days earlier, Garrett had cleverly come aboard on the pilot-ship before his vessel had docked.

He was in Regent Street one day when he heard a voice behind him cry out: 'Hullo Garrett, when did you arrive?' Some say that Inspector Webb had called out with the bush cry 'Coo-ee!', but whatever the cry, Garrett was caught unawares, turned and gave himself away. Taken back to his hotel a large amount of the stolen property was discovered in his room. He was brought back to Melbourne to stand trial.

The four Ballarat bank robbers were each sentenced to ten years hard labour. When questioned by counsel if he was in Geelong when the governor had arrived, Quinn answered, as quick as a flash:

Deep Sinking Ballarat

BAIL UP!

OPPOSITE:
The Battle at the Eureka Stockade, 3 December 1854
Engraving from *Picturesque Atlas of Australasia*
(Private Collection)

'I don't associate much with governors except governors of gaols...I don't care much for their society.' They all were destined to spend the next decade in the company of one governor at least.

Garrett was eventually granted a ticket-of-leave in August 1861, and he departed the colony for the goldfields in New Zealand, where he earned himself the honour of becoming that colony's first bushranger.

The account given here was recorded in Craig's *Adventures on the Goldfields*. There are, however, variations to the pattern of events. Some suggest that Marriot lay low in Ballarat for a while, and it was Quinn and Bolton (Boulton) who headed down to Geelong, then onto Melbourne where they sold their share to the London Chartered Bank in Collins Street.

From they there went back to Geelong and then back up to Ballarat where Bolton was arrested after attempting to obtain a bank-draft for £1450 from the very bank he had robbed only weeks earlier. When he passed his bundle of cash over the counter, the teller recognised the numbers and he was nabbed.

It is certain, however, that Garrett was caught in Regent Street in that most amusing manner.

The Eureka Gang

In June 1851 *The Geelong Advertiser* warned that 'large numbers of men – half bushranger, half gold-seeker – are travelling along the roads – robbing all who are unprotected'. They were attacking hopefuls heading for the New South Wales goldfields. By the end of the year the same newspapers were warning of the huge number of 't'other siders' coming into the colony from Tasmania, attacking those on their way to the diggings.

John Baylie, Charles Bow, John Donovan, John Finegan and Henry Johnstone were just such characters, and they adopted the name 'The Eureka Gang', sticking up diggers on the road at Aitken's Gap to the north of Melbourne.

When they were eventually brought to ground they stood accused of robberies all over the district. In court one of the prisoners exclaimed in their defence:

> Here's one man says we stuck him up at Aitken's Gap, another at the Porcupine, another near Mount Egerton, and others at other places, and the police says they caught us in the Crown hotel, Buninyong. Why, your honour, horses couldn't get over the ground in the time, what do you think we are, crows?

They were soon to be gaol-birds anyway!

A Decisive Moment – 3 December 1854

From the beginning of the gold rushes in both Victoria and New South Wales, thousands of people came from all over the world to try their luck and to make a fresh start.

Ships choked the harbours, many unable to sail away again as their crews abandoned them for the rush to the diggings. Across the diggings there are countless Sailor's Gullies, Sailor's Creeks or Sailor's Flats that indicate the spot where these crews had slung their swag.

Sailors were treated much the same as convicted labour; they had very few rights to personal freedom and suffered the lash or the noose at the whim of their master, just as the convicts did who were assigned to a station or shepherd's hut far away on the edge of a run.

These 'absconders' were joined on the diggings by hundreds of refugees from all the European wars. These were the wars of revolution, wars of the commoner rising up against the aristocrat and railing against the destruction of their livelihood in the face of the machine.

Add to this a liberal dose of Californian '49ers, topped off with boatloads of radical Irish lawyers and political activists, Scottish chartists, Welsh orators, Wesleyan preachers, Catholic priests and hundreds of bolters from Tasmania, and the diggings were about to explode.

No longer could the colonial governors and the military commanders expect to rule with an iron fist and take from the digger as if the goldfields were their own personal fiefdom. There were too many people abroad without any need to defer to military rule or government decree, who demanded a right to live, work and die as they wished. The common man was about to demand to be treated as a citizen.

The government imposed a heavy licence fee on all those who were on the goldfields, whether or not they were there to dig. Many unfortunate 'diggers' were arrested just as they arrived before they had even had any opportunity to do the right thing. Those unable to pay were either 'chained to the logs', sometimes for weeks in all kinds of weather or sent to work on the roads. The government had not forgotten the value of enforced labour, only this time no one could be put in chains.

December 1851: Only weeks after the Victorian diggings had begun, over 14 000 attended an anti-licence protest meeting at the

THE EUREKA STOCKADE, BALLARAT.

old shepherds' hut at Chewton on the Forest Creek goldfield.

August 1853: Following two years of constant bickering, petitioning the governor and altercations with the troops, a mass meeting was held in Bendigo. Thousands of armed diggers marched on the government camp, ready to do battle. They wore a red-ribbon in protest, 'as a sign that those who wore it were pledged no longer to pay the license-fee.'

December 1854: One more year had passed with the government doing nothing but intensifying the frequency of licence hunts and increasing hardship and dissatisfaction across the colony.

While the diggers were angry at the government's persistence with the licence fee, they also complained that they got little back for this heavy tax impost. They complained of the poor condition of the roads, the high cost of provisions, the treatment at the hands of the military, corruption of officials and the lack of protection against bushrangers.

Into the middle of all this argument stepped yet another Irishman, Peter Lalor. On the morning of 30 November 1854, he stepped upon a stump at the centre of a stockade built on the Eureka diggings, beneath a fluttering blue banner emblazoned with a white cross and five white stars, and in unison with the diggers massed before him declared the diggers' oath: 'We swear by the Southern Cross to stand truly by each other, and defend our rights and our liberties'.

3 December 1854, just before dawn: The crude stockade that had been constructed around some tents with the fluttering blue standard at their centre was attacked by the troops of the 40th Regiment who had been building their numbers in Ballarat over the previous few days. In the short but vicious battle that ensued, some twenty-two diggers were killed and six troopers lay dead or dying. Lalor had his left armed shattered with a musket ball and it was amputated in secret at the Presbytery of Father Smyth later that afternoon.

All of the protagonists of the Ballarat Reform League were brought to trial for treason under the watchful eye of the Protestant Irish judge, Redmond Barry.

The battle for constitutional freedom, democratic process and equality of opportunity which had its beginnings in the transportation of the Scottish chartists, the Tolpuddle unionists, the Irish revolutionists and the diaspora of the unwanted English criminal poor was once again fought on colonial soil.

Again the Irish were in the vanguard of revolution, but this time they were aided and abetted by the gentlemen of 'the California brigade' who, with their glistening colts tucked into their belts, were just as eager for a 'right Royal tussle' as any old lag.

In the end this battle may have been lost but the war was eventually won.

BAIL UP!

'Horse-Trading' in the High Country – Gentleman 'Bogong Jack'

John Payne (or Paynter) remains an almost uncelebrated bushranger of the high country, compared to the Kellys who roamed the same inaccessible country decades after he had opened the route across the mountains from Gippsland.

Payne was born in Leicestershire, the son of John Griefotheran Payne, the prominent road and railway construction engineer who had served with the Duke of Wellington's army in the Peninsular war.

Young John Payne enjoyed a privileged childhood, but he was such an energetic and sporting young man that he seemed to spend almost as much time in the saddle as with his books.

He went up to Cambridge to further his opportunities but again spent his time carousing, often in the pursuit of horse-flesh. He joined the Cambridge Coaching Club, and it was an unfortunate incident while driving the mail coach on the Great North Road that precipitated his departure for Australia.

The appointed driver of the coach was asleep inside, taking the place of the young lady seated beside the carefree Payne. The horses, frightened by the noise of a passing steam-powered three-wheeled vehicle, reared up and the coach was overturned.

Now, this was indeed an unfortunate accident for young John Payne. Although little damage had been done, the young lady, who suffered a broken collarbone, was the daughter of a local squire with connections to parliament and it was across his lands that the railways were hoping to run. He insisted that John Payne had been spending far too much time in the pursuits of pleasures, including the pursuit of his daughter, and not enough at his studies.

To avoid a stalemate in the future prospects of the railways, Payne senior decided that it would be a good idea if Payne junior spent some time away from Cambridge and took employment in the open air that he enjoyed so much – but in Australia.

In 1853 John Payne set out to London to kit himself out for his trip to the Antipodes where he expected to find a position as a trooper in the gold escort company of the Port Phillip District of New South Wales. Captain Payne had send money to London for his son's kit and a small amount to cover only the cost of the voyage, as it had been agreed that John should make his own way when in the colonies.

While in London, Payne visited a Mr Barlow, the engineer of the Midland Railway, who was meeting with the great engineer of steel and steam, Thomas Brunel, at the time. Young John was invited to inspect the construction site of the Great Exhibition Building, known as the Crystal Palace, on which the two men of steel had been working with the architect Sir James Paxton.

When he finally arrived in Port Phillip, Payne was dismayed to find that there was no position for him. The persons with whom he had arranged letters of introduction had gone on to Port Jackson and there was no possibility of his appointment.

He soon found his way around the town, enjoying the horse bazaar up the eastern end of Bourke Street where he had offers of work building fences up the bush. However, Payne was largely unused to any manual labour and not keen to start.

By chance he heard the landlord of Harper's Hotel, where he was staying, complain that his 'Boots' had left for the diggings without warning and the job was up for grabs. University educated (partly), son of a prominent Army Captain (Rtd), intimate of the greatest engineers of his day, John Payne was soon to be found up at six a.m., lighting the house fires, boiling the kettles for the servants, watering, feeding and grooming the horses and cleaning the muddied boots of the guests for £2 a week plus keep and 5/- tips. The landlord found it hard to believe that such a gentleman would take to such work, but this was just the first of many changes in the fortunes of young 'Jack'. Before long, however, a visitor from home who was shocked at the position accepted by his young friend advised him of an opportunity that had recently presented itself — joining in the driving of a mob of cattle brought down from Campbelltown in New South Wales to Gippsland, and then on to Omeo where they would be slaughtered to supply meat for the hundreds of miners who had rushed to join the diggings there.

Payne jumped at the chance to get back into the saddle and be paid for it. He sailed to Sydney with drovers he had met in Melbourne. One, 'Orfear Ferdie',* remembered him from Leicestershire, where he had been employed as a kennel hand and John was 'Mr. Payne of the Quorn Hunt Club' — how the world had turned 'topsy-turvy'.

John took to life in the bush with great relish, sleeping out under the stars with his saddle for a pillow. He delighted in campfire life, his strong baritone voice entertaining his droving mates with rollicking songs of home.

It was not long before he became aware of the carelessness with which some cattle owners counted their herds:

> John noticed that Doleful Dave (Drover) was not too particular in accounting for the numbers and any mistake was always in favour of the drovers and against the owners.[15]

There was cattle wandering, often unbranded, across the high plains. The numbers arriving at the slaughtering pens would often be quite different from the numbers counted at departure, what with natural attrition, run-aways and other unforeseen occurrences. The cattle owners could do little to keep track of the situation and trusted their drovers to furnish honest reports.

---

* 'Orfear Ferdie' had gained his nickname from the unfortunate occasion when he stood a little to close to a pony he was appropriating.

The horse was startled and as a consequence took a piece out of one of his ears. Ferdie suffered a loss of hearing as well, and requested that people spoke into his good ear, and not his 'orfear'.

ABOVE:
Bushrangers' Camp
Watercolour by S.T. Gill, c.1871
Two mates bed down for the night under the stars, their fire blazing, billy boiled, and horses hobbled safely until morning breaks. The bushranging life had some pleasures to share.
(Rex Nan Kivell Collection NK2043. National Library of Australia Collection)

BAIL UP!

* Major General Sir Robert Nickle took command of the goldfields of Ballarat, after martial law was declared in 1854, following the battle at the Eureka Stockade.

In 1856 John received a letter from Major General Sir Edward [Robert?] Nickle,* commander of the 12th and 40th regiments at Port Phillip, offering him temporary command of the Castlemaine gold escorts, but it seems that he had already decided on a life that was veering away from the law. He had made up his mind to join up with his mates, live a life free under the stars and make his fortune selling cattle. The only problem was that he didn't think that the cattle had necessarily to belong to him.

> In their present environment it did not impress them greatly that cattle stealing was a serious crime in this, a remote outpost of the British Empire, where the laws were made 13,000 miles away ... it was the environment that prevailed over ethical considerations, an environment that had similarity to the scenes of successful cattle raids in the old country ... [16]

Along with his new droving mates, John disappeared into the bush and gradually began a highly profitable enterprise, stealing Gippsland horses and driving them over the ranges to sell in the north. There were always horse-traders around the bustling goldfields of Beechworth, Yackanandah and Wangaratta, eager for a bit of prize Gippsland horse-flesh. The gang stole good horses from the north and drove them back over the ranges to sell to miners around the Omeo and Wood's Point diggings.

John Payne, now bushman Jack, was popular wherever he went. He was quick witted and charming, and his fine baritone voice held him in good stead wherever miners or traders gathered. He had a repertoire of old coaching songs, of highwaymen and brigands that entertained his fellow bushmen around the campfire or crowded pubs and rooming-houses.

Chinese Stick-em-ups!

There were some incidents during which some of the thousands of Chinese who came to the diggings took to the roads. A large and stout Chinaman held up a Mr Ball of Cathcart in New South Wales in 1859. Ball chased the man with his bull-whip, and he ran away.

Chinese laundry-man, Sam Poo, was one of the unlucky ones. Giving the laundry business away, he bailed up several people in the Mudgee district, but he shot the policeman who went to arrest him. He soon faced the same retribution as his European brothers-in-arms, and had his neck stretched on the gallows.

But it wasn't long before the police in Melbourne became concerned at the constant reports of stock losses, and a close eye was cast over the activities of all those seen going in and out of the mountains. Jack had developed an intimate knowledge of the bush and was one of the best judges of horse-flesh in the colony, but even he was not able to control the events that surrounded him.

Two of his companions, George Chamberlain and William Armstrong, were planning to attack and rob a gold trader who was taking a case of gold worth £20 000 to the Gippsland coast. Although Jack wanted nothing to do with the robbery, it was not his style, he was after all a gentleman thief, a liberator of 'homeless' animals. The robbery went ahead. Fifteen miles out of Omeo the gold trader was attacked. The bandits opened fire on the escort party, Cornelius Green was killed, the trooper guarding the party was shot in the arm and his horse bolted for the bush. A storeman was wounded and a female in company with them was so traumatised that she was never able to give a coherent account of the affair.

When Green's body was recovered, his body had been mutilated. He had been shot through the chest, his skull smashed in with a tomahawk, his nose sliced off, and one hand almost cut from the arm. It seems that the thieves were angered that the horse carrying the gold had bolted for the bush.

Chamberlain and Armstrong were under suspicion of the murder of Green. A local storekeeper had seen them at the same lodging-house as Green and suspected that they may have learned of the gold escort unbenownst to him. After the aborted attempt on the escort, they had stolen some good horses belonging to local farmers to make their escape, and although the local police reckoned that they could easily have covered 100 miles before the next day, it didn't take long before they were apprehended. Chamberlain and Armstrong were found hiding up a tree behind a shanty fifty miles from Omeo.

Both Sydney Penny and John Payne* were also taken into custody, but subsequently released.

*John Payne earned the soubriquet 'Bogong Jack' simply because he rode the trails of the Bogong Ranges. In fact, he was one of the first Europeans to cross those rugged mountains, and certainly one of the few who knew the way back again.

When the police where searching, in vain, for the Kelly gang some twenty years later, they believed that Ned had learnt the escape routes from Harry Power who had in turn been instructed by 'Bogong Jack'.

88

Chamberlain and Armstrong were found not guilty of the murder of Cornelius Green, but of manslaughter and wounding, and were hanged, just the same, on 12 July 1859.

Jack tried to retire from his unlawful ways, but he was never forgotten. He was under constant surveillance, as much as could be maintained in the darkened, steep tracks of the heavily wooded high country. He was charged with horse-stealing several times but remained free to roam his beloved mountains.

The facts of his demise are unknown. It is said that he was murdered while searching for gold in the vicinity of the hut he had built on the spur at Mt Fainter, but there are those who argued that this was unlikely as Bogong Jack was a 'horseman' not a 'prospector'.

A fellow who called himself 'Paddy Hekir' reported that he spent some time up in the high country with a man who would only identify himself as Jack.

Hekir apparently stayed in Jack's company for a while until one day he rode down into Beechworth where he told some men in the Magpie Hotel that his mate Jack had been lost in the fog. They thought that it must have been Bogong Jack as no one had seen him around for a month or so, nor had he been in to Yackandandah or Wangaratta.

A few months later a prospector, after a few drinks, told how he had discovered a skeleton deep in a gully below a high cliff near Mt Fainter. The back of the skull appeared as if it had been struck a blow from a miner's pick. The prospector had picked up a sovereign belt hanging from a ti-tree and had found another sovereign not far from the body. Nothing was said about the leather bag of sovereigns in the hut, the books in the pack saddle or the bundle of letters with a Leicestershire postmark.

The hut, once used by drovers and cattlemen, is used no more. It is rumoured that, around midnight, a tall lean figure, booted and spurred, strides out from the tall timber and across the camp and holding yards, causing 'the cattle to leap to their feet and rush down the spur in terror'.[17]

RIGHT:
The prison hulk Success

The prisoners from the *Success* were responsible for the vicious attack on the hated John Price as he walked unarmed among them at the Gellibrand Quarries. He was felled by a blow from a shovel to the back of his head. The prisoners then stoned him and kicked him to death. Not one mourned his passing.

(La Trobe Picture Collection, State Library of Victoria)

The Death of Price

John Price was appointed as Inspector-General of Convicts to Victoria in 1854 at a time when there was an unexpected demand for police services as thousands joined the rush for gold.

Prior to this appointment Price had been 'Civil Commandant for Norfolk Island' from 1846 to 1853, where his insistent harshness had him earned the soubriquet 'The Monster of Norfolk Island'. Before he had been 'Muster Master of Convicts in Van Diemen's Land' where he had, again, earned a reputation for 'carrying out his duties with exceptional rigour and cruelty'.

It was in Van Diemen's Land that Martin Cash had suffered at Price's cruel hand, and Price's departure was felt warmly by the convicts there.

Price's brutality followed him to Victoria where men of the cloth and others protested at his appointment. His reputation had preceded him.

There was such a demand for prisons at that time that Port Phillip Bay began to resemble the English ports before transportation. Ships were again turned into floating prisons, and some hardened and desperate men were 'rotting' in these hulks. It was the prisoners from the *Success* who brought an end to the career of Inspector-General Price. As he walked, unarmed, among them, the prisoners had downed tools in protest at the appalling conditions in which they were held, the less than adequate rations they received and the harshness of their labours at the Gellibrand quarries. Price refused to accommodate their requests, demanding that they should make their complaints 'in the proper form'.

The men gathered had had enough. One struck Price over the back of the head with a shovel, and the rest picked up the rocks they had been breaking and brought Price down. He was bashed and stoned to death by prisoners in the quarry at Port Gellibrand in March 1857. There were few who mourned his passing.

BAIL UP!

FLASH COVES & CURRENCY

Above:
*Robbery of the Gold Escort from the Lachlan,
New South Wales*
Wood engraving by Frederick Grosse,
published in *Illustrated Australian Mail*, 25 June 1862
(La Trobe Picture Collection, State Library of Victoria)

John Piesley, the First Truly 'Australian' Bushranger

John Piesley was possibly the first of the truly Australian bushrangers. He was born in the Abercrombie district of New South Wales in 1834, and was first in trouble aged twenty when he came up before the Bathurst Quarter Sessions charged with cattle-stealing. This was a misdeed so common that most didn't consider it a crime at all: it was simply unauthorised re-distribution of the bovine gene-pool.

Piesley was sentenced to five years, but managed to escape on his way down to Darlinghurst. He was at large long enough to steal a few horses, then he was captured again and sent down to Cockatoo Island where he was to meet one fellow with whom his name was to become inextricably entwined – Frank Gardiner.

Piesley attempted to escape from the island 'taking to the water', but was recaptured and served out his time until he was released on a ticket-of-leave on 23 November 1860. Upon Gardiner's release the pair took to the roads, terrorising travellers from Yass to Cowra.

On 16 July 1861 Sergeant Middleton and Trooper Hosie of the Western Patrol were out looking for the bushrangers when they were attacked and wounded at a homestead on the Fish River where they had interrupted a meeting of two scoundrels, Gardiner and an old acquaintance Fogg. After a struggle in which Middleton was shot in the face by Gardiner, who was also wounded as the stricken officer flailed at him with the handle of his hunting-whip, and Hosie felled by shots to his body, Fogg brought Gardiner to the floor and restrained him with Hosie's handcuffs.

As Hosie and Fogg were escorting Gardiner to the nearby town of Bigga, they were again attacked by two men, one they asserted to be Piesley and the other a fellow known as Zahn from Abercrombie. They shouted at them to free Gardiner or they would shoot his horse. When they did they turned their attention to the now faint Hosie who, having fired his last shot, was at the bushrangers' mercy.

ABOVE:

The Australian Dick Turpin – Bushranger's Flight
Lithograph by J.J Blundell & Co., from a drawing by S.T. Gill, c. 1862
Gardiner, the 'King of the Road', is in full flight, hotly pursued by the police.
(Rex Nan Kivell Collection NK9841/7B, National Library of Australia)

BAIL UP!

The bushrangers would have dispatched Hosie had it not been for the entreaties by Fogg to spare the stricken trooper's life.

In January 1862 the government offered a total of £175 for information that would lead to the capture of Piesley and Gardiner. On the reward poster the following description of Piesley indicates that he was 'one flash and fearsome looking cove':

> John Piesley ... labourer, about 28 years of age, about 5 ft. 10 in. high, stout and well made, fresh complexion, very small light whiskers, quite bald on top of head and forehead, several marks on face, and a mark from a blow of a spade on top of head; puffed and dissipated-looking from hard drinking, invariably wears fashionable Napoleon boots, dark cloth breeches, dark vest buttoned up in the front, large albert gold guard, cabbage-tree hat and duck coat. Sometimes wears a dark wig and always carries a brace of revolvers.

Piesley was not pleased with being held to account for Gardiner's rescue. He maintained that Fogg, who had been a partner with Gardiner in a butchery on the Lambing Flat diggings, had paid Trooper Hosie £50 to let him go. He was so infuriated by the implication that he had been involved that he wrote to the *Bathurst Free Press* denying any involvement in the shooting of the troopers and the subsequent battle for Gardiner's freedom.

He insisted that, although there were many who thought him 'a desperado in the eyes of the law', he 'never in no instance did I ever use violence, nor did I ever use rudeness to any of the fair sex ... I must certainly be the Invisible Prince to commit one-tenth of what is laid to my charge'. He added at the end of his letter that he '[loved his] native hills, I love freedom and detest cruelty to man or beast'.

Unfortunately, Piesley did use violence at least once when he shot a man in a drunken brawl. He was tracked down near Tarcutta and hanged at Bathurst on 23 March 1862. Standing on the scaffold, facing the moment of his death, with the hangman standing patiently by, he again declaimed the accusations made against him. He may have been a notorious bushranger, but at least he loved his country.

The Boldest Gang of All

The most sensational hold-up in Cobb and Co.'s coaching history was the attack on the Eugowra Gold Escort on the Forbes–Orange road on 15 June 1862.

The highly organised gang of eight bushrangers stopped the coach at Eugowra Rocks some twenty-seven miles from Forbes. The attackers had blackened* faces and were wearing red serge shirts and red comforters, drawn back like night-caps over their heads, as they appeared alongside the coach. One of the party shouted 'Fire', and a volley of shots rang out as bullets splintered the side of the coach.

After the first volley had shattered the peaceful silence of the bush, the men stepped back and their compatriots stepped forward taking their line. They too fired into the coach, then the military-style action was repeated.

Two of the guards were wounded as Fagan, the coach driver, felt a bullet whistle through his hat. He claimed later that he was knocked from the coach and stood beside his frightened beasts holding tight the reins as he walked them forward slowly. The rest of the guard took to the bush, seeking refuge from their determined attackers.

The noise of the repeated gunfire caused the horses to bolt, capsizing the coach and spilling its contents across the roadway.

The haul from this short affray netted the robbers 2717 ounces of gold, £3700 in cash and several mailbags. In all the haul was worth over £14 000.

Sergeant Condell, who was in charge of the escort, wrote in his official report one week later:

> The bushrangers were commanded by one man, who gave orders to fire and load. I believe it to have been the voice of Gardiner, as I know his voice well. I cannot identify any of them with the exception of the voice I heard.[1]

---

*When attacking a coach Australian bushrangers rarely wore masks as was the fashion of 'Turpinesque' highwaymen or in the American west.
 They often wore calico sacks over their heads with obvious eye holes cut in them. Sometimes, they simply pulled a comforter (scarf) over the lower part of their face (comforters being a common item of clothing in those days) or blackened their faces with soot. While this may have been a very effective disguise, many a wanted man has been discovered for the mistake of, simply, not washing his neck properly.

Sergeant Condell was in no doubt that it was the ex-butcher from Lambing Flat who was the leader of this well-drilled gang.

Gardiner, Hall and Gilbert were high-profile bandits and the rest of the gang had also made a fair name for themselves in one way or another.

The news of this robbery caused a sensation right across the country. It was the biggest haul ever taken in a daring daylight attack on one of Cobb's coaches.

One extraordinary result of the fracas at Eugowra Rocks was the wounding of Constable Haviland who, after recovering the untouched mail that had been of no interest to the bandits, delivered them to the Postmaster in Orange. The coach then proceeded to Dalton's Inn where the escorts usually had their billett. About halfway between the Post Office and the Inn, the other passengers noticed that Haviland was wounded and that blood was pouring from his chest. One of the female passengers held him until they reached the hotel where as they lifted him from the coach they saw that he was dead. It appears that Haviland had placed a loaded revolver beneath his seat and it had gone off unexpectedly, shooting him through the throat and spine.

There were others who, less generously, intimated that Haviland may have attempted to wound himself as he had not sustained any injury in the attack and feared that he would have been held to ridicule by his fellow officers. The death of Haviland was just another mark against the record of Gardiner and his now long-departed mates.

Gardiner headed north, taking Katherine, Ben Hall's sister-in-law and wife of settler John Brown, with him. They settled at Apis Creek in Queensland where they opened a store, and apparently went straight for some time, until Kate wrote a note to her sister Bridget (Ben Hall's sister) back home which, carelessly, threw a light on the trail to Gardiner that the police had thought was long cold.

Bridget foolishly showed her sister Kate's letter to her husband who, one night a little worse for the

RIGHT:
The Ubiquitous Frank 'Darkie' Gardiner
In 1862 the *Lachlan Observer* commented that Gardiner and his mates had 'held up every coach and dray on every road on the Lachlan'.
(Police Museum Melbourne Collection)

'Darkie' Gardiner

Frank 'Darkie' Gardiner had assumed the soubriquet 'Darkie' for no apparent obvious reason. Although he did have dark hair, his otherwise sallow complexion did not give any hint that he may have had native blood flowing through his veins.

Gardiner was, in fact, pure Hebridian. Although not technically a 'currency lad', he did spend his formative years in Australia. Four-year-old Frank Christie (aka Gardiner) emigrated from Rosshire with his parents, brother and two sisters, arriving in Sydney in November 1834.

They moved up into the rich farming land around Goulburn in south-central New South Wales, a lovely spot to bring up a young family and right in the heart of bushranging country.

Frank first got into trouble when he was twenty years old. He was arrested for horse-stealing and spent some time in prison.

Butcher, horse-thief, cattle-duffer and a leader of men, Gardiner earned himself the reputation of the 'King of the Road'. His daring exploits led large groups of likely lads to terrorise the highways across the New South Wales goldfields.

Gardiner did, at times, try to make an honest go of things, although his attempts do seem rather half-hearted. He first rode onto the Kiandra goldfield astride a stolen horse. It was at Lambing Flat that he set up a butchery with Fogg who later turned against him to save his own neck at Fish Creek, and the pair did think it more profitable to steal their meat than to buy it. Gardiner was arrested for cattle-duffing and, while on bail, absconded and left the district for a while.

He rode with some other notorious characters – John Bow, Dan Charters, Charles Darcy, Alexander Fordyce, John Gilbert and Harry Manns.

BAIL UP!

drink, boasted of his knowing the whereabouts of the infamous 'King of the Road'.

The police followed the trail back up to Apis Creek. Gardiner was finally taken into custody and brought back to trial in Sydney in May 1864. He was sentenced to spend the next thirty-two years in prison.

However, Gardiner only had to spend the next decade inside as he received a pardon in 1874, granted by the premier of New South Wales, Henry Parkes, who was eager to regain public approval and support after his government was forced to resign. Parliament had dissolved over the Gardiner issue the previous year. There had been increasing public pressure brought to bear on the government to rescind the harsh punishments served on the 'Knights of the Roads' when the public's fear of bushrangers was at its height in the earliest days of the gold rushes.

There were plenty who demanded that the convicted remain inside, but there were enough of those who saw the bold young men as folk-heroes, whose dash, daring and charismatic charm added some excitement to their otherwise ordinary lives. They also protested that the sentences issued under Sir Hercules Robinson had been unneccesarily severe and that leniency be considered.

Gardiner was released with one proviso – that he be deported to China. That didn't suit Frank at all. He did sail as far as Hong Kong where, as was his usual fashion, he absconded. This time he jumped aboard

---

ABOVE:
Bailed Up
Oil on canvas by Tom Roberts, 1895

When Roberts was in the Riverina district of New South Wales painting his *Shearing the Rams*, he was intrigued by the story of the Eugowra robbery as told by a former coach driver, 'Silent Bob Bates'. Obviously, 'Silent Bob' wasn't all that quiet as his account inspired Roberts to execute this iconic work. In order that his work capture the exact feel of the event Roberts had a platform built opposite the spot on the Forbes–Orange road where the robbery had taken place. It was here that he painted the landscape, then he worked on the coach back at the station, with 'Silent Bob' as one of his characters. This painting took several years to complete, but it was not popular at the time. Its easy-going manner may have been viewed as approving of the bushrangers, who do seem to be charming the pretty lass inside the coach.

(Art Gallery of New South Wales Collection)

GARDINER'S HOUSE AND SCENE OF HIS CAPTURE AT APIS CREEK.—(SEE PAGE 11.)

ABOVE:
The Capture of Gardiner at Apis Creek, Queensland
Engraving published in *Ilustrated Sydney News*, 16 June 1864
(National Library of Australia Collection)

an American ship bound for San Francisco. Gardiner was to set himself down in the very city where, only years before, the Californians had formed vigilante groups to rid the port of the Australian criminal menace, but times must have changed.

Gardiner established 'The Twilight Star', a saloon and restaurant on Kearney Street where, under his new name, Frank Smith, he lived until his death from pneumonia in 1904. Some would like to believe that Frank Gardiner was shot in a card game in Colorado. Others believe that his twin American sons travelled to Australia in 1912, under the guise of mining engineers, to dig up his loot from the Eugowra robbery which he had supposedly hidden somewhere near the summit of Mount Wheogo.

LEFT:
The 'King of the Road', the dashing folk-hero Francis Christie, aka Frank Clarke, Frank Gardiner, 'Darkie' Gardiner, Smith, Jones and even Reverend Christie
Engraving
(La Trobe Picture Collection, State Library of Victoria)

GARDINER, THE BUSHRANGER.

BAIL UP!

Lambing Flat Riot, 'No Chinese – Roll Up! Roll Up!'

Many of the notorious names of bushranging fame also spent their time in other 'worthwhile' pursuits, although few managed to keep out of trouble for long at all.

The goldfields were almost a magnet for trouble. New townships of tents and bark-huts were being thrown up all over the colonies as thousands of diggers poured in from around the globe. The Victorian diggings were in previously uninhabited districts, save for a few squatters and their flocks of sheep who had taken up runs north and west of the divide after Mitchell had opened up the district in 1836. Ballarat was really the only inland settlement.

The New South Wales goldfields were more well established. Bathurst was the oldest inland township in the country, and the region from the Goulburn to New England had seen the prints of leather boots, cloven hooves and horse shoes track backwards and forwards across the rolling hills for decades before the rush.

It was the sons of the sheep-herder and the released convict who had settled the New South Wales hinterland who, upon reaching their teens, began to feel their oats. Obviously, they had something to prove, and once they were all together on the diggings, far away from the restraining influence of family, they ran amok.

On 30 June 1861, an angry band of armed young white diggers, liquored up and ready to go, marched through the Chinese camp on the Lambing Flat diggings at Young, driving everything before them. Rallying behind a blue and white starred banner, similar to that flown at Eureka, which bore the words 'No Chinese – Roll Up! Roll Up!' they smashed and destroyed as they went. Unfortunate Chinese were buried in their holes. They killed those who refused to declare the whereabouts of their gold, and wounded others as they went about destroying the camp.

The police came in from surrounding districts and arrested only three men, but the diggers were so fired up they attacked the police, demanding that their mates be released. The police fired back, and one poor digger dropped dead in his tracks – a bullet had tapped his skull. Even though the affair caused great concern to the government, only one European was ever brought to justice for the murderous affray.

'Bold' Ben Hall, Mickey Bourke, 'Darkie' Gardiner, Johnnie Gilbert and young John Dunn were all there that day.

Left:
Morgan the Bushranger
Wood engraving by Samuel Calvert
Daniel Morgan earned the nickname 'Mad Dan' for the seemingly unwarranted brutality of his behaviour. It seemed that prison had truly sent him insane.
(National Library of Australia Collection)

MORGAN, THE BUSHRANGER. — SEE PAGE 10.

'Mad Dan' Morgan

In 1854 Daniel Morgan was arrested in Barker's Creek, near Castlemaine, on the diggings around Mt Alexander, where he kept a butcher's shambles. It was the one and only arrest for Morgan in what was to become a short, but very bloody, career. He was arrested for sticking-up a hawker, brought before the nemesis of all bushrangers, Judge Redmond Barry, and was sentenced to twelve years hard labour.

The bastard son of a Sydney prostitute and a London barrow-boy, born in Campbelltown, New South Wales, brought discredit to the popular 'currency' heroes with his mixture of violence, abuse and seemingly meaningless murders. It is believed that he took the name Morgan from his boyhood hero, the boldly bearded buccaneer, 'Captain Morgan'.

Morgan always maintained his innocence of the crime for which he was incarcerated, protesting that he had been framed by a squatter who was not fond of him. He was sent to the Victorian prison, Pentridge, to serve his sentence.

Once imprisoned Morgan developed a hatred of all authority, developing an especially violent dislike for the police. This was probably not the best frame of mind for someone who faced the prospect of over a decade in judicial company. He did, however, serve out his time and was granted a ticket-of-leave to the Ovens–Yackandandah district in 1860. The unfortunate squatters of the Ovens Valley would not have had any idea of the madness that had been released into their midst.

Morgan's time in prison had not gone well, and upon his release he began a long and bitter campaign of retribution against society at large, and the constabulary in particular.

This large brooding man, with a dark, luxuriant beard that flowed across his chest, hair swept to his shoulders in gypsy ringlets, aquiline nose that tipped almost over his upper lip, and deep-set hawk-like, bright blue eyes was a sure sight to strike fear in any who met him. Morgan ranged far and wide, and although his deeds seemed mindless and unnecessarily brutal, he did enjoy some degree of popularity among the settlers and old transportees who were still living in the north-east. Maybe the settlers preferred to allow him some slack to keep themselves out of trouble, and he certainly created plenty of that.

Morgan held up Bayliss, the Wagga magistrate, but let him go as he complimented him on his bravery. When Bayliss brought the police after Morgan, he risked discovery by stealing close enough to the search party to shoot Bayliss in the hand and shoulder, just to teach him a lesson no one should have ever forgotten.

Angry with one overseer whom he considered too familiar with the police, Morgan arrived at the overseer's homestead intending to shoot him. When he discovered that his quarry was away mustering cattle, he turned his attention to the man's wife. He demanded money, but the woman replied that there was very little kept on the station. Morgan didn't accept this answer but ordered her to boil him some eggs as he was hungry. He refused to eat anything else as he feared there was too much strychnine and arsenic used around stations and was wary about his diet. The eggs were boiled, and after inspecting the

Opposite:
Might versus Right
Watercolour by S.T. Gill, c. 1851
Diggers attack the Chinese in an attempt to drive them from the diggings.
(La Trobe Picture Collection, State Library of Victoria)

BAIL UP!

Morgan Sticking Up the Navvies, Burning their Tents, and Shooting the Chinaman. —[SEE PAGE 11.]

shells, he ate heartily. Then he again turned his attention to his cook. He built up the fire until it was blazing furiously, then forced the woman back against the flames all the time demanding money. She continued to refuse until Morgan caused her clothes to catch alight. When she had learned her lesson, he threw a bucket of water over her, but she had still suffered severe burns to her back and legs.

Morgan tried to burn squatter Isaac Vincent by tying him to a fence by his woolshed and setting the shed alight. Vincent had informed on him to the police.

One day, Morgan was riding past a policeman on the Tumbarumba Road. The policeman did not recognise Morgan and greeted him with a polite 'hello'. Morgan turned and answered, 'You're one of the bastards looking for bushrangers, are you!' and shot him dead. When more police came out to look for him, he crept up on another officer, Sergeant Smith, and murdered him as he lay in his tent.

Morgan bailed up some navvies working in the Albury district and made them empty out their tents for him, taking whatever he fancied. Then he burned their tents. Discovering that there were five Chinese among them he made them dance and sing for him then, summarily, shot one, breaking his arm. The poor man died later in Albury of blood poisoning.

A CHASE AFTER MORGAN—[DRAWN BY N. CHEVALIER, ESQ.]

LEFT:
Morgan Chased by Troopers
(La Trobe Picture Collection, State Library of Victoria)

OPPOSITE:
Morgan Sticking-up the Navvies, Burning Their Tents, and Shooting the Chinaman
Wood engraving by Samuel Calvert,
published in *Melbourne Illustrated Post*, 25 January 1865
(La Trobe Picture Collection, State Library of Victoria)

BELOW:
Morgan at Round Hill Station
Wood engraving by Frederick Grosse, c.1864
Morgan shot a station-hand named Heriot during a drunken meal at Round Hill. He apologised for his mistake, then shot another.
(National Library of Australia Collection)

Morgan bailed up coaches, too. After instructing the drivers to get inside, he would then stampede the horses, sending them careering down the road to their eventual destruction.

He shot a station-hand during a drunken meal, and then apologised for his mistake. He sent another to fetch a doctor, then shot him as he hurried away. However, he felt some remorse for this action so he nursed the poor fellow until he, too, lay dead.

Morgan seemed unassailable as he rampaged across New South Wales; however, the Victoria Police boasted that they could bring him to justice within two days if he ever dared to cross the border.

Morgan could not resist this challenge. He replied by stating that he would take 'the bloody flashness out of the [Victorian] police' and crossed the river.

Morgan announced his arrival in Victoria on 5 April 1865 by holding-up a station at Whitfield, where he terrorised the station-hands and set fire to a haystack as revenge for a wound he had suffered at the hand of its owner when he had worked there four years earlier. He added to his bounty by holding up every carriage he saw on the roads, taking sums from £3 to £50 from the poor travellers.

On 8 April, Morgan came upon Peechelba Station, twenty miles out from Wangaratta on the Ovens River. The police were hot on his blazing trail and were only a few hours behind him. He bailed up the occupants of the station, forcing them into one room. He had eight female and four male hostages. One of the women, nursemaid Alice McDonald, said she had heard one of the children crying in an adjoining room and she demanded to be able to attend to her charge. Morgan refused, so she slapped his face and told him that she would go in spite of him. Morgan was not used to feisty female display and amused the lass by letting her go. She left the room and was able to alert one of the station-hands who had not been locked-up with Morgan. He went to warn the police.

MORGAN AT THE ROUND HILL STATION—SEE PAGE 12.

BAIL UP!

As tea was already on the table Morgan invited everybody to sit down together and 'tuck in'. He chatted with the owners of the station, regaling them with tales of his trials and tribulations, how he was blamed for more than he had ever done, talked of his mother and father whom he said were still alive, and invited Mrs McPherson, the squatter's wife, to sit and play the piano for him.

He said that he hadn't slept for five days, but could sleep with one eye open. As he sat by the piano with a 'borrowed' cigar between his teeth, he dozed but never let his revolver go from his hand.

The young station-hand had by now reached a neighbouring station. When they heard the news, the men armed themselves and headed out to Peechelba to cover Morgan in case he tried to escape and to wait for the Wangaratta police. In the darkness the police swelled the number of men lying armed, waiting for Morgan to show himself.

At around daybreak, Morgan stepped out onto the verandah and looked about as if he sensed that danger was at hand. He went back into the room and drank a glass of whisky. He then reappeared, this time with the squatter, McPherson, and three others whom he made step through the door in front of him. He ordered them to walk ahead of him towards the stables. As McPherson turned to Morgan, he spied one fellow in the bush who had just stepped forward to take aim from behind a tree. He stepped away from the bushranger, and a shot rang out. A bullet ripped into Morgan's back. He fell to the ground, and was immediately set-upon and taken. He cried out, 'Why didn't you challenge me fair, and give me a chance?', but it was all over for 'Mad Dan' Morgan.

It was 8 o'clock in the morning when Morgan was laid low, and he lingered until 2 o'clock in the afternoon when, pointing to his throat as if he were choking, he died. The bullet had gone in at his upper shoulder and up and out his windpipe.

He had two revolvers in his possession at the time of his death. One belonged to Sergeant McGinnerty whom he had killed on the road some months earlier, and the other belonged to John Kirk, a digger from Barker's Creek near Castlemaine.

Morgan was placed on a wooden pallet and carried into the woodshed where he was propped up for

ABOVE:
Morgan Enjoying Mrs McPherson's Music
Engraving from *Cassell's Picturesque Australasia,* published 1889
Morgan passed his last evening pleasantly, while keeping the McPherson household locked together in one room. He said he hadn't slept for five days but never let his revolver fall from his grasp all night.
(Private Collection)

OPPOSITE TOP:
Death of Morgan
Engraving from *Cassell's Picturesque Australasia,* published 1889
Morgan was shot in the back by a rifleman who stepped from behind a tree as he went to take a horse he had been promised to make his getaway.
(Private Collection)

photographers and artists to record his impressively hirsute corpse.

After Morgan's death his body was mutilated. His head was cut off at the request of Dr Dobbyn, the coroner, who wanted to study the skull for phrenological research. Locks of his once luxuriant beard and ringlets from his hair were souvenired. His facial skin was flayed from his skull so that Police Superintendent Cobham could 'peg it out and dry it like a possum skin', and his balls were cut off to be manufactured into a souvenir money pouch.

The police treated Morgan's body with the disrespect for another human being that had been his trademark. Morgan, a once proudly defiant individual, had been reduced to a curiosity, as all those he had resented took their amusement from his lifeless body.

RIGHT:
Daniel 'Mad Dan' Morgan, post-mortem
Photograph by Henry Pohl, 9 April 1865
(Mitchell Library Collection, State Library of New South Wales)

BAIL UP!

Brave Ben Hall

*That settles it . . . there's no getting out of this.
May as well have the game as the blame.
– Ben Hall while under pursuit for Daly's theft*

Ben Hall was born at Breeza on the Liverpool Plains in north-central New South Wales in 1837, the son of transportees to Van Diemen's Land. It is believed that Ben's father selected his mother from the Female Convict Factory at Parramatta.

Hall's father had become a free-holder and a successful farmer. He had taken a job as overseer of a property in the Lachlan district and took Ben with him. Young Ben spent his teen years working with horses and cattle and developed a love and expertise with both. Like so many other young lads on the Lachlan, Ben was brought undone by four-legged beasts.

His father returned to Murrurundi and left Ben behind, very much against his wishes. Then aged eighteen, Ben was smitten with young Bridget Walsh of Wheogo, and even wild horses couldn't drag him away from her. Just before his father left and without his father's knowledge, Ben took a job as a stock-keeper for Bridget's father and within a year the young couple was married.

The following year Ben and Bridget took a lease on a property in the Sandy Creek and set up home, where they soon built a fine herd of their own. Ben's knowledge of stock and the astute manner in which he managed his affairs meant that people thought well of him in the region. Nothing he did over the next few years ever seemed to change that opinion.

Just after they had been married a year and she had born him two fine children, Bridget ran away with John Taylor, a former policeman. Ben was away mustering cattle at the time, and had no idea at all that she was intending to bolt. It seemed that the tables had certainly turned against Ben Hall.

Not long after this calamity, in April 1862, he was at the races when he was arrested for robbery under arms by none other than the English Baronet, 'new chum' Sir Frederick Pottinger, who had begun a long, but not very fruitful, career in hunting bushrangers. Ben was arrested on suspicion of being an accomplice of Gardiner in the sticking-up of William Bacon's wagons just outside of Forbes.

Ben's arrest shocked the other settlers in the district because it was known that he didn't have any sympathy with the likes of Gardiner and his mates at that time. He had even put up police overnight in his home when they were out looking for the gangs. Maybe it was on such evenings that Bridget was romanced into running away with Taylor.

Hall was thrown into the Forbes lock-up and sat there for four or five weeks until, due to lack of evidence, he was released. He went back to his farm and continued in his work mustering his horses. But he was arrested again almost immediately, charged with robbery under arms, and taken down to Forbes where he spent another six or seven weeks in the lock-up. Once again there was insufficient evidence to convict him, no matter how hard they tried, so he

ABOVE:
Ben Hall
Ben Hall was twenty-two when his wife ran away with a former policeman. He is reported to have said that he took up bushranging to meet the man who ruined his happiness.
(Forbes Historical Museum)

*Although Pottinger first arrested Hall for suspicion of the robbery of the Eugowra Escort, Hall was never convicted of that offence, nor even listed in official records as one of the culprits.

was released on bail of £500, a surety of £250 and required to appear when called on.

Pottinger was dubious of Hall's period spent mustering and had suspected him of participating in the robbery at Eugowra* Rocks only a few weeks earlier. Pottinger was keeping an eagle eye on any likely lads who had the misfortune to pass his way, but his total lack of bush-sense and ignorance of local ways caused much derision among the settlers and homesteaders who wished for a speedy end to the days of bushranging.

When Hall returned once again to Wheogo, he was devastated to discover that his house had burned down and his stock lay dead, perished in the yards from lack of water. This, added to the loss of his wife, must have made him feel that all his efforts over the past few years to make a decent life for himself and his young family had gone up in smoke.

It was this disaster which had inadvertantly cast Hall in with Gardiner's lot, and the die was cast. Ben Hall, the smart young settler from Sandy Creek, decided to take his revenge and become a bushranger.

It was not long before the gang of 'currency lads' – Gardiner, Hall, O'Meally, Gilbert and Dunn – were making a nuisance of themselves along the roads of New South Wales as they ranged and robbed from Yass to the Wedden Ranges. They moved with incredible speed from one side of the region to the other. Like so many other young Australian-born lads, they had an excellent knowlege of the territory, were great judges of horse-flesh and could ride like the wind.

After the Eugowra robbery and Gardiner absconding to his new life in the north, Ben Hall took over as leader of the band. With Johnny Gilbert and John Dunn, and various others from time to time, they held up nearly every coach and traveller that came their way.

The night the Pinnacle Police Station was held up, in February 1863, Hall had stopped at the home of Mr Allport on the Lambing Flat Road, and it was to this house that the stick-up merchant Patsy Daley ran to make his escape. Hall knew that Daley was an accomplice of 'Darkie' Gardiner, and when Ben was made aware of the circumstances of Daley's hurried arrival and hasty departure, with the police hot on his trail, he feared that he would be implicated. So he, too, ran. Whether or not he was there, Ben Hall's horse was recognised and the rest is history.

Ben Hall explained his actions when he told Inspector Morton:

I'm not a criminal. I've been driven to this life, Pottinger arrested me on Forbes racecourse last year in April; and I was held for a month in the gaol, an innocent man.

While I was away me wife ran away – with a policeman. Well, with a cove who used to be in the force. Then I was arrested for the mail-coach robbery and held another month before I was out on bail. When I came home, I found my house burned down and my cattle perished of thirst, left locked in the yards.

Pottinger has threatened and bullied everybody in this district just because he can't catch Gardiner. Next thing I know that the troopers fired on me three weeks ago for robbing the Pinnacle police station, when I had nothing to do with that little joke.

Trooper Hollister has skited that he'll shoot me on sight. Can you wonder why I'm wild?

By Gawd, Mr Norton, it's your mob have driven me to it and, I tell you straight, you'll never catch me alive!

LEFT:
Just the Sort to Catch Gardiner
The popular press were dismissive of the attempts by police to catch the gang. Satirical cartoons took pot-shots at Baronet Sir Frederick Pottinger and his band of hapless troopers, who didn't seem to have any luck at all.
(Private Collection)

BAIL UP!

While the gang attacked the roads, sometimes holding up as many as sixty travellers at gun-point in the one spot as they waited for an expected mail-coach to come through, they began to turn their attention to other venues for amusement.

A Party at Canowindra

The gang attained new heights of daring and bravado when, in October 1863, they bailed-up the entire town of Canowindra and held a 'bushrangers jubilee'.

The whole gang, including Hall, Gilbert, Michael Bourke, O'Meally and John Vane, rode into town on Sunday night and held up Robinson's Hotel. They placed guards at each end of the street and shepherded everybody in town into the hotel, where they instructed them to eat and drink all they wished – at the bushrangers' expense.

They stayed in town for three days, taking hostage every dray and traveller who passed along the road. Eventually, fourteen drays were pulled up in the street, and at no stage did the gang attempt to rob any of them.

Gilbert bought cigars for everyone, and sweetmeats were laid out on the tables for all to enjoy. As a precaution the bushrangers drank ale and porter, only from unopened bottles, the corks being drawn in their presence.

They entertained their 'guests' with displays of target shooting, and if any wanted to visit their homes, they were given 'leave of absence passes' first signed by one of the gang.

At one point, Hall rode down to the police barracks, picked up the only officer there and drove him along the road ahead of him and back to the hotel where he was told to go in and join the party.

Opposite:
Portrait of Bushrangers – Mickey Bourke, Ben Hall, the 'King of the Road' Frank Gardiner, Johnnie Gilbert and John Dunn[e]
Oil on canvas by Patrick William Maroney, c. 1894
(Rex Nan Kivell Collection, R4408. National Library of Australia)

Above:
Bushrangers Holding Up Coach Passengers
Oil on canvas by Patrick William Maroney, 1894
Hall and his boys would sometimes hold as many as sixty travellers at a time at the side of the road as they waited for a mail-coach to arrive. They couldn't let them pass, even though they had finished with them, as the alarm would be raised as soon as they got to their destination.
(National Library of Australia Collection)

BAIL UP!

Mickey Bourke

Mickey Bourke was shot when the gang held up Mr Keightley at Rockley, twenty miles out of Bathurst. Keightley was standing on his verandah when he saw five men ride up; when he noticed they were armed, he cried out, 'Here are the bushrangers!' and bolted for the door. Prepared for such an event with loaded guns at the ready, both he and his guest, Dr Pechey, fought it out for as long as they could until Keightley killed Bourke with a shotgun blast to the abdomen.

Keightley had climbed onto his roof to be able to fire down on the gang, but after having spent all his ammunition and unable to reload, he was directed by the bushrangers to come down. Fearing that they would set fire to his house, he climbed down from the roof.

John Vane was aggravated at the death of his friend, Mickey Bourke, and wanted to take his revenge and execute Keightley with the very gun that had caused Bourke's demise, but Keightley's wife pleaded for her husband's life. Hall and Gilbert ordered Vane to put his gun down, and seething with rage and remorse at Mickey's miserable death, he dropped the gun.

The gang allowed Keightley to ransom himself for £500, and Mrs Keightley and Dr Pechey had to ride into Bathurst to withdraw the ransom from the Commercial Bank – on a Sunday morning. This was not at all an easy task. First they had to raise the bank manager from his bed, then put a large some of money together without him becoming aware of its intended use. In such a rush on a Sunday morning, he must have become a bit suspicious but the job was eventually done.

John Vane

John Vane, the son of a devout Protestant family, was the only one of the gang to give himself up to the police. After his mate Bourke's death, Vane was resentful of the way in which he had been denied his satisfaction. He fought with the others and left. They may also have argued over the split of the ransom as Vane was to complain later that 'he got not a sixpence of Keightley's ransom money'.

After Vane left the others, he was riding alone on the road one day when he fell in with Reverend Father McCarthy, a popular Catholic priest well known in the district. At the end of their journey the priest had convinced Vane to give himself up. On 18 November 1863, Vane presented himself, as agreed, to the Bathurst police. He was locked away but didn't appear in court until April 1864. The lucky young man had escaped being outlawed but did not escape his punishment. He was sentenced to fifteen years on the roads.

He was released fourteen years later. Although he was in and out of gaol for the rest of his life, he did outlive his old master, the 'King of the Roads', by two years. He died in Cowra Hospital in 1906.

When three of the fourteen bullockies detained warned Hall that a nearby river was on the rise, he considered this a reasonable request and allowed them to leave after being told that if they didn't get across pretty soon they could be trapped for weeks.

It seemed that with this departure the party was over. The forty 'guests' of Mr Robinson and the bushranging gang were bid farewell and Hall and the boys headed out of town. They went searching for a man who had informed on them to the police. Whoever he was, he could be sure that he would not find the gang quite so accommodating.

The only losses in this raid were £3 taken from Robinson and a revolver from one of the guests.

The Attack on Bathurst

On the evening of 3 October 1863, five mounted horsemen dashed into the town of Bathurst. One was left as armed sentry, while the rest proceeded to Pedrotta the gunsmith's and asked to see some repeating rifles. When the owner informed them that he was out of stock, they left and went into McMinns the jewellers. They entered through the back door and surprised the McMinn family who were sitting down to tea as they burst throught the door, waving their pistols in the air. One of the women at the table became hysterical, and the bushrangers quickly made their exit, but not before they attempted to help themselves from the shop. Although this also proved unfruitful, they hopped back on their horses and galloped down the street fearing that someone would soon raise the alarm.

Two of them galloped straight up towards the police barracks, only turning back when the leader of the gang, realising their mistake, fired his pistol in the air. They galloped back down the street where the sentry rejoined them, and all sped to the edge of town, where it seemed they vanished into the dark. By now the police had joined in the fray. They mountd up and clattered after them. Getting to the edge of the town, they stopped and listened for the

SOMETHING FROM SYDNEY (FROM MELBOURNE PUNCH)
"The Police are Scouring the Country After Bushrangers."—VIDE A LATE TELEGRAPH.

sound of hooves in the distance, before they took chase into the night. In the darkness was silence.

The bushranging gang had turned back again and were now sticking-up De Clouet's Public House. Again, they entered through the back door, pushing their way into the bar where they first took £2 from one of the patrons. Hall pushed open the bedroom door to find Mrs Clouet washing her baby. Thinking he was just a drunken customer, she ordered him to leave, but Hall soon left her in no doubt of his intentions. He demanded the cash-box as he rummaged through the room. 'Here,' she exclaimed, 'I'll find it for you if you'll hold the baby.' Hall smiled and indicated his inability to help her, as he had his hands already filled with his revolvers.

He helped himself to the notes and some gold, then demanded of the publican that he hand over his prize racing horse Pacha. As they were jostling the ostler towards the stables, the police rode by. Hall decided it was better to leave while he was still ahead, rather than endanger the gang for his love of

ABOVE:
Something from Sydney – The Police are Scouring the Country After Bushrangers
Cartoon from *The Melbourne Punch*, c. 1864
No matter how hard they tried the police had no luck at all until the *Felon's Act* was passed and the gang were made outlaws.
(National Library of Australia Collection)

John O'Meally

John O'Meally was just a boy when Gardiner began his career on the roads. He lived at the Weddin Mountains where his father kept a shanty, and it was here that he first made the acquaintance of the famous bushranger. The boy soon fell in with Gardiner and cut his teeth at the Eugowra Rocks. From then on he became one of Gardiner's most reliable young lieutenants.

O'Meally did not have the courtesy displayed by the older man. Once he met a Mr Barnes on the road; now Barnes had previously been robbed by the gang and didn't think it fair to have to go through another stick-up. When O'Meally demanded that Barnes hand over his saddle and bridle, he refused, dug in his spurs and rode off. O'Meally was not to be thrown off quite so easily; he took aim and shot Barnes in the back. Barnes fell from his horse and died as he lay on the road. O'Meally later rode into Barnes's station and took the saddle and bridle from the store. He got what he wanted in the end.

O'Meally died on 19 November 1863, the day after Vane gave himself up. Hall, Gilbert and O'Meally had attacked the Campbell homestead at Goimbla Station. They first set fire to the haystack, and then attempted to break into the homestead. Mr and Mrs Campbell were both defending themselves with great valour when a man in a cabbage-tree hat stood looking in at the window at the lady of the house. Campbell took up his gun, aimed at the intruder's throat and opened fire. Silence fell on the deathly still night air.

BAIL UP!

a good horse. He then leapt upon his own mount and galloped away.

But the gang hadn't finished with Bathurst yet. As they trotted down the street, they saw a large group of mounted police on a rise before them. They turned and sped away towards Vale Creek, a suburb of Bathurst. There, they went from house to house along the creek, stealing from everyone they met. The police chased them along the street but as they entered one house the robbers were already sticking-up the next.

When they had had their fun, the gang disappeared into the night, unharmed. The bushrangers were always better mounted than the police, as they helped themselves to the best horses in the district. The taking of horses was stock-in-trade to them, and they stole and changed horses more regularly than they changed their socks. A fresh mount meant life or death to them, and all had an excellent eye for the finest stock.

Sticking-up the Mails

The coaches that travelled up and down the roads, day by day, provided the gang with the perfect opportunity for some entertainment. They knew the timetables of the coaching companies and simply lay in wait for their arrival. At times they held up scores of other travellers who were on the roads just ahead of the coach. The gang had no trouble at all extracting money from these hapless travellers as they kept them under guard at the side of the road. In fact, on that fateful day in November 1864 that Sergeant Parry was shot in a raid on the Binalong coach which was carrying mail from Gundagai to Yass, those detained off the side of the road all moved out of the bush where they had been hidden in order to get a better view of the fight.

The gang took their time opening the mail-bags. They ripped open envelopes in search of cash, bank-drafts and cheques. They spent their time in the

---

ABOVE:
Night Raid on Bathurst
Oil on canvas by Patrick William Maroney, 1894
The gang galloped into Bathurst in the early evening, hoping to be able to appropriate some repeating rifles. When this proved not possible, they helped themselves as they rode from house to house, robbing as they pleased.

Although the police mounted a gallant chase, the bushrangers simply rode to the edge of town and disappeared into the night. They were always better mounted than the troopers as they rode only the best horses in the district – stolen, of course.
(National Library of Australia Collection)

leisurely inspection of private mail, reading letters out to one another, then more often than not destroying what they left behind. Hall even set fire to the papers and letters on the Binalong coach, announcing that he would 'put a stop to this bloody English correspondence'.

There were plenty of sympathisers who shared the same views. They also had no love for the system, and continued to aid and abet the bandits' every move. They supplied information about the whereabouts of the police, they offered them safe hiding places, and in turn were often rewarded with a share of the goods that the gang managed to secure. Ben Hall had become almost a modern-day 'Robin Hood', but he stole from the rich and the poor alike, distributing the booty among his supporters, his family and his friends.

Over his few short years on the rampage Hall committed over 600 robberies. He never killed anyone, and this may have been the reason why he remained a popular folk hero.

There was one small boy in the Victorian northeast, only a few miles out of Beechworth, who grew up with the tales of 'bold' Ben Hall ringing in his ears. To him Hall was 'his' handsome young Australian-born horse-back hero, who was defending his family against the troopers and in turn, the English social system, a system that had always denied the Irish their own birthright. And it was this young Ned Kelly who was outraged when he too was 'outlawed', just as his hero Ben Hall had been.

ABOVE:
Bushrangers Pass the Time Reading the Mails...
On one occasion Ben Hall even set fire to the papers on one mail-coach, stating that he would 'put a stop to this bloody English correspondence'.

BAIL UP!

'Bold' Ben Hall's pistol.
Colt's Patent Firearms manufacturing Co., c. 1850
(National Library of Australia Collection)

The Streets of Forbes

Come all you Lachlan men, and a sorrowful tale I'll tell.
Concerning of a hero bold who through misfortune fell.
His name it was Ben Hall, a man of good renown,
Who was hunted from his station, and like a dog shot down.

Three years he roamed the roads, and he showed the traps some fun;
A thousand pound was on his head, with Gilbert and John Dunn.
Ben parted from his comrades, the outlaws did agree
To give away bushranging and to cross the briny sea.

Ben went to Goobang Creek, and that was his downfall;
For riddled like a sieve was valiant Ben Hall.
'Twas early in the morning upon the fifth of May
When the seven police surrounded him as fast asleep he lay.

Dargin he was chosen to shoot the outlaw dead;
The troopers then fired madly, and filled him full of lead.
They rolled him in a blanket, and strapped him to his prad,
And led him through the streets of Forbes to show the prize they had.

– ATTRIBUTED TO JOHN MCQUIRE

The Felon's Act

The gang had been so active and the police so inefficient that the government was demanding an end to the Ben Hall bushranging menace. Not a day went by without Parliament being regaled with the affairs of the gang. The government wanted to put a decisive end to the matter, so an Act for the destruction of the bandits known as the *Felon's Apprehension Act* was rushed through Parliament. This Act enabled the gang to be outlawed, making it possible for anyone who came across them to shoot them down like mad dogs. All it required to outlaw such persons was to place a general summons in the *Government Gazette*.

The Act demanded that the persons named in the summons should give themselves up on or before a certain date, and to stand trial for the crimes of which they were accused. If they failed to do this or had done so, and then escaped, it was lawful for any other person to bring them in – dead or alive.

Anyone found to be harbouring or assisting the accused in any way would also be considered to be a felon and, if convicted, be forced to surrender all his lands and goods, and then be imprisoned for a maximum of fifteen years.

The police had virtually *carte blanche* to enter any dwelling or home where they suspected a bushranger was hiding and arrest any person they suspected of being a bushranger, or helping a bushranger, and were able to confiscate any weapons that were found inside.

The government had succeeded in tying up almost all avenues of escape. The terms of the Act were so onerous that they believed that there was nobody abroad who would put their future at risk for the sake of a few bandits, who were all going to die before long, one way or another.

On 8 April 1865 John Gilbert, Benjamin Hall and John Dunn were outlawed.

God save the Queen!

The Death of Hall

Once outlawed the end came fast for Ben Hall, and it was a mate of his who hastened his demise. Mick Connelly had been keeping Hall's money safe for him, and when he asked for it back he betrayed him to the police. Hall had told Mick that he had had enough, that he wanted to get away from the district and disappear, possibly jump aboard a ship headed for California. But it was too late for him: the die was already cast.

It was just before dawn when troopers came upon a camp in the trees where Connelly had told them the bushranger was hiding out. They saw a figure come out from the thicket and move two horses a couple of hundred feet to a spot with better grass. After hobbling them again, the figure returned to what appeared to be a bed among some fallen leaves. It was too dark to see whether the figure was, in fact, the man they were seeking, so the police decided to await the sunrise.

CAPTURE AND DEATH OF BEN HALL, THE BUSHRANGER.—See Page

Above:
Capture and Death of Ben Hall the Bushranger
Wood engraving by Oswald Campbell,
published in *Australian News for Home Readers*, 1865
Hall was killed at daybreak on 6 May 1865. His body was riddled with bullets as he tried to escape his attackers.
(National Library of Australia Collection)

BAIL UP!

At about 6.30 a.m., the figure came out again from the trees, with a bridle in his hand, and made towards the horses. Seeing this the police began to run towards him when, on hearing their approach, he turned and sprinted in the opposite direction towards five other policemen.

Sergeant Condell, who by this time was sure it was Hall, cried out to him several times and ordered him 'to stand', but Hall kept running in the vain attempt to secure his escape. Although over 100 yards behind the running bushranger, Condell raised his shotgun, took careful aim, and pulled the trigger. The shot hit Hall in the shoulder. He staggered a little, then turned and continued to run on towards the trees. He grabbed out at a sapling and held himself up as he cried out to his old friend Billy Dargin, the black-tracker who had led the police to his camp, 'I am dying! I am dying! Shoot me dead!' He had once before vowed: 'They'll never hang Ben Hall'.

The other troopers now began to open fire, and bullets rang through the air as they found their mark. Hall staggered, threw out his feet as if in a convulsion and rolled over, dead.

His body was riddled with lead. The police report stated that the thirty bullets had done their job. Three had hit him in the head, four in the left shoulder, two in the right and the rest were scattered all over his lifeless form. Another report given later by Billy Dargin, who had once been a friend of Hall and had tried to get close enough so that he could be taken alive, said that he had sustained most of these wounds after he had hit the ground.

On the morning of 6 May 1865, Ben Hall, the feared bushranger, who had never shot anybody in all his wild career, was brought down in an unseemly barrage of fire.

ABOVE:
Death of Ben Hall
Oil on canvas by Patrick William Maroney, 1894
After Hall's death his body was wrapped in a blanket, strapped to one of the horses and taken into Forbes, where he was buried two days later.
(National Library of Australia Collection)

The Demise of 'Blind Freddy'

Sir Frederick Pottinger was recalled to Sydney, charged with having neglected his duty. He had ridden in a gentleman's race at the Wowingragong track and was totally unawares that the men who he was supposed to be arresting were there on the course as well. He simply had not taken any notice of the crowd. The Baronet was obviously otherwise occupied that day. Although his constant patrols of the Lachlan district did bring the bushrangers to heel, it was really the *Felon's Act*, rather than the efforts of 'blind Freddy', that took the credit.

After an inquiry into his behaviour, Pottinger resigned from the force. He was heading down to Sydney on 5 March 1865, to seek redress when he died from a pistol shot from his own gun. He was only thirty-four.

Poor Freddy was subjected to such public ridicule that the derisive term 'even blind Freddy couldn't see it' was coined in his dubious 'honour'.

ABOVE:
Sir Frederick Pottinger
Poor 'blind Freddy' couldn't take a trick. Just before the gang was brought to pay for its crimes, he was charged for neglect of his duty, and then shot himself with his own gun — accidentally?
(Mitchell Library Collection, State Library of New South Wales)

Johnnie Gilbert

John Gilbert arrived in Australia, aged ten years old, on 15 October 1852. His family had came out from England, first to Canada, where John was born, then on to Australia at the height of gold fever.

The family went first to the Lauriston area on the fringe of the Forest Creek–Mt Alexander diggings. From there John went to work as a stableboy at the Kilmore Inn on the road to the diggings in the north-east of Victoria.

A long way from the influence of his family, the twelve-year-old boy soon fell in with a bad crowd. He travelled around the diggings in the company of a group of con-men, and the easy pickings from this illicit trade soon seduced the boy.

He did not go unnoticed by the authorities – this flash young lad about the place, playing tricks and helping himself whenever he could get away with it. But he didn't get away every time. He was caught horse-stealing and sent down to Cockatoo Island, at

---

ABOVE:
John Gilbert, the Bushranger
Wood engraving, published in *Illustrated Sydney News*,
16 June 1865
(National Library of Australia Collection)

BAIL UP!

Hall, Gilbert, and Dunn Sticking Up the Mail at the Black Springs.
[From a Sketch by W. Rose, Esq., Police Magistrate, who was present at the Encounter.—SEE PAGE 11.]

ABOVE:
Hall, Gilbert and Dunn Sticking-up the Mail at Black Springs
Wood engraving by Oswald Campbell,
published in *Illustrated Melbourne Post*, 25 January 1865
It was the killing of Sergeant Parry that rang the death knell for the gang. The police always reacted decisively after the killing of one of their own.
(National Library of Australia Collection)

what was for him probably a very inopportune time. It was there that he met Frank Gardiner, and as they say, the rest is history. After their release from Cockatoo, both took to ranging the bush around the goldfields of central New South Wales.

This small gang ranged so far and wide in country that both Gardiner and O'Meally (and later Hall) knew so well that it was incredible that they were able to commit so many crimes in so many different places, within apparently impossible spaces of time.

The gang had sympathetic public support even though they, at times, proved an inconvenience when they held up the roads for hours on end waiting for the 'mail'. When they took over inns and commanded the townsfolk to join them for celebrations and shooting displays, they were admired for their bravado and cheeky larrikin spirit. But when Gilbert shot and killed Sergeant Parry while they were sticking-up the mail coach at Black Springs, the tide soon turned for the cocky young 'Canadian'.

After Gardiner had been imprisoned and Hall killed, Gilbert and Dunn, now outlawed and the only ones of the old gang left, decided to keep their heads down. They holed up at Binalong, in the hut of John Kelly, a close relative of Dunn and the murderous Clarke brothers. Dunn assured Gilbert that he could be trusted. Kelly must have been wary of the terms of the *Felon's Act*, or enticed by the huge reward on the boys' heads and led the police to his hut.

It was on 13 May 1865 when the police arrived suddenly at Kelly's hut. Gilbert and Dunn escaped through a back window of the hut but Gilbert

The Scene of Gilbert's Death.

turned and decided to shoot it out. He rushed the police at the front of the hut and shouldered his rifle to cover Dunn as he made his getaway. His gun wouldn't fire, so he reached for his pistol, but before he could get a shot away a bullet ripped through his chest and tore through the left ventricle of his heart.

Gilbert lay dead on the open ground in front of Kelly's hut. He had made his last stand. Dunn had got away to stand and fight another day, and he soon did.

Gilbert was taken into Binalong Police Station and exhibited there for three days. People came from miles around to gaze at the body of the lifeless young bushranger. His shirt was torn into strips and locks of his hair cut for souvenirs. Then, on 16 May, without ceremony, John Gilbert was buried on a slight rise beside the road in the police station horse paddock at Binalong on the road from Young to Yass.

ABOVE:
Capture and death of Gilbert the bushranger
Wood engraving by Oswald Campbell,
published in *Australian News for Home Readers*, 24 June 1865
(National Library of Australia Collection)

RIGHT:
Gilbert's lonely grave at Binalong, New South Wales
(Author's photograph)

BAIL UP!

John Dunn

John Dunn was another of the Roman Catholic 'currency boys' who took to the roads to make a name for themselves.

He was only seventeen years old when he joined up with Ben Hall's gang and was present when that other youngster, Johnnie Gilbert, was killed. He escaped from that shoot-out and headed north for the Queensland border. It was only by chance that some policemen were attracted to a campfire he was sharing with two stockmen on Christmas Eve 1865. They were out searching for some sheep-stealers who had been reported to be in the region. Dunn, unable to account properly for himself, took a shot at the policemen, wounding one, and received a wound in the foot in reply.

He was captured and taken into Dubbo Gaol hospital where he somehow managed to escape, but as he was weakened by his injuries he collapsed in the bush before he got very far. He was recaptured and taken to stand trial for his shooting of Constable Nelson at Collector when he was standing look-out while Ben Hall and Gilbert were engaged in a hold-up at Kimberley's Inn.

Nelson, the only policeman in town, had come running up the street towards the Inn when Dunn stepped down from the verandah, popped behind a paling fence and opened fire. The shotgun blast hit Nelson in the stomach and he fell to the ground. Dunn stepped out from behind the fence and finished him off with two revolver shots in the face.

Over sixty people came to see the demise of the last of Ben Hall's gang when 'the day', 19 March 1866, finally came. As he mounted the scaffold, arms bound to his sides, the white hood drawn down over his face, his short and bloody career came to an abrupt end when he dropped to his death and was left to swing for ten minutes, on the gallows at Darlinghurst Gaol. He was only twenty years old.

ABOVE:
Recapture of John Dunn, the Notorious Bushranger, at Dubbo
John Dunn had been betrayed by his own grandfather, when he went to his hut to hide away with Johnnie Gilbert. Dunn must have been a fit young fellow; even though he was badly wounded he continued to escape to the bush, and put up a terrific fight before he was finally taken.
(National Library of Australia Collection)

From Dunn to His Father

These letters are from John Dunn to his father Michael. He wrote them from Darlinghurst Gaol. They are unexpectedly cheerful as Dunn predicts his demise in a matter-of-fact way. The Irish certainly had a great respect for family, but there was only one mourner at Dunn's interment when his body was finally lowered into the ground.

13 February 1866:
My dear Father
I would have written to you before this only that I was under remand for the murder of Constable Nelson, but that now I am committed to take my trial . . . I hasten to let you know.

I was defended by Mr Greer, solicitor, who promises to get Mr Dalley to defend me at my trial before the Judge, but I may be tried at this sitting as I believe Mr Greer has made application to have my trial postponed to give him an opportunity to look through the depositions and prepare a defense. I would with to get 50 pounds for my lawyer if possible which might be sent here to me, or if you are coming down, maybe brought with you. — I have had one hearing on another charge of shooting at with intent to kill and murder at the time of my apprehension.

Mr Read the Gaoler wan all the officers are particularly kind to me under the circumstances, and it would be ungrateful of me to pass over the kind and considerate attention of the Sisters of Charity who come to visit me frequently — also several priests.

Since you saw me last I cannot say that I am better. I am still very weak, but every care and attention to my comfort seems to be made for me. I am in very tolerable spirits, and if all comes to the worst I hope I will have sufficient fortitude to bear it, indeed I am sure I will.

I would [like?] soon to hear from you and my dear mother, brothers and sisters to whom you will give my love — Tell them not to fret on my account that I do not intend to let the most hopeless result affect me in any other way that in a sincere and ? effort to prepare myself for a happier future —
Believe me my dear father, your affectionate son,
John Dunn

2 March 1866
My dear Father
I received your very welcome second letter a few days ago — I say welcome although it conveyed to me the death of my sister. I can sincerely condole with you on this bereavement coming too at such a time, but you will remember that I never saw my little sister and therefore it is why I state that any letter from you under any circumstances is welcome.

I have not yet heard what day is fixed for my execution but it cannot be far off as I was told by Father Dwyer last evening that he had an interview with the Prime Minister and that the law is to take its course.

Under the circumstances it will be advisable for you to come down with my brother without delay — Mother knows how gratified I would be to see her before I die, but don't let her come. It is best not. I can bid her goodbye to you for her, and send her a keepsake by you also. So reason with her about it and persuade her to remain at home.

I have no more to say in this letter. As soon as I hear of "the day" I will let you know.
With love to all believe me dear father, your affectionate Son,
John Dunn

(John Dunn's letters to his father are reproduced by permission of the Mitchell Library, State Library of New South Wales)

Above:
Dunn the bushranger
Wood engraving by Arthur Levett Jackson
Published in *Illustrated Melbourne Post*, 23 February 1866
John Dunn was a native-born lad who met his maker sooner than even he would have expected. A life on the roads with a loaded shotgun across the saddle could only lead to one thing — premature death, usually dangling at the end of a rope.

(La Trobe Picture Collection, State Library of Victoria)

BAIL UP!

Fred Lowry: 'Tell 'em I died game'

Fred Lowry, John Foley and Larry Cummins stuck-up the Mudgee Mail as it laboured up the Big Hill crossing the Blue Mountains.

The gang had got wind of the news that Mr Kater, a Mudgee bank accountant, was travelling to Sydney with £5700 in old banknotes that were destined to be destroyed. When Lowry and his team rode into the path of the coach and shouted 'Bail up!', Lowry demanded that the banker hand over the mail bag filled with notes. Then he said, 'We can make a bonfire of them just as well as you can'.

There was only one other passenger in the coach, and she started to scream when the trio ordered them out onto the road. Lowry stepped forward and assured her politely, 'We never rob women, ma'am'. This act of courtesy cost them the other £200 that Mrs Smith was carrying in her handbag.

When Lowry helped himself to Kater's pistol, he stuck it into his belt and exclaimed, 'Now I have eight of these, all got in the same way'.

They cleaned out all the cash, unharnessed the horses, smacked them on the backsides and left the coaching party to trundle their way into the next town. By the time Mr Kater had walked into Hartley and raised the alarm, the bushrangers were already long gone.

It took the police another seven weeks to catch up with the robbers of the Mudgee Mail. They had been given a tip-off about some fellows who were already known to them. One was Lowry who had, earlier, enjoyed some notoriety as the man who had escaped from Bathurst Gaol when he cut a hole through its massive brick walls and got clean away with five other prisoners. The other fellow was Foley, who was captured not long after the tip-off.

By August, the police had scoured the ground around the Goulburn area thoroughly and were out around Campbell's River when they decided to shelter at Mackie's public house to get out of the weather. As they came near the pub, they saw a woman push a man hurriedly into one of the rooms and slam the door. Their suspicions were aroused. While one watched the house, another went to the stables where there was a horse saddled up ready to ride. They went back and banged on the door of the room, but the man inside refused to open it. After they had fired a few shots into the timber, the door was opened and Foley surrendered.

He had on him at that time £60, later identified as taken from the Mudgee Mail, plus two fine pistols and a massive gold watch and chain.

The police had a bit of luck as they continued their search for Lowry. They had put up at an inn for the night some thirty miles out from Goulburn. The next morning, the landlord tipped them the wink that the man they may be seeking was at another hotel only fifteen miles away.

They arrived just on daybreak and Senior Sergeant Stephensen of the Goulburn Police went up to the front door. His uniform was hidden beneath a great coat, and the girl who opened the door looked at him and exclaimed at first, 'Oh! we'll all be shot'. Stephensen calmed her down, and then asked of the

LOWERY THE BUSHRANGER.—SEE PAGE 11.

ABOVE:
Fred Lowry
Lowry was another Australian-born New South Welshman who once challenged Gardiner and Hall for supremacy of the roads, but his career was pitifully short. He expired uttering the immortal words, 'Tell 'em I died game'.

hotel-keeper, who came running out with his trousers over his arm, 'Do you have any strangers staying in the house?' The hotel-keeper pointed to a room opening out onto the verandah and said, 'In there, in there'.

Stephensen went up to the door and demanded it be opened. There was no reply. He put his shoulder to the door and it burst open. He found Lowry standing facing the doorway, his two pistols aimed at the officer. Lowry fired first, and a bullet just missed Stephensen's head. The officer replied but missed, hitting the door handle, Lowry fired again, this time hitting Stephensen in the knuckles, and Stephensen replied with a shot that hit its mark tearing through Lowry's throat. Lowry was taken by dray to Goulburn, dying of his terrible wound almost twenty-four hours after he had been hit. His last words were: 'Tell 'em I died game'.

Cummins was found hiding in his locked hotel bedroom. He was arrested, tried and sentenced to fifteen years. Both Lowry and Cummins had £160 on them when they were taken. Foley eventually surrendered his share of the loot, the bank regaining over £2000 of the original £5700.

A lot of this unaccounted-for cash was recycled around the Goulburn district for years after the skirmish in Lowry's hotel bedroom on 29 August 1863. Although it was against the law to spend the old banknotes, no one was ever convicted of passing Lowry's 'legal' tender.

ABOVE:
Sticking up the Mudgee Mail, 30 May 1874
Lithograph by Gibbs, Stallard & Co., published in *Illustrated Sydney News*, June 1874
When Lowry and his mates held up the Mudgee Mail, they were not wearing masks at all. This engraving depicts another one of the many occasions when the Mudgee Mail was robbed. Many blamed the influence of the American West for the proliferation of headgear . . . sacks with eye-holes, masks and comforters. But the best disguise was yet to come.
(Rex Nan Kivell Collection NK1234, National Library of Australia)

BAIL UP!

The Brothers Clarke

Since 1863 . . . the murders believed to have been committed by you bushrangers are appalling to think of. How many wives have been made widows, how many children orphans, what loss of property, what sorrow you have caused! . . . and yet these bushrangers, the scum of the earth, the lowest of the low, the most wicked of the wicked, are occasionally held up for our admiration!

But better days are coming. It is the old leaven of convictism not yet worked out, but brighter days are coming. You will not live to see them but others will. — CHIEF JUSTICE ALFRED STEPHENSON WHEN SENTENCING THE CLARKES, JULY 1867

The list of crimes committed by the Clarkes is extraordinary. Between October 1865 and April 1867, they must have been the busiest crooks in all of New South Wales.

The Clarkes' territory ranged from Yass to Goulburn, centring around Braidwood. They were so active that by January 1867 the reward for their capture stood at £5000, making them second only to the brothers Kelly in the high reward stakes.

The brothers, Thomas and John, were aided by a huge army of family, friends, and supporters — all crooked.

Their father, John Senior, died in Goulburn Gaol where he was being held for the murder of a blacktracker. Their mother, *née* Connell, had four brothers, one of whom was serving ten years in Darlinghurst for highway robbery, and she was also in Darlinghurst for receiving stolen property. Another brother was charged with being an accessory to killing a party of policemen, a third had been shot dead by the police and the fourth was under sentence of death for highway robbery and murder.

The entire family and numerous friends from brother James Clarke, uncle Patrick Connell, Jane, Ellen, Patrick and Margaret Clarke, John, Michael, Jane and Ellen Connell, James Fletcher, William Berriman, William Scott, James Dornan to James Griffin were, to put it simply, a bad lot.

Together they robbed banks, held up coaches, stuck-up stores, stole cattle, pinched horses, robbed post offices and anyone else they came across.

Their story really begins with Thomas Clarke, who escaped from Braidwood Gaol on 3 October 1865, where he had been awaiting trial, charged with robbery under arms. His escape and subsequent career kept the entire police force of the region busy for the next eighteen months. His crimes included:

Horse theft, Jembaicumbene, 27 October
Horse theft from Mulligan, 1 December
Horse theft, Mr Mallon Mericumbene, 13 December
Robberies
Mr Hosking, Foxlow, 29 December
Summer's Store, Jembaicumbene, 30 January 1866
Frazer & Mathison, Major's Creek Mt, 15 January
Michelago Post Office, 3 February
John McElroy, Manar, 10 February
Edward Seaton, Crown Flat, 13 February
Morris' Store, Mudmelong, 23 February
Cullen & Harnett, Cooma, 22 March
Nerrigundah Mail, 9 April
Murdered Miles O'Grady, 9 April*
Robbery, Armstrong's Store, Araleun, 22 May

*Thomas was outlawed for the murder of Miles O'Grady. It was not long after this that he was joined on the roads by his younger brother John, and together, they went on a rampage, as follows:

Robberies
Levy (and others) Michalego, 1 June
Thomas Well, Jindera, 4 June
Moruya Mail, 4 June, also stole mailboy's horse
King & Morris's Stores, Mudmelong, 16 July
Fired at Ballalaba Police, 17 July
Robbery, F. H. Wilson, Manar station, 24 July
Yass Mail, 27 July
Queanbeyan Mail, 30 July
Hosking's at Foxlow, 22 August, and again 10 September

SURRENDER OF THE CLARKES, THE BUSHRANGERS. — SEE NEXT PAGE.

Myers & Badgery, Jembaicumbene, 27 August
A number of Chinamen, Araleun, 27 August
A Chinaman, Jembaicumbene, 20 November
A number of Chinamen, Major's Creek, same day
Yass Mail, Razorback, 7 December
Chinaman, Mudmelong, 31 December
James Hyland, Crown Flat, same day
Suspected of murdering four special constables at Jindera, 9 January 1867
Robbery, John Hornby, Araleun, 13 January
Chowdry & Lamb, Mongarlo, 14 January
Yass Mail, 22 January
James Meyers, Jembaicumbene, 26 January
The Goulburn Mail, 22 February
Frazer's Store, Gundaroo, 7 March

They were also charged with the felonious wounding of Constable Walsh and Sir Watkin the black tracker when they were finally brought to heel in the shoot-out at Jindera on 27 April 1867.

As was the case with most bushranging gangs, the police were working against an almost invisible wall of local sympathy, silence and intelligence which alerted the criminals to their every move. In order to capture the brothers, four special constables infiltrated the district under the guise of a survey party. They camped near the Clarke homestead and, over time, became friendly with Thomas and John's mother and sisters. But the girls were not taken that easily. One slipped away to warn her brothers.

When police came again into the area on 5 January 1867, they found the four policeman dead in the bush. An all-out attack followed on the Clarke brothers, and they were outlawed and £5000 offered for their capture. The brothers replied by going on a rampage again, bailing-up mail coaches, and doing stick-ups and stores.

Working on a tip-off a party of heavily armed police caught the boys in a hut at Nurregundah in the Jindera Ranges. After a brief battle they both surrendered. Twenty-two-year-old John and twenty-eight-year-old Thomas were hanged together at Darlinghurst Gaol on 25 July 1867.

Although there were pleas for a reprieve for young John, as it was doubtful that he ever killed anyone, the public wanted revenge — and they took it.

ABOVE:
Surrender of the Clarkes, the Bushrangers
Wood engraving, published in *The Illustrated Melboure Post*, 27 June 1867
There was no more criminal band than the Clarkes. No one was sorry when they finally laid down their guns. They were not 'folk-heroes', these boys, just nasty little criminals.

The public were shocked to see two simple country lads when they were brought to trial in Sydney. There had been so much said about the evil deeds of the murderous Clarkes that they expected monsters.
(La Trobe Picture Collection, State Library of Victoria)

BAIL UP!

Andrew Scott, or Was It 'Captain Moonlite'?

William Scott was a most unlikely candidate for the hangman's noose. He came from a well-off family, and his father had been an Anglican cleric and had hoped that Andrew would follow him into the church, but he had ideas of his own. He trained as a civil engineer before he left County Down to chase adventure wherever he could find it.

It seems that Scott may have had trouble telling truth from fiction, but he did claim to have fought with Garibaldi in the Italian Civil War. He also claimed to have fought in the American one as well, but this would have been awkward as he was also in New Zealand, where he claimed he fought in the Maori wars between 1861 and 1867.

After he had had enough of fighting, or dreaming of fighting, he travelled to Australia, landing in Sydney in 1868. He then moved down to Melbourne, then on out to Bacchus Marsh on the road to the Ballarat goldfields.

He took a position as a lay preacher, and combined this with some work as an engineer. Scott was a learned man, and a passionate and engaging speaker who settled himself well into the local community.

The church moved him out to Mt Egerton where he was to work with the gold-miners, but he found this experience less than satisfying. He persisted at his work, however, and again settled in well with the local community.

Scott always sought out the friendship of younger men in the community, and he soon struck up an acquaintance with 18-year-old Ludwig Brunn, a local agent of the London Chartered bank.

On 8 May 1869, young Brunn was surprised as he went to open up the bank. As he approached the door he felt an object pressed into the small of his back.

'Don't make a sound or you're a dead man,' said a voice that sounded familiar to him. He turned and saw a masked man behind him who ushered him into the bank with a wave of his pistol.

He was sure it was the preacher, and said, 'This is no time for jokes.' But Scott was in no mood to delay, and he moved quickly inside where Brunn became convinced that he knew who his black-masked burglar was. Scott took over £1000 in notes, sovereigns and gold cake from the safe, then marched Brunn to the schoolhouse where he dictated a note that explained to the police that it was 'Captain Moonlite' who had held up the bank, expecting that this would let his young friend off the hook.

Poor Brunn! Moonlite tied him to a chair and left him in the schoolhouse with his signed alibi on the table beside him. It didn't do any good at all, as no one accepted the ruse and the police arrested young Brunn for the burglary, as was the school teacher John Simpson. In a twist of perfect irony, Scott was called to give witness against them. Although they

Opposite:
The Moonliters: Bennett, Rogan, Captain Moonlite, Nesbitt and Williams
Oil on canvas by Patrick William Maroney, 1894
Scott had a certain proclivity for attracting young men and even boys to ride with him. Maybe Moonlite was more the gay blade than he was ever considered in polite society?
(National Library of Australia Collection)

Above:
Andrew Scott or Captain Moonlite
Andrew Scott was probably schizoprenic. He was well educated and well liked in the community wherever he went. After Moonlite stuck-up the bank at Mt Egerton no one would have ever considered that the preacher, Mr Scott, could have been involved.
(Police Records Victoria Collection)

BAIL UP!

Opposite, Top:
The capture of Moonlite and his gang
Engraving, published in *Illustrated Australian News*,
28 November 1879
(La Trobe Picture Collection, State Library of Victoria)

James Nesbitt

Nesbitt was born at Buninyong on the Victorian goldfields in 1857. He first came to the attention of the courts when he was tried for 'robbery in company' when he was eighteen. The judge sentenced him to four years hard labour and he was sent down to Pentridge Gaol. He served his time and was out back on the streets by September 1878.

During his time inside, he had made the acquaintance of Andrew Scott, and like several other young lads fell under Scott's spell.

When Scott was released in March 1879, he was joined by Nesbitt and they soon got up to their old tricks again.

In the police attack on Moonlite and the gang at Wantabadgery Station, near Wagga Wagga, in November of that year, and the subsequent battle at McGlede's Selection, it was Nesbitt who sacrificed himself in a vain attempt to help his master get away. Nesbitt ran from the homestead, with guns blazing, but was killed even before Moonlight could make a break.

After he had been taken, Moonlite asked to see the body of his young friend. Looking at Nesbitt lying still on the floor of a shed behind the house, Moonlite said, 'He died trying to save me, he had a heart of gold'. Nesbitt was only twenty-two years old.

Above:
James Nesbitt
Wood engraving, published in *Illustrated Melbourne Post*,
22 November 1879
(La Trobe Picture Collection, State Library of Victoria)

were dismissed due to lack of evidence, both suffered from Moonlite's little game and remained under suspicion, losing their jobs.

Moonlite was well away. He travelled up to New South Wales where he soon cut a fashionable swath through Sydney society. He used the gold from the Mt. Egerton robbery to establish his *bona fides* with the Sydney banks and bought a yacht on which he planned to travel to the South Seas with his new friends. Unfortunately he had paid for the yacht with a bad cheque and didn't even get through the Heads before he was overtaken by the police.

He was sent to Maitland Gaol, and also spent a few months in the Parramatta Lunatic Asylum when he pretended to be insane. Although he was no doubt very convincing, he couldn't keep the act up, and was sent back to Maitland.

When Moonlite was released in March 1872, he was immediately re-arrested by the Victoria Police and taken back to Ballarat to stand trial for the Mt Egerton bank robbery. The 'preacher' from Mt. Egerton stood in the dock before Judge Redmond Barry, who had no time at all for a man who wantonly betrayed the trust of his friends. Barry sentenced Scott to ten years in Pentridge.

After serving half his time, Moonlite was again at large and went on the lecture circuit, 'preaching' against the inadequacies of the prison system, the conditions of the gaols and the treatment of prisoners. He did well from the collections taken at his lectures, but the other side of Andrew Scott soon demanded his renaissance.

Captain Moonlite hit the roads again in 1879 in a spate of horse-thefts and robberies around northern Victoria. He travelled with a number of younger men; his charismatic charm, eloquence and the convincing surety of his actions attracted impressionable boys to his side.

When Moonlite attacked Wantabadgery Station near Wagga Wagga in November 1879, he had in his company Graham Bennett, twenty, James Nesbitt, twenty, Thomas Rogan, twenty-three, Thomas

Opposite, Below:
Augustus Wernicke
Wood engraving, published in *Australasian Sketcher*,
22 November 1879
Fifteen-year-old Gus Wernicke died trying to cover Moonlite's escape from McGlede's hut. As he fell he cried out, 'Oh God! I'm hit, and I'm only fifteen.' After two days of agony he was dead.
(La Trobe Picture Collection, State Library of Victoria)

ARRIVAL OF THE WAGGA POLICE AT WANTABADGERY STATION.

Williams, nineteen, and the fifteen-year-old Augustus Wernicke.

For two days the gang held a large number of people imprisoned inside the homestead. Moonlite found it increasingly difficult to control them all. He suffered from intense headaches whenever he was under stress, and his behaviour at Wantabadgery would suggest that he wasn't operating at full pace. At times he was good-humoured and polite and at others totally irrational.

Moonlite was infuriated when one man, having made his escape, sent another back to try and release the prisoners. Moonlite captured him and held a mock trial of three men whom he accused of carrying arms against him. Naturally, the trio were found to be guilty and were sentenced to death, but the women in the group pleaded so passionately for their lives that Moonlite gave them up.

Moonlite knew it was time to get out and the gang prepared for their exit. Four policemen had failed to take the bushrangers in a surprise attack just before dawn, and considering the large number of people still inside, they decided to wait for reinforcements. Moonlite and his boys managed to escape without injury.

Around midday more police arrived and the hunt for Moonlite resumed. It didn't take them long to find the gang, who had stuck-up a Mr McGlede on the road and forced him back to his selection nearby, where they partook of breakfast prepared by their unwilling host.

Over 300 people walked over the paddocks from Wantabadgery to see the shoot-out at McGlede's hut. The fifteen strong police contingent had formed

FROM A PHOTOGRAPH TAKEN TWO YEARS AGO.

. . . I intend going to Melbourne first ship which will leave this before this letter leaves for you as this Colony is no longer a safe place for me a man once convicted the police are all professional perjurers would swear anything against him.

The Convict Blood is in the population nothing will efface it from this colony is a fearful place for crime within the last few days a series of most dreadful murders have been discovered in Sydney every one is excited about the affair It is believed that hundreds are missing and that there is a larger gang of murders yet at large.

— *Extract from a letter written by Scott to his father. Obviously Scott was in 'preacher' mode at the time.*

BAIL UP!

a circle around the hut when Moonlite and his boys tried to make their escape.

Wernicke made the break first, drawing fire away from Moonlite, but he was gunned down. Screaming in agony from the wounds to his abdomen, the young lad cried out, 'Oh God, I am shot, and I'm only fifteen'. He died two days later. Bennett was standing at the window as Wernicke was felled, and he too fell back as a bullet ripped through the window and shattered his arm. Nesbitt was next, and Constable Bowen dropped him before he got very far. Bowen was shot in reply with a bullet in the neck from Moonlite.

Thomas Rogan hid beneath a bed, and after the fight, he was found cowering in fear with guns that hadn't even been fired. There was only Moonlite and Williams still left to fight, and they could see that they were well and truly out-numbered and that escape was impossible. They both surrendered.

Charged with the murder of Constable Bowen, 'the preacher' seemed to take over from Moonlite on his 'day in court'. Andrew Scott harangued the courtroom with long and passionate speeches that defended his actions. He pleaded for mercy for his young friends, but all his rhetoric and eloquence were to no avail. Justice Windeyer sentenced all four to the gallows. Bennett and Williams escaped death as their sentences were commuted to life in prison.

Andrew George Scott and Thomas Rogan took the drop together at Darlinghurst Gaol on 20 January 1880.

The Bulletin recorded his fateful end: 'A fixed appearance of utter helplessness and despair. The convict's wasted frame, his sunken eyes, his white face, the helpless doubled-up appearance ...'

His fashionable Sydney friends would not have recognised the flash, charming and erudite Andrew Scott at his miserable end.

ABOVE:
The Shooting of Constable Bowen
Wood engraving, published in *Illustrated Sydney News*, 29 November 1879
The last moments of the fight between Moonlite and the police was particularly vicious. Constable Bowen had shot Nesbitt as he ran from the house, and Moonlite avenged his death by shooting Bowen in the neck. Bowen died the following day. It was the killing of Bowen that convicted Moonlite and sent him to the gallows.
(National Library of Australia Collection)

LEFT:
Frederick Ward, 'Captain Thunderbolt'
Engraving from *Illustrated Australasian News*, c. 1870
Born at Windsor, New England in 1836, Ward soon earned the name 'Thunderbolt', because of the way the he rode about the district – 'like a bloody Thunderbolt'.
(Private Collection)

Captain Thunderbolt

Frederick Ward (aka Captain Thunderbolt) was born in Windsor, New South Wales in 1836. He grew up with such a fondness for horse-flesh that it soon played a significant role in his quick decline.

Ward began working as a groom, horse-breaker and stockman and earned a local reputation as a jockey. In fact he was to gain the 'honoured' title of 'Captain Thunderbolt' because of the way he rode when in the saddle – 'like a bloody thunderbolt'.[2]

Like so many other young men, Ward soon fell foul of the law for engaging in the time-honoured practice of horse-stealing. In 1856 he was sent down to Cockatoo Island for ten years for taking illegal possession of seventy-five horses. After four years he was out again, on a ticket to the Mudgee district where he soon got back to business. He broke parole and stole two horses, and was away.

A £25 reward was posted for the apprehension of the bolter. He was caught and returned to Cockatoo Island with a further three years added to his sentence. Ward was one of the few who escaped from what must have seemed like a training camp for the 'currency boys' of New England. Before long he escaped again from Cockatoo with another prisoner named Britton. This time Ward simply vanished – until Captain Thunderbolt took to the highway.

Once again Ward was at large; like Dan Morgan, he preferred to work alone, although he did gradually attract to his side a succession of young lads eager for the game and, no doubt, the fame. One by one they were picked off, arrested, gaoled or killed. Ward attacked mail coaches, stuck-up travellers, hawkers and even hotels. In fact, so many attacks in the New England area were attributed to him that he could not possibly have committed them all.

Ward's skill on horse-back was legendary; the police could not keep up with him. He knew the landscape like the back of his hand, every gully, every outcrop, and flew through the bush just 'like a thunderbolt'.

He would travel over two hundred miles to help himself to a prize beast, stealing for his pleasure some of the finest race horses in New England. He took John Brown from Samuel Clift, a prized animal that had run in the Maitland and Sydney races. He had taken Tallyrand from Mr Wyndham, who had offered £100 for his return, but Ward had to abandon the animal to avoid capture.

One day out at the Goonoo Goonoo Gap, Ward held up a German band, making them play for him as he rifled their pockets. Although the Germans protested that their families would suffer if Ward cleaned them out, he did so just the same, promising that he would give them back their money if the horse he fancied, running in the Tamworth races, did the right thing. The band went away empty-handed as they kissed their purses goodbye. When they got home back to Warwick, they were surprised to find a Post Office Order for £20 waiting for them. 'Thunderbolt' was as good as his word – he must have picked the winner.

After the death of his devoted companion 'Yellow Long', Thunderbolt was believed to have left the

… driving for Cobb's on the run
up from Tamworth – Thunderbolt at the top of Hungry Hill,
and I give him a wink. I wouldn't wait long, Fred,
not if I was you; the troopers are just behind,
coming for that job at the Hillgrove.
He went like a luny, him on his big black horse.

– From South of My days, a poem by Judith Wright

BAIL UP!

district, but after a few quiet months reports were made that 'The Captain' was back in business. A couple of policemen caught up with him as they were riding along the Namoi River near Manila. A vigorous chase over two miles followed, but as Thunderbolt was riding the fine-blood mount stolen from Mr Clift, he soon outran the police.

In May 1870, two years after this spirited chase and the escape of Thunderbolt, more news was about to come to hand. Constables Walker and Mulhall were in Uralla when a hawker came into town boasting that he had been stuck-up by Thunderbolt at Blanche's Inn three miles out of the town, and he had been allowed to continue on his way.

Mulhall mounted up, instructed lock-up keeper Walker to do the same as soon as he was able to change into civilian clothing – and the chase was on.

The Half-Caste Accomplice, 'Yellow Long'

Mary-Ann Bugg was an intelligent, well-educated, and civilised half-caste woman who rode with Captain Thunderbolt. Her aboriginal name was Yellilong, It is believed that her aversion to violence may have been a significant influence on Ward. He claimed that he never shot anyone, and when his body was recovered from the waters of the Rocky River, his revolver was not even loaded.

Yellilong was also an accomplished horsewoman, and it appears that she had been well trained in ways of survival in the bush. When supplies ran short, she could help herself to a young calf, kill and carve it, carrying it back to the bushrangers, camp.

She spent hours and days in the outdoors, in all weathers, looking out for Ward and gathering information about the whereabouts of the police.

At times she travelled with a number of her children, but she was utterly devoted to Ward who was similarly devoted to her well-being. She entrusted her children to Ward's friends.

When Yellilong was near the end of her life, Ward arrived at the door of a station at Muswellbrook and asked if the mistress of the house could care for her in her last moments. Knowing that he was not able bring her down, he showed Mrs Bradford the way to his hideaway where Yellilong was lying close to death. She was brought down to the station where she died in peace and with dignity. 'Yellow Long's' children were adopted by sympathetic farmers after her death from pneumonia in 1868.

When the policeman arrived near Blanche's Inn he saw two well-mounted horsemen in a garden at one end. The policeman immediately took the horsemen to be the bushrangers, and Mulhall let fire as he galloped towards his quarry. His horse was frightened by the report, and turned tail and bolted back towards Uralla for a few hundred yards where he met Walker as he rode onto the scene. As they came towards the Inn, the two bushrangers turned and, at the same moment, dug in their spurs and galloped away, one headed down the road, the other to the bush. Walker chose the horseman heading for the bush and sped after him. He was thrown from his horse when a low branch had struck him in the chest, but he leapt back into the saddle, dug his spurs into the flanks of his mount and resumed the chase.

Ward was trying to gallop around the paddock at the rear of the Inn, then head back for the road, but the brave Walker blocked his escape. Ward was forced to tackle a small gully through some swampy ground, then back up a hill on the other side. He was now above Walker so he steadied his mount and fired at the officer, but to no avail, and the chase resumed. Ward drove his horse around some granite rocks on the edge of a pool and leapt into the water. Walker saw what Ward was up to; he expected the horse to gallop around the pool and meet him on the other side. Walker took aim and dropped the horse with a bullet to the brain. Ward was now without any means of escape.

The two men stopped and surveyed one another.

'Who are you?' asked the bushranger.

'Never mind; surrender,' replied the constable.

'Are you a policeman?' asked the bushranger.

'I am; you surrender,' replied the constable.

'What's your name?' queried the bushranger.

'My name is Walker.'

'Have you a wife and family?'

'I thought of that before I came here; you [must] surrender.'

'No! I'll die first,' exploded Thunderbolt.[3]

OPPOSITE, TOP:

Capture of 'Thunderbolt', near Uralla, by Constable Walker

Lithograph published in *Illustrated Sydney News*, 1870

Captain Thunderbolt (aka Frederick Ward) was killed in a pond on the Rocky River at Kentucky Creek by Constable Walker on 27 May 1870, bringing to end more than a decade of horse-theiving around the Armidale district of northern New South Wales.

(National Library of Australia Collection)

CAPTURE OF "THUNDERBOLT," NEAR URALLA, BY CONSTABLE WALKER.
SEE PAGE 106.

With that Walker dug in his heels and drove his horse into the water to close in on Thunderbolt, but the horse slipped and tumbled into the water, giving the bushranger an opportunity to lunge forward and pull Walker from his saddle. The two men struggled hand-in-hand until Walker, who had the presence of mind to keep his pistol charged and powder dry, brought the gun up against Thunderbolt's chest, pulled the trigger, and a bullet ripped through his lungs and out his back. Although Thunderbolt was mortally wounded, he rallied and fought back at Walker. Knowing that he had fired his last shot, he swung his revolver around and clubbed Thunderbolt until he fell back into the waist-deep pond. Walker dragged him to the surface, but he was past saving.

On 25 May 1870, Captain Thunderbolt lay dead.

RIGHT:
Frederick Wordsworth Ward, post-mortem
Ward was an excellent horseman, whose love of horse-flesh ultimately brought him undone. His biggest problem seemed to be that he never actually bought a horse, and only stole the very best.
(Courtesy Armidale Folk Museum Collection)

BAIL UP!

RIGHT:
Portrait of Rolf Boldrewood, aka Thomas A. Brown[e]
Photograph by S. Milbourn. Jnr., c. 1890–94
(La Trobe Picture Collection, State Library of Victoria)

The Legendary Starlight

The media played a huge part in bringing the deeds of bushrangers into the ordinary homes of bush and city dweller alike. While the early days of the bolters and the hard-men from Tasmania filled the papers with unspeakable horrors, it was the second generation of bushrangers who became media stars. When Gardiner and his gang roamed the Weddin Mountains, the media mounted sustained and cynical attacks on the efforts of the police. When the Kellys rode through the Strathbogies, the telegraph lines crackled with news of their every move.

Just one year after Ned Kelly had faced the noose, a real 'pot-boiler' of a novel appeared, serialised in the *Sydney Mail*. The rollicking tale of bush life and banditry enthralled a public whose taste for adventure was not extinguished with Ned's demise.

Robbery Under Arms by Rolf Boldrewood first appeared in 1881, and became an instant Australian classic tale of 'Life and Adventure in the Bush and in the Goldfields'.

Rolf Boldrewood, born Thomas Alexander Brown[e], came to Australia at the age of four when his father, a ships-master with the East-India Company, sailed in his own ship, the *Proteus,* to establish the family as squatters at Enmore near Sydney. Thomas followed in his father's footsteps and was himself a squatter until a number of years of drought forced him off the land.

In 1870 Thomas took a position as Police Magistrate and Warden of the Goldfields. His bailiwick included Gulgong, Dubbo, Armidale and Albany. This district was rich in the stories of true Australian pioneering life, and Thomas began to collect and write some of them. He was even bailed up, at least once, by the bushranger known as 'Blue Cap' and used this event as the basis of one of his stories.

When *Robbery Under Arms* started to appear in the newspaper, the public couldn't get enough of the tale, and the book, which was published in 1888 was a great success.

The public, brought up on the writings of Walter Scott, the buccaneers and the highwaymen, were ready for an Australian story to rival the English.

Robbery Under Arms had all the ingredients of the classic adventure: the hero wronged, the thwarted lover, the reluctant outlaw, the good boy simply gone wrong, with echoes of the Australian bush 'bird-song at dawn, creeks in the sunlight, ranges under the moon, the sight and sound and smell of horses, mobs of cattle, shearing sheds, billy tea, damper, fried-steaks and billy-tea again; Cornstalks and bush-whackers, diggers and cobbers and goldfields and gold'.[4] All of this was mixed in with a reckless disregard of authority and Boldrewood had the Kelly saga and the Ben Hall story down pat.

When Thomas wrote his story, it was not long since the demise of Captain Moonlite and Thunderbolt and it is easy to see where his 'fictional' character Starlight had his genesis.

OPPOSITE:
Portraits of Charles White, author of Story of Australian Bushranging
Oil on canvas by Patrick William Maroney, c.1894
(Rex Nan Kivell Collection NK4396. National Library of Australia)

RIGHT:
Robbery Under Arms
Photographic tableau by Alfred Dampier, 1899
(La Trobe Picture Collection, State Library of Victoria)

BAIL UP!

Young Johnny Gilbert is also immortalised in the story in the guise of young Jim Marsden, the flash lad whose foolish recklessness brought himself, and others, undone.

It was not long since the most engrossing real-life drama had drawn to its fiery conclusion with the dramatic burning of the Glenrowan Hotel, the garrulous man in the iron mask taken away to be hanged, and the public taste for danger left longing for more.

Robbery Under Arms begins with the biggest cattle theft in all history; more than 1000 cattle are stolen from a squatter and driven down to Adelaide, a distance of more than 500 miles.* The boss of the drive is 'Captain Starlight', a titled English gentleman who has teamed up with the old Irishman, Marsden, an ex-convict from Van Diemen's Land transported as a lad for poaching a few rabbits.

Two brothers, Jim and Dick Marsden, are called to help their father muster the cattle, and although their long-suffering mother begs them not go, they can't resist the call of adventure.

When he is questioned by his youngest son, Dick, why he just doesn't give the outlaw life away, old Marsden replies, '"I have had the iron on my legs and will never have it again."' Old Marsden has a hide-out in the hills, a safe place called 'Terrible Hollow', where no one has been able to track him down. Starlight and Marsden also travel with Warrigal, an Aboriginal man, who is not only a good tracker but has a close bond of true friendship with Starlight.

After the drive, Jim and Dick travel to Melbourne, then on to the goldfields where they decide to keep their noses clean, win some gold, save their money and be able to go home, marry the lasses they fell in love with on the boat trip from Adelaide, and raise decent Australian families. But Jim, the older brother, does have a hankering for California, where many an old Australian bushranger retired to spend the rest of his days.

This story has all the right elements; the details of the most notorious of all the Australian bushrangers are neatly woven into one fictional family saga. One fateful day, just as the brothers Marsden have decided to get away, they go into the bank and withdraw all their cash. Jim is recognised in the bank by the brother of his childhood sweetheart, whom he had promised to marry, until she turned him down when he took to crime.

Unbenownst to the brothers, Starlight sticks-up the bank, making off with all the gold in the safe. As they make their getaway, they carelessly kill a woman, whose weeping child is left alone outside the bank on the boardwalk.

Jim is shot down in the street before he is able to make his break, undone by a thwarted lover who identifies him when he is met by his first true-love, who has, by now, forgiven him due to his hard work on the diggings. Old Marsden was seen outside the bank on the getaway cart, and their complicity with Starlight's gang is 'proven' by association.

Dick is jumped by an angry mob, even though he was not involved at all, but he is found with a large wad of cash. Narrowly escaping a lynching, and taking leave of his heart-broken bride, Dick is escorted along the road to gaol when Starlight attacks, killing the troopers and freeing the young prisoner.

Then they are all outlawed. After some coach hold-ups and a few other skirmishes, the police, using black-trackers, follow them to their hideaway at Terrible Hollow. In the shoot-out that follows all but young Dick is killed. He returns home to give himself up to the police, take his medicine and eventually start a new life in the bush.

No wonder this story had such resonance with the reading public; it was, after all, their story as well.

---

* The cattle-heist is based on an actual event. In 1870 cattle-thief Henry Radford drove a herd of stolen cattle from Roma in Queensland down to Adelaide.

There was a real 'Starlight'; he was an Englishman who arrived in the colonies in 1866. His name was Frank Pearson, or Dr Pearson, Major Lacy or Major Gordon. He sounds a bit like 'Bogong Jack' as well.

Above:
Robbery Under Arms
A postcard illustrated by Charles Hammond, c.1907
'Starlight and his gang sticking up the Turon Gold Escort.
"Fire", the order was given in Starlight's clear, bold voice.'
Even the fictional account demanded its souvenirs.
(La Trobe Picture Collection, State Library of Victoria)

'What would England do if America declared war and hoisted a green flag, as it's all Irish-men that has got command of her armies' forts and batteries, even her very life guards and beef tasters are Irish, would they not slew around and fight her with their own arms for the sake of the colour they dare not wear?' — EDWARD 'NED' KELLY, THE JERILDERIE LETTER, PAGE 48

1860 – 1880

THE WAR AGAINST THE KELLYS

BAIL UP!

A lazy loafing cowardly billet ... deserted the shamrock, the emblem of true wit and beauty to serve under a flag and nation that has destroyed massacred and murdered their fore-fathers by the greatest of torture ... – NED KELLY ON IRISH POLICEMEN

The Kelly Gang, a Family Saga

In the 1880s the Australian illustrated newspapers were still in their infancy, and they were searching for truly Australian stories, stories of Australian heroes or anti-heroes to counter the tales of derring-do that pervaded the English popular press. After the gold rushes Australia seemed a new and exciting land, and its free men and women were bound to be as capable as English heroes and explorers, generals and martyrs who made the news of their day.

Unlike earlier days when news took a long time to travel from town to town, by the 1860s the electric telegraph had made communication very fast indeed. In fact, the deeds of the Kellys even made their way into the English morning papers, and the folks 'back home' became obsessed with this fascinating 'fenian' melodrama.

When the Kelly gang rode onto the north-eastern Victorian stage, they arrived at just the right time, with the right mix of derring-do and dastardly deeds to give them instant and international fame. The saga of the Kellys had all the right ingredients: a family drama with sex, violence, betrayal, lust, drunkenness, police corruption, robberies, murders, hold-ups, runaways, and the big and strong, bold and handsome, feisty and proud 'sons of old Ireland' who galloped

---

ABOVE:
The Kelly gang, from an original photograph,
Steve Hart, Dan Kelly, Ned Kelly
Photographic postcard, published by *Regal Post Card Co.*, series, Sydney, c. 1870
The publicity surrounding the Kellys was constant; all kinds of souvenirs were manufactured both before and after Ned's death and the destruction of the gang in 1880.
(National Library of Australia Collection)

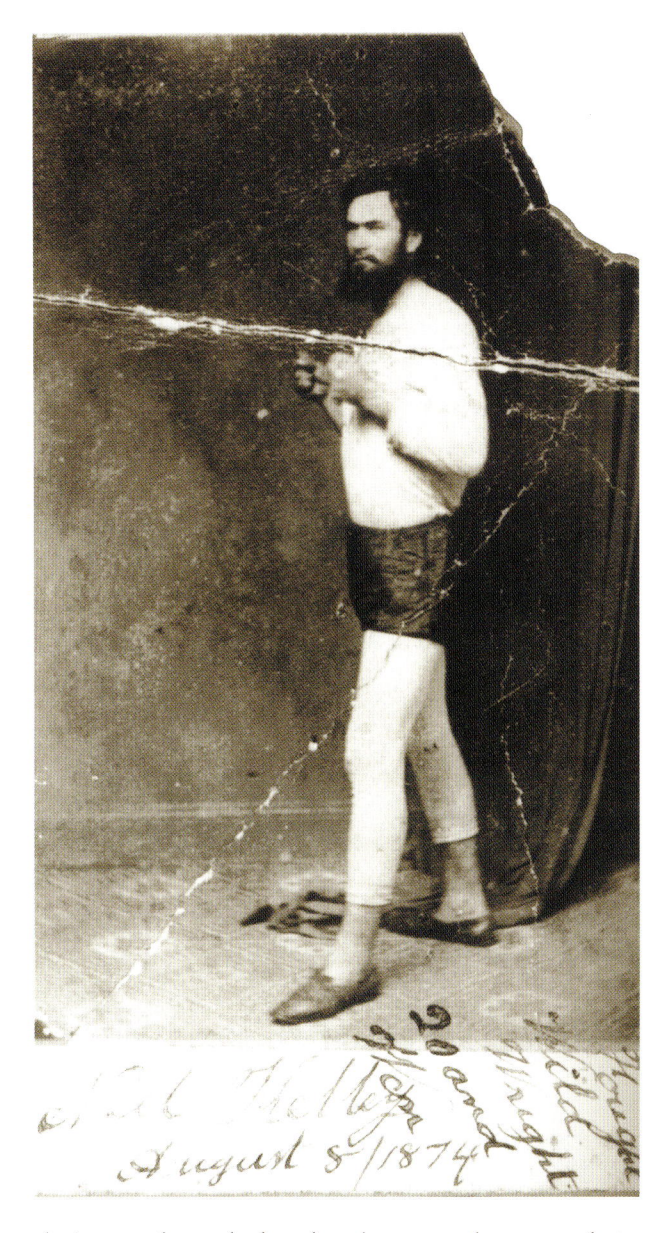

their way through the ghostly gums, always ready to defend the honour of the family, against all odds, and, what's more, they loved their mother!

Like most 'micks' cast out on the edges of respectable society, the Kellys were bound together by the independence of their Catholic faith and the bonds of family. Ned was fiercely protective of his mother and his sisters, and it was the bonds of family and Irish pride that would eventually bring him, and almost all his kind, undone. Ned may have been born free, but he was deeply washed with the convict stain.

Ned came into this world at Beveridge (Wallan-Wallan) in 1854, the son of Irish convict John 'Red' Kelly, who had been transported in 1842 to Van Diemen's Land for the theft of two pigs; and Irish 'bounty migrant'* Ellen Quinn, who was also connected to that other pioneering criminal clan, the Lloyds. Red had done his time, seven years, before he eloped with Ellen in a marriage that bore them eight children, of whom Ned was the eldest son.

Because the Quinns objected to the marriage, Red and Ellen left Van Diemen's Land for Port Phillip, arriving just before the discovery of gold in the colony. Red settled in the Victorian ranges to the north of Melbourne where, like so many others, he eked out a living from the poor land left at the edges of the squatters' rich spreads, and supplemented his income by engaging in the fine old art of horse-stealing.

He was eventually arrested and gaoled for horse-stealing, and died before finishing his sentence. Ellen moved the family to a slab-hut on the Eleven Mile Creek in the north-east of the colony, near to where the rest of her family, the Quinns and the Lloyds, were living. It was here that Ned was cast in the role of bread-winner, taking jobs as a timber-cutter and rural worker, earning praise for his diligence and aptitude for hard work. It was also here that Ned would first be in trouble with the police.

Ellen had taken her children and moved them into the middle of a hot-bed of horse-stealing, cattle-duffing, petty theft, drunkenness, indecent assault and even manslaughter – and these were just the crimes for which her own family would stand accused. There also Ned was to become all too acutely aware of inequality of opportunity enjoyed by the squatters and denied to the predominantly Irish settlers.

At the age of fourteen, Ned was arrested for 'sticking up a chinaman' and stealing ten shillings from him. Hitting the poor man with a stick, Ned is reported to have announced that '[he] was going to be a bushranger'.

The Kellys were also acquainted with the old man of the ranges, the infamous Harry Power, and Ned was sent with Harry as a kind of 'apprentice'.

ABOVE:
Twenty-year-old Ned Kelly, 'the boxer'
Photograph taken 8 August 1874
Ned's notoriety grew as he gained a reputation as a fighter. This photograph was taken just after his famous twenty-round, bare-knuckle scrap with Isaiah Wright. Ned won, of course!
(Courtesy, Ian Jones Collection)

*A 'bounty migrant' was so called because emigration agents were paid a bounty of £15 for every adult landed 'alive' in Australia during the 1840s. A shortage of labour, which followed the abolition of transportation of convicts, meant that muscle, unchained, was worth the price of assisted passage.

BAIL UP!

One year after the 'Chinese stick-up', the 'Boy Bushranger' was again arrested, this time charged with robbery under arms. He was freed due to lack of evidence only days before his fifteenth birthday.

A few months later Ned was back in the Beechworth lock-up, sentenced this time for assault and indecent behaviour after a fight with hawker, Jeremiah McCormack, over a horse and a parcel he had delivered to Mrs McCormack. The parcel contained a pair of calf's testicles and an indecent note; the gist of it was that a competitor of McCormack's had sent the childless couple the bull's testicles suggesting that they were not doing their bit in helping Australia's population to grow. Insulted, McCormack accused Ned of theft and challenged him to a fight. Ned was a 'champion' boxer in the Beechworth district so he easily knocked him to the ground.

The Attack on Fitzpatrick

Ned's real troubles began after his mother was arrested for the shooting of Constable Fitzpatrick. Fitzpatrick was later dismissed from the police force, and was accused by Chief Commissioner Standish of being 'a liar and a larrikin'. He had headed out to the Kelly hut, having heard that the youngest of the clan, Dan Kelly, was visiting his mother. Dan had just spent three months in prison for house-breaking and was wanted now for horse-stealing, but he had done a runner into the bush.

Fitzpatrick had been sent to take charge of the police station at Greta for a few days, and had been warned to stay away from the Kellys. On the way he stopped at several hotels, bragging that he was the man 'to fix the Greta mob'. Full of courage he decided to arrest Ned and Dan, so he headed out to the Eleven Mile Creek area.

It seems that Fitzpatrick also had an eye for Kate, Ned's older sister, and may have done a little more than allude to his desire in his inebriated state.* The facts of the ensuing affray are both contradictory and confusing, but the upshot was that Fitzpatrick was shot in the wrist as he attempted to arrest Dan. No one could really tell who shot who.

Mrs Kelly is known to have told him that 'if my son Ned was here, he'd throw you out the window'.+ but by now she wanted to avoid any repercussions ensuing from this unfortunate 'accident'. So, in an attempt to placate Fitzpatrick, she attended to his

---

On Taking Horses

Horse-thieving was not considered a serious crime by the working classes. There were so many horses and cattle wandering all over the often unfenced countryside that rich and poor alike found it hard to keep track of all their stock.

Wealthy squatters would impound any beast that wandered onto their properties, and the poor settler, who was probably unable to afford to fence his farm properly, would have to pay the police a fine for the beast's retrieval.

In his *Jerilderie Letter*, Ned Kelly explained the reason why he stole horses as restitution for horses taken from him:

I started wholesale and retail horse and cattle dealing Whitty and Burns not being satisfied with all the picked land on the Boggy Creek and King River and the run of their stock on the certificate ground free and no one interfering with them paid heavy rent to the banks for all the open ground so as a poor man could keep no stock, and impounded every beast they could get, even off Government roads.

If a poor man happened to leave his horse or bit of a poddy calf outside his paddock they would be impounded. I have known over 60 head of horses impounded in one day by Whitty and Burns all belonging to poor farmers they would have to leave their ploughing or harvest or other employment to go to Oxley.

When they would get there perhaps not have money enough to release them and have to give a bill of sale or borrow the money which is no easy matter.

And along with this sort of work, Farrell the Policeman stole a horse from George King and had him in Whitty and Farrells Paddocks until he left the force. And all this was the cause of me and my step-father George King taking their horses and selling them …

—*Jerilderie Letter*, pages 16—17

---

* Some suggest that he raped Kate and, as a consequence, was the father of her child.

+ Other records suggest she said: 'If my son Ned was here, he'd ram your revolver down your throat'.

wounds, fed him, gave him something to drink, and then they all decided that nothing more was to be said about the affray. Fitzpatrick agreed and went on his way.

Fitzpatrick told a completely different story when he got back to the station. He said that both Ned and Dan had burst into the hut shouting: 'Out of this, you bastard', then shot him twice at blank range. Ellen Kelly hit him over the head with a shovel, Dan stole his revolver, and next he was ambushed by two other Kelly sympathisers who burst in waving their pistols at him. Ned was supposed to have shot at him three times before he recognised the constable and apologised to him.

Ned was actually 400 miles away at the time.

Ellen Kelly was sentenced to three years in gaol for the attempted murder of Constable Fitzpatrick, and the two sympathetic neighbours got six years each. When Judge Redmond Barry passed sentence on Ellen, he added: 'If your son Ned was here, I would make an example of him. I would give him a sentence of five years.'

Ned, who by this time was also in the hills with Dan, were joined by their mates Joe Byrne and Steve Hart. He was so enraged by the treatment of his mother that he wanted to stage a break-out on the Beechworth Gaol to rescue her. His friends managed to convince him of the futility of this action, so he offered an ultimatum to the government:

> It will pay the Government to give justice and liberty to those people who are suffering innocently. If not I will be compelled to show such colonial stratagems which will open the eyes of not only the police and inhabitants of Victoria but also the whole British Army ... Fitzpatrick will also be the cause of greater slaughter to the Union Jack than Saint Patrick was to the snakes and toads of Ireland ...[1]

Like so many other sons of dispossessed Irish parents, Ned Kelly, a native-born free Australian, was being forged in a rebel mould.

The Unfortunate Deaths of Constables Lonigan, Scanlan and Kennedy

The boys had made a hide-out in the ranges at the head of the King River, a place where Harry Power had long eluded escape. The district was virtually impenetrable to all but those in the know.

The police were determined to hunt down the Kelly gang. In October 1878 a party of police were sent out from Mansfield to bring the boys to heel. They carried with them a powerful arsenal intent on Ned and Dan's destruction; armed with revolvers, a double-barrelled gun and a Spencer rifle, the party, under the command of Sergeant Kennedy, made their way up into the hills and camped at Stringey Bark Creek for the night.

There were so many 'informers' in the bush who sympathised with the Kellys that they were constantly informed of police activities. Hearing some rifle shots in the distance, when one of the police search party began taking pot-shots at some parrots, Ned rode down to Stringey Bark Creek to confirm who had made their way up into his ranges.

ABOVE:
Constable Thomas Lonigan
Lonigan, thirty-seven, was from Violet Town. He knew the Kellys by sight, and was the first to die in the ambush laid by Ned and his mates at Stringey Bark Creek.

Lonigan went for his revolver and was shot down by one of the gang. 'Oh Christ! I'm shot,' he cried out, and dropped to the cold gumleaf-strewn ground.

He was one of four policemen who had fought with Ned in a Benalla bootshop. Ned is supposed to have said, 'If I ever have to shoot a man, Lonigan, you will be the first.'
(Courtesy Victoria Police Records)

BAIL UP!

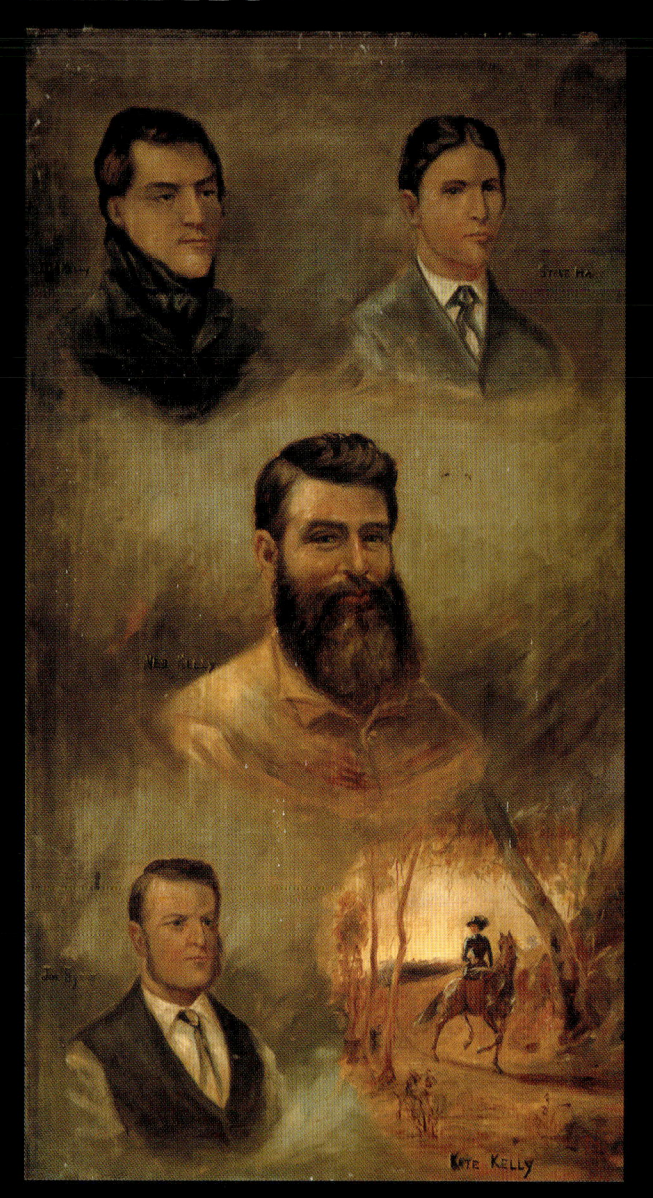

LEFT:
(Clockwise from top) Dan Kelly, Steve Hart, Ned Kelly, Kate Kelly and Joe Byrne
Oil painting by Patrick Marony, c. 1894
Marony was an illustrator for popular newspapers, and was able to observe events at close hand.
(National Library of Australia Collection)

BELOW:
Kate Kelly
(Latrobe Picture Library Collection, State Library of Victoria)

This old picture of the 'eighties looks impressive. It portrays Kate Kelly, sister of Ned and Dan, and has been for many years in the possession of the family of Mr. A. Skinner, 309 Sussex street, Merlynston, N.14. 10/6.

EDWARD AND DANIEL KELLY, THE OUTLAWED BUSHRANGERS.

There were only two men in the police camp when, late in the day, around five o'clock, they were surprised by a visit from the Kellys. Ned strode in with two rifles at the ready; Dan, Steve Hart and Joe Byrne were all armed for a fight too. Ned bellowed a command to the astonished policemen: 'Bail up! Throw up your arms'. Unarmed, Constable McIntyre put up his hands in surrender, but Lonigan went for his revolver in reply. Ned swiftly put one bullet through his temple, and Lonigan fell dead.

The short fight was over. As the gunsmoke slowly dissipated among the damp gumtrees, Ned suggested that McIntyre sit down, make some tea and wait for the return of the others. When Constable Scanlan and Sergeant Kennedy rode back into their camp, they saw McIntyre sitting alone on a log. He cried out to them: 'You better surrender Sergeant, we're surrounded'. Thinking McIntyre was joking, Kennedy put his hand to his revolver in jest and a shot rang out from the trees. Although this volley missed him, Kennedy did not have long to live. He dismounted as his horse bolted, but McIntyre was able to leap on its back and escape. Scanlan was the first to die while trying to drag his rifle from its holster. Kennedy was then mortally wounded, shot in a running battle with Ned, who chased him for over half a mile from the camp until he collapsed, exhausted.

ABOVE:
A Search Party in the Wombat Ranges
Wood engraving from the *Australasian Sketcher*, December 1878
Ned showed nothing but distaste for the police sent out to track him. He railed against them as the gang moved from place to place. Informants kept him aware of their movements.

If they were in one place he moved to another; if they followed him there he moved again; if they followed him again he was already on his way to his hideaway in the hills. The gang was never afraid of betrayal until Aaron Sherritt turned.
(La Trobe Picture Collection, State Library of Victoria)

BAIL UP!

Ned knew that Kennedy could not live and believed that, right or wrong, the best thing was to put an end to his misery. He shot him in the head. As a mark of respect to his foe, Ned leaned down and covered Kennedy's body with his cloak.

When the sergeant's body was discovered some weeks later, the public were horrified by the report of his wounds; Ned's bullet through the back of his head had passed through the skull and torn away most of his face. There were also several other bullets found in his body.

Three Irish policemen, 'brutal and cowardly... parcel of big ugly fat-necked wombat headed big bellied magpie legged narrow hipped splay footed sons of Irish Bailiffs or english landlords which is better known as officers of Justice or Victoria Police who some calls honest gentlemen', [2] lay dead, murdered by four young Irish-Australians, avenging their bloodied history — or that is how Ned saw it.

As Ned continued in the *Jerilderie Letter*: 'I would like to know what business an honest man would have in the Police as it is an old saying "It takes a rogue to catch a rogue"'. [3]

TOP:
Constable Michael Scanlan
Scanlan, thirty-six, came across from Mooroopna at the specific request of Kennedy. He was regarded as one of the best 'bushmen' in the police force.

ABOVE:
Constable Michael Kennedy
Kennedy, thirty-six, was thirteen years in the Mansfield district. Liked by everyone, he was shot in the head by Ned who was later to describe this act as a 'mercy killing'.

ABOVE:
Constable Thomas McIntyre
McIntyre, thirty-two, was taken with the search party because he was a good bush cook. He survived by escaping on Kennedy's bolting horse. He later led a party back into the ranges to retrieve the bodies of the three slain policemen. Kennedy's body was not found until four days after the others as he had run into the bush, chased by Kelly until his luck ran out.

£8000 REWARD

ROBBERY and MURDER.

WHEREAS EDWARD KELLY, DANIEL KELLY, STEPHEN HART, and JOSEPH BYRNE have been declared OUTLAWS in the Colony of Victoria, and whereas warrants have been issued charging the aforesaid men with the WILFUL MURDER of MICHAEL SCANLON, Police Constable of the Colony of VICTORIA, and whereas the above-named offenders are STILL at LARGE, and have recently committed divers felonies in the Colony of NEW SOUTH WALES: Now, therefore, I, SIR HERCULES GEORGE ROBERT ROBINSON, the GOVERNOR, do, by this, my proclamation issued with the advice of the Executive Council, hereby notify that a REWARD of £4,000 will be paid, three-fourths by the Government of NEW SOUTH WALES, and one-fourth by certain Banks trading in the Colony, for the apprehension of the above-named Four Offenders, or a reward of £1000 for the apprehension of any one of them, and that in ADDITION to the above reward, a similar REWARD of £4000 has been offered by the Government of VICTORIA, and I further notify that the said REWARD will be equitably apportioned between any persons giving information which shall lead to the apprehension of the offenders and any members of the police force or other persons who may actually effect such apprehension or assist thereat.

(Signed) HENRY PARKES,
Colonial Secretary, New South Wales.

Illegal Withdrawals

Now the gang were really on the run. The murder of the three policemen and the condition of Kennedy's corpse* when it was discovered led the authorities to 'declare war' on the Kellys.

Plenty of Kelly sympathisers in the north-east were in constant fear of arrest, and they kept the Kellys aware of police activity:

> If, for instance, the police made up their minds to search the interminable ranges at the back of Greta, extending for over one hundred miles, the outlaws would, through their sisters, get the information furnished to them that the police were in that district, and they would shift their position during the night to the Warby Ranges, at the back of Hart's place; if parties of police were sent there, they would move over to Byrnes friends.
>
> In this manner they could find retreats over hundreds of miles of impenetrable mountains, amongst which they had been brought up all their lives, and where they knew every road, gully and hiding place. – SUPERINTENDENT FRANCIS HARE [4]

Ned was furious about being made an outlaw. The *Felon's Act* had been resurrected to bring Ned's boyhood hero, brave Ben Hall, to justice. He was also enraged at the use of native trackers, brought down

---

*When Kennedy's body was recovered on 31 October 1878, four and a half days after the shooting, his corpse was already partly decomposed and had been got at by native animals. Ned was accused of the mutilation of Kennedy's corpse which he denied in the *Jerilderie Letter*: 'If Kennedy's ear was cut off it was not done by me ... after he was shot I put my cloak over him and left him as well as I could and were they my own brothers I could not have been more sorry for them ...' *Jerilderie Letter*, p. 41–42.

ABOVE:
£8000 Reward, Robbery and Murder
This reward poster was issued by New South Wales Governor Robinson, and was signed off by Henry Parkes, Colonial Secretary of New South Wales. There are many names connected to the Kelly saga that have been written into the history books in one way or another.
(La Trobe Picture Collection, State Library of Victoria)

BAIL UP!

> MURDE
> Of Police, near Ma
> £2000
> REWA
> For Capture of offenders K
> others, increased to £50
> offender.
>
> THE FOUR OFFENDERS ARE
>
> By Order
> *Manly*
>
> Printed by Thomas Still, at the "Chronicle" Office

ABOVE:
Outlawed!!
'I was forced without any cause and cannot be no worse and have but once to die,' cried Ned on being otlawed. He was infuriated. He was not a common criminal, and he believed he had done no wrong, but that wrong had been done to him and his family, and to the generations of wronged Irishmen that had gone before.

By now Ned was thinking like a revolutionary. His deeds were a legitimate struggle against the forces of English repression, and he was the rebel leader, and his gang a tiny revolutionary army. For him, it remained a pity that the opposing forces were backed by centuries-old British law.

As outlaws they could be shot on sight, no questions asked, none to answer. The *Felon's Apprehension Act* of 1878 was an ancient English law, dusted off, to bring Ben Hall to justice; it was now turned on Ned.

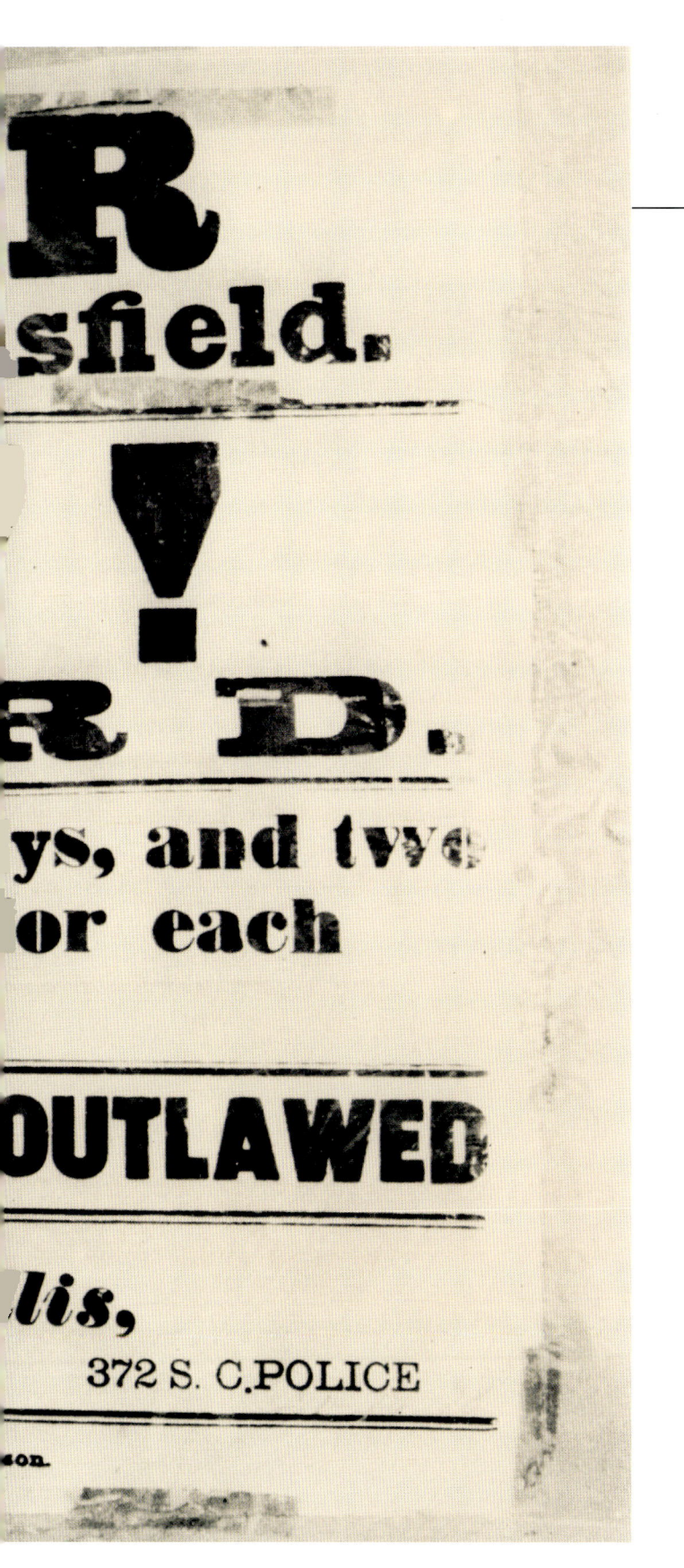

from Queensland. He felt that the English law was not playing it fair.

As outlaws, they would have everything thrown against them until they, too, were gunned down, just like Ben Hall before them. That wronged man, who had never killed anybody, was gunned down like a dog. Ned feared that he, too, would never have the opportunity to tell his own tale.

10 December 1878, Euroa

Ned thought that he and the gang should show the police what stuff they were made of. First, they held-up the National Bank at Euroa. After raiding the Faithful Creek Station four miles out of Euroa, imprisoning the station manager, farm hands and their families overnight, they drove in a 'borrowed' hawker's wagon into town, arriving at around four p.m. They robbed they bank of about £2000 in notes and gold, and left, taking the manager, his family and clerks back to Faithful Station with them. There, they enjoyed a picnic tea with the twenty-two persons who were now held hostage,* gave them a spirited exhibition of fancy riding and, as darkness fell, politely took their leave.

The hostages were, however, warned that if any attempted to follow or to inform the police within three hours of their departure they would return to take their revenge.

After this raid, New South Wales Governor Sir Hercules George Robert Robinson offered a reward for the sum of £1000 on the head of each of the gang, £4000 for them all and a further £4000 was to be added by the Government of Victoria.

11 February 1879, Jerilderie

Ned and the gang crossed the border and struck again; this time it was the Bank of New South Wales at Jerilderie that was their target. First, they entered the police station, stuck-up the officers stationed there, and then locked them in the cells. Dressed in police uniforms and taking one constable with them, they strode into the Royal Hotel where Ned asked

---

* Among the hostages were some telegraph linesmen sent up to Euroa to repair the lines that Ned had previously cut down.

BAIL UP!

Aaron Sherritt

Detective Michael Ward was obsessed with bringing down the Kelly gang. He watched Joe Byrne and Aaron Sherritt like a hawk, and it was Ward whose scheming caused Sherritt's death. It was also Ward who had attempted to create a spy ring to inform on Kelly, but when that proved unsuccessful he resorted to more nefarious means.

Ward duped Sherritt's brother Jack into stealing a saddle, planting it at Byrne's and falsifying the report of its theft. For this Mrs Byrne would be arrested, bringing Joe, and hopefully, the Kellys out of hiding.

Ned was suspicious of Sherritt's loyalty to the gang, but his worst fears were confirmed when they leaked false information of a raid planned on a bank in Goulburn. Sherritt warned the police and received £2 for his troubles. When Joe's mother saw Sherritt lying in wait for the gang alongside the police, she proved the gang's suspicions.

Aaron Sherritt knew his time was running out; he told Superintendent Hare that ... 'I am a dead man'. How right he was. Although the Kellys would have known that four armed police were stationed at the hut on the Woolshed Creek that Sherritt shared with his fifteen-year-old bride, they called upon him just the same. Dan Kelly and Byrne tapped on Sherritt's door on the evening of 26 June 1880; standing ahead of them was Sherrit's neighbour, Anton Weekes, who was known to Sherritt. Seeing his neighbour, Sherritt opened the door to be met with a volley from Joe's gun. Sherritt fell back, dead.

The police had scrambled under Sherritt's bed and refused to come out until the next morning, even though Kelly and Byrne had stayed at the hut for almost an hour after the shooting, challenging them to come out and fight.

Cox the landlord for rooms as he was going to rob the bank next door. Dan stood guard at the door of the Royal, and as people entered, they were politely shown to the dining room and the key turned after them. Ned moved into the bank. When the bank employees were made aware of the identity of the tall, bearded gentleman in the stolen uniform, they put up no resistance at all. Some are said to have almost fainted at the knowledge. Ned took £2141 from the bank, and then destroyed all the record books and deeds. This act may well have benefitted scores of poor farmers indebted to the Bank of New South Wales.

While sixty people were now held up in the dining room of the Royal, Ned dictated the now famous *Jerilderie Letter*, an essay of over 7500 words, an expressive, at times poetic, at others rambling, account of his life, crimes and misdeeds. Ned wanted to set the record straight. He tried to find the editor of the local newspaper as he wanted him to print his account, which ended with the paragraph:

> I give fair warning to all those who has reason to fear me to sell out and give £10 out of every hundred towards the widow and orphan fund and do not attempt to reside in Victoria but as short a time as possible after reading this notice, neglect this and abide by the consequences, which shall be worse than the rust in the wheat in Victoria or the druth of a dry season to the grasshoppers in New South Wales I do not wish to give the order full force without giving timely warning. But I am a widows son outlawed and my orders must be obeyed.

However, the editor could not be found. He was in hiding, fearing that Ned would take retribution for some editorial comment made by him in earlier editions of his paper. Ned placed the 'letter' into the keeping of one of the tellers with instructions for its publication. Ned knew the power of the media; he also knew of the role it had played in bringing his crimes to public attention, and how much interest there was in his story. The reward was upped to £2000.

ABOVE LEFT:
Aaron Sherritt
Sherritt had been a close friend of Joe Byrne and always tried to keep his name out of any reports he passed to the police. He had once been sweet on Kate Kelly and engaged to Joe's sister. He took up his own selection, aged eighteen, where Ned and Joe helped him fence the property; this marked him as an accomplice of the gang. He colluded with the police to help keep him out of trouble – his ruse failed.
(La Trobe Picture Collection, State Library of Victoria)

The Murder of Sherritt

On the night of 26 June 1880, Joe Byrne and Dan Kelly, believing that their old friend Aaron Sherritt had betrayed them to the police, rapped on the back door of Sherritt's hut on the Woolshed Creek. When he appeared Byrne shot him twice, once in the chest, and the second blast hitting him in the stomach. He fell back into the hut and died instantly.

Four policemen were secreted inside the hut, along with Sherritt's young wife and her mother, Mrs Barry. The police had taken refuge in the bedroom, leaving the two women in the only other room of the hut to take their chances with the killers. But Joe Byrne and Dan Kelly were interested only in Aaron Sherritt and his complicity with the police.

The bushrangers taunted the police, demanding that they crawl out and fight, but the policemen hid beneath the bed and refused to come out.

The two women argued that the police should appear. They went into the bedroom, and the police grabbed them and held them hostage, to protect themselves from attack by the boys. Dan threatened to set fire to the hut and force them into the open, but their job had been done and eventually they gave that game away. The police remained under the bed until morning when they were sure that Byrne and Dan Kelly were long gone.

The killing of Sherritt redoubled the police's attempts to capture the Kellys, who now seemed to be able to move about the district and dish out their own kind of justice 'as they wished', with impunity.

The gang had been outlawed after the shootings of the police at Stringey Bark Creek and the terms of the *Felon's Act* should have put an end to their reign. But the bonds of police hatred bound tight in the north-eastern ranges, even after the police began to round up anyone they suspected of having sympathy for the gang. And, in the north-east, the gaols, were not big enough to begin to house them all.

The Final Showdown

Ned decided to bring the whole affair to a head. He believed that he could bring down the Victoria Police in a hail of fire, if he could only entice them into a decisive battle where he dictated the terms of engagement. He believed that he would ultimately prevail. However, he underestimated the dogged determination of the 'bulldog breed'. The Crown had been denied its victory for too long, and the rule of law had to be seen to be obeyed.

Ned and the gang took over the railway settlement of Glenrowan. They held up the station-master's house, and took hostage a team of plate-layers who were camped by the railway line. Ned instructed the men to move down the line and pull up the railway tracks. However, the telegraph wire was left untouched between the station and Melbourne, Ned wanting to ensure that the police were not going to miss this little escapade. He relied on the electric telegraph to bring his quarry to within his sights.

A special train was arranged to carry a contingent of police and their horses up to Beechworth to mount a raid on Kelly's hideaways in the ranges. It left Melbourne on Sunday morning, 28 June 1880. At first it was decided to strap a police officer to the brass rail that ran around the engine where he would act as a forward scout, keeping an eye out for any danger on the line, but this was considered too dangerous. Another engine was secured and it was to run, without carriages, some distance ahead of the

> *These homicidal outlaws must be tracked to their lair, and shot down there like wild animals.*
> — The *Weekly Times*,*
> 2 November 1878

---

*A media event
When the news of the siege of the Glenrowan Hotel reached Melbourne by electric telegraph, there was so much public interest that businesses closed their shutters, workers dropped their tools and Parliament was abandoned so that everybody could keep abreast of the succession of despatches coming down the wire from Glenrowan.

The *Weekly Times* devoted five full pages to the story, unbroken by illustrations or advertisements; the paper wrote: 'Taken in all its details, the sensation created by this event is quite unparalleled in the history of this country'.

BAIL UP!

passenger train, which by this time was to carry a large number of detectives, journalists, artists and photographers, and horses, on board. There was even one woman who, taking her daughter along, joined the party for a bit of excitement on a Sunday afternoon.

The train picked up extra police from Benalla and continued on its journey heading for the centre of the Kelly 'outbreak' at Beechworth. The police didn't know what Ned had planned for them and that they wouldn't get far down the line before they met with their adversary.

During the day Ned and Dan detained seventeen passers-by in the station-master's house. Even children on their way to Sunday School were kept away from church and spent the day, captive, with the Kellys.

The train was already on its way from Melbourne, a showdown in its sights, when Ned was putting his plan into action. Ned was convinced that he could attack the train as it spilled off the broken tracks, and those not killed in the crash could be picked off as they scrambled away up the embankment.

Ned was preparing to murder all the black trackers whom he knew had joined the police on the train. He had a personal dislike for black trackers, whose kind had been used in the eventual discovery and death of his boyhood hero. Ned was planning to summon his supporters from all over the district by sending up rockets, and then his loyal army would storm down and line the railway track for this deadly attack.

Ned's plan was to take a fresh supply of guns and ammunition from the wrecked train, ride to Benalla and set fire to the court-house, then attack the gaol and release all the prisoners held there, rob the banks and the stores and disappear to his hideaways in the Strathbogies. It is impossible to conceive what Ned may have thought he was able to do after that,

---

ABOVE:
The Dance at the Glenrowan Hotel
Wood engraving, published in *The Australasian Sketcher*,
17 July 1880
More than sixty people were held at the Glenrowan Hotel the night before the battle with the police. One of the 'captives' had a squeeze-box, and the crowd danced, sang and even had long-jumping contests to while away the time.

Ned, who was always very athletic, failed to win his contest, but explained away his lack of form when he revealed the heavy iron armour worn beneath his coat.
(La Trobe Picture Collection, State Library of Victoria)

but it seemed as if he believed he could mastermind an armed insurrection from his fastness in those hills. He reckoned without taking into account the scheming school teacher, the intrepid Mr Curnow.

After Steve Hart and Joe Byrne arrived down from Beechworth the entire party moved across the line to Jones' Glenrowan Hotel, where more 'guests' were invited to join them as the afternoon drew on.

Ned took one of his prisoners, who was known to the only policeman in town, to the police house where the lad was instructed to call out to Constable Bracken, telling him that his father wanted to see him. When Bracken answered the door, he found to his dismay that he was staring into the barrel of one of Ned's revolvers. Unarmed, the officer had no option but to join Ned, who warned Mrs Bracken that she would never see her husband alive again if she raised the alarm.

When Bracken entered the hotel, he saw that over sixty people were already inside. He recognised many of them as sympathisers of the Kellys. They partied all afternoon and into the night. Ned was never one to put fear into the hearts of his 'prisoners', and as many of those he detained that night were friends, and sympathetic to his problems with the law, he demanded that this night be as light-hearted as possible.

The crowd helped themselves to Jones's liquor. One of the prisoners had a squeeze-box, and people danced and sang as the night drew on. During the evening, Ned gave several speeches explaining his troubles with the police. He always seemed at pains to explain himself, as he didn't believe it was right that he should have been outlawed. He continued to emphasise that he was not a common criminal, but claimed that he was forced to this life by the constant pressure put on his family by the discriminatory police.

Mr Curnow persuaded Ned to allow him to take his wife and child home. This was Ned's first mistake. Once his family were safely back in their home, Curnow rushed down the line and waited for the oncoming train. When the first steam-engine came into view at around three a.m., Curnow stepped forward onto the line and lit a bundle of matches, which he held inside a lantern wrapped in a red silk handkerchief.

The advance guard in the first engine saw the school teacher's ingenious danger signal weaving about on the track and pulled his engine to a halt. In a blast of steam, he leapt from the plate and rushed back along the line to warn his commander in the second train coming along behind of the danger waiting ahead of them.

Ned's first skirmish was lost without his ever being aware of this disastrous alteration to his plans.

The Siege

Saved from certain destruction by the decisive actions of the quick-thinking school teacher, the police left the trains and headed for Glenrowan, which still lay half a mile up the track. When they came to the small settlement they were quickly made aware of Ned's battle strategy. They began making their own plans to get their horses from the train, in case the bandits made a run for it, when Bracken, having made his escape from the confusion inside the hotel, rushed back into the station-master's house where Superintendent Hare was considering his next move.

LEFT:
Stopping the Special Train by Mr. Curnow
Wood engraving, published in *The Australasian Sketcher,*
31 July 1880
School teacher Curnow was able to excuse himself from the hotel on the pretext that he had to take his daughter home. Once freed he rushed to the railway line, and signalled the train to stop using a flare made from some matches, aflame, behind a red silk handkerchief. Curnow avoided certain disaster as Ned had had the rails torn up.
(La Trobe Picture Collection, State Library of Victoria)

BAIL UP!

Bracken convinced Hare that the Kellys were just about to make a run from the hotel, and the police knew from past experience that, once the gang were mounted, there was little they could do to bring them back to justice.

Hare gave the order and the police made haste towards the hotel. When they were about twenty metres from the building, their progress was checked as a volley of fire rang out from the front verandah. They had run straight into a line of fire. Superintendent Hare was the first to be hit — a bullet struck and shattered the bones of his left wrist.

Ned had taken first blood, and cried out, 'Fire away you beggars, you can't hurt us', as he retired back towards the building. The police fired back but couldn't see anything in the shadow of the hotel verandah as it was dark still before the dawn. The police took what cover they could find, and ontinued the barrage of shots that splintered the hotel walls.

Inside the hotel was pandemonium. After such a pleasant evening of dance and song, the guests were rudely wakened to an incessant barrage of gunfire from outside. The police seemed to be oblivious to the peril in which they placed the innocent people inside, but as Bracken believed most inside were sympathisers anyway, the police may not have been concerned about who got shot. Confusion reigned inside the hotel, and as the Kellys struggled to regained order, a few more of their guests managed to slip away.

At the beginning of the siege, the police had been told to aim high, but as the battle raged on they lowered their sights, pouring lead into the building. Some of those inside still tried to get away but the police fired upon them as they ran from the building. When Mrs Reardon ran with her two children, one a babe in arms, her son was shot in the back.

Ned broke away from the hotel in what some say was an attempt to escape, but it seems more likely that he was planning to get out and get behind the police lines and attack them from the rear. He did get away into the trees to begin his rear-guard action but fainted from both loss of blood and the exhaustion of carrying his heavy metal armour about for so long.

There was a break in the shooting, and the people inside the hotel were allowed to leave one by one. The police challenged each as they left, fearful that the Kelly gang would attempt to escape in disguise.

I have often spoken to respectable farmers, and pointed out to them that it was their duty to assist the police, and their reply was, "I want to stand aloof from everything connected with the Kellys; if they hear the police have been to my place, my stacks will be burnt down, my fences broken, and probably all my cattle and horses will be stolen."

— FRANCIS HARE, THE LAST OF THE BUSHRANGERS

When Ned regained consciousness, and even though he was wounded and had taken lead in his arm and foot, he turned back and began a vain attempt to defend his brother, his mates and the honour of the Kellys. But, for Dan, Steve and Joe Byrne, it was already too late. Joe had been felled when he stood up at the bar to take a drink; the heat of the battle and the weight of the steel armour he was wearing had taken its toll. He removed his helmet, and as he raised his head to press the glass to his lips, a shot hit him in the groin. He was spun around by the impact, crashed to the floor and slowly bled to death.

Dan and Steve already lay dead on the floor.

ABOVE:
The Seige of the Glenrown Hotel
Engraving from *Cassell's Picturesque Australasia,* published 1889
The first shots came from the four bushrangers who were standing on the verandah of the hotel as the police rushed forward. Superintendent Hare was the first to be hit; a bullet smashed through the bones in his left wrist. He retired for the rest of the fight.
(Private Collection)

BAIL UP!

Joseph Byrne

Byrne grew up on the Beechworth goldfields, close to where Chinese miners had a camp. He acquired a rudimentary knowledge of Cantonese from the Chinese but also shared another of their habits. He had acquired a taste for opium. His knowledge of gold-seeking was useful for a time.

He is said to have been killed during the seige at the Glenrowan Hotel when, wearying from the heat, he went to the bar to take a drink. Unable to raise the glass to his lips, he removed his heavy iron helmet, and as he took a draught, he was shot in the groin, spun around and fell to the floor with a crash, and slowly bled to death.

Joe was found on the floor of the burning hotel: 'His body ... lying there in a strangled kind of way, [and] quite stiff.' The police dragged his slightly scorched body clear of the flames.

This photograph was taken the following day, when Joe's stiffened body was strapped to the door of the Benalla lock-up for souvenir photographs.

The man looking into the camera is the artist Julian Ashton, who wrote for several newspapers under the *nom-de-plume* of 'The Vagabond'. He later founded the Julian Ashton School of Art in Sydney, where many of the greatest Australian painters of the following generation were to train.

(La Trobe Picture Collection, State Library of Victoria)

BAIL UP!

LEFT:
Ned Kelly at Bay
Wood engraving by T. Carrington,
published in *The Australasian Sketcher*, 3 July 1880
Ned's left arm was hit, so he was unable to hold
a pistol. He began shooting with his right arm.
(La Trobe Picture Collection, State Library of Victoria)

NED KELLY AT BAY.
FROM A SKETCH DRAWN ON THE SPOT BY MR. T. CARRINGTON.

A Strange Apparition

Just after daybreak on the morning of 28 June 1880, Ned clambered to his feet and stepped into the damp and foggy morning. He looked a strange sight; beneath a large grey cloak he was encased in a crude suit of steel armour that a local blacksmith had fashioned from mouldboards from a plough.

Ned's revolutionary dream was about to be realised. He had become a 'colonial knight' in rusting armour about to defend his honour. Alone, he stepped away from the hotel. Bullets rang off his body as he moved among the trees, and he seemed unassailable:

> We were watching the attack from the rear of the station at the west-end when we suddenly noticed one or two of the men on the extreme right, with their backs turned to the hotel, firing at something in the bush. Presently we noticed a very tall figure in white stalking slowly along in the direction of the hotel. There was no head visible, and in the dim light of the morning, with the steam rising from the ground, it looked for all the world like the ghost of Hamlet's father with no head, only a very long thick neck … the figure continued gradually to advance, stopping every now and then, and moving what looked like its headless neck slowly and mechanically round, and then raising one foot on to a log, and aiming and firing a revolver.
>
> Shot after shot was fired at it, but without effect … the blows ringing out with the clearness and distinctness of a bell in the morning air … Presently the figure moved to a dip in the ground near to some dead white timber … at this moment I noticed a man in a small round tweed hat stealing up on the left of the figure, and when about thirty paces of it firing two shots in quick succession.
>
> The figure staggered and reeled like a drunken man, and in a few moments … fell near the dead timber … we were upon him, the mask was torn off, and there in the broad light of day, were the features of the veritable bloodthirsty Ned Kelly himself. – *The Australasian Sketcher*

Ned had been shot twice in the legs by Victoria Police Sergeant Steele (the man in the small tweed hat). He was saved from immediate execution for, when Steele placed his revolver against Ned's head, Bracken cried out: 'shoot him now and I shoot you'.

Throughout the entire affray at the Glenrowan Hotel hundreds of onlookers had gathered in the bush. Some had even placed a ladder against the verandah of the Railway Station and climbed onto its roof, to afford themselves of a better view of the fight.

A team of railway gangers had gone back out to the track under cover of darkness, and in the early morning they had replaced the up-rooted rails. Trains came and went all day, bringing in sightseers who took their turn to view the dangerous spectacle.

Among those who had come to witness the terrible conflict were Isaiah 'Wild' Wright, the man whose actions over a stolen horse had first got Ned into trouble with the police; and Ned's sister, Mrs Skillion, who had come out for the day dressed in a dark riding habit trimmed in scarlet and a 'jaunty' white-feathered 'Gainsborough' styled hat.

OPPOSITE TOP:
Capture of Ned Kelly
Oil on canvas by Patrick W. Maroney, 1894
Ned fell in a hail of fire near a log one hundred metres from the hotel. It was not long after Ned was taken that the hotel was set alight, bringing an end to the whole affair.
(National Library of Australia Collection)

OPPOSITE BELOW:
The Capture of Ned Kelly
Wood engraving,
published in *The Illustrated Australian News*, 3 July 1880
Sergeant Steele of the Victoria Police grapples with Ned as he lies beside the trunk where he fell. Steele would have executed Ned on the spot but for the swift action of Constable Bracken who warned him: 'Shoot him now and I shoot you'.
(La Trobe Picture Collection, State Library of Victoria)

— 1860—1880 THE WAR AGAINST THE KELLYS —

THE CAPTURE OF NED KELLY.

BAIL UP!

The police had decided to set fire to the hotel at three p.m. on Monday, 29 June, one constable running to the south side of the building with a torch of kerosene-soaked straw that he placed against the wall. The flames leapt up at first, then died away, bringing a cheer from the crowd as the police's attempt to fire the building had clearly failed. As the constable ran around the back of the building, he saw four horses standing away in the trees, saddled and ready for flight. The police shot them to cut off any avenue of escape.

Mrs Skillion rode up to the hotel demanding that she be allowed to talk with her brother Dan and persuade him to surrender, but before a decision could be made, the fire had finally taken hold and flames leapt up and out from the roof of the building.

Father Gibney, a Catholic priest from Perth, was on his way to Melbourne when he heard news of the affray at the hotel. He had disembarked the train he was travelling on at Glenrowan Station, believing that he may be of some use in a clerical capacity. Once the fire had taken hold he called for the police to help remove the men still left inside the hotel and rushed into the burning building, crucifix in hand, to try and rescue the three bushrangers. When Gibney and some other bystanders burst into a small parlour off the bar, they found the bodies of Dan Kelly and Steve Hart, but before they could remove them the fire blew up and they had to retreat to save their own lives.

Only the scorched body of Joe Byrne was retrieved; he was found lying dead in the bar. After the fire had died away, one man, Martin Cherry, was found in a kitchen at the rear, but unfortunately he was very badly burned. Both he and the young lad who had been hit in the back died sometime later.

ABOVE:
Jones's Hotel just beginning to burn
Photograph by John Bray, 29 June 1880
Bray's photograph shows the hotel at left with smoke just beginning to appear, rising above the roof.

The fire was set at around three p.m. Ned had already been captured and everybody else had been able to get away – except old Martin Cherry who was trapped, wounded, in a kitchen at the rear. The gangers' tents can be seen in the foreground, and it is apparent that there was not too much cover for the police in front of the hotel.

It is surprising that the photographer seemed so close to the action. A large crowd had gathered to watch the fight; obviously none feared the Kelly fire-power from even this short distance.
(La Trobe Picture Collection, State Library of Victoria)

Dan Kelly and Hart were both burned beyond recognition.

After the fight was over, the police swept up the remains of Dan Kelly and Steve Hart and placed their charred and mangled bodies onto bark strips. Mrs Skillion went to look at the blackened remains of her brother and his mate, and she was heard to say, 'Thank God they are burned. I would rather see them burned than shot by police.'

Although the bodies were placed in elaborate coffins and taken to Greta by hearse, where on the following day a wake was held at the home of Jack Lloyd, the police still wanted to seize the remains for a coronial inquest. There were so many armed Kelly sympathisers at the wake that the police were warned to stay well away. An inquest was never held.

It was not possible to confirm how the boys died. There were rumours that they may have poisoned themselves to avoid capture; others suggested that they may have shot one another simultaneously, or

ABOVE:
The charred remains of Dan Kelly and Steve Hart
Photographs by John Bray *(top)* and Oswald Madeley *(bottom)*, 29 June 1880
Dan Kelly and Steve Hart were dead before the fire raged through the hotel. Although police rushed in to try to move them, the fire blew up and the heat forced them out. Only the body of Joe Byrne was saved from the flames.
(La Trobe Picture Collection, State Library of Victoria)

AT TOP:
Ned Kelly's log at Glenrowan
Photograph taken 8 August 1880
It was not long before souvenir hunters were on the scene. All kinds of onlookers lined up to have their portraits taken before important relics of the fiercesome battle.
(La Trobe Picture Collection, State Library of Victoria)

BAIL UP!

EXAMINATION AND REMAND OF KELLY IN MELBOURNE GAOL.

they may have simply been overtaken by the heat and smoke and not been able to getaway. It is unlikely that the gang sacrificed themselves to the flames, but these were very unusual times, indeed.

After Ned had been captured and was told of the fate of Dan, his brother, and Steve Hart, he said that they had all made a pact to shoot one another before they could be taken, better to die by their own hand in battle than hang from a rope at the behest of the 'splaw-footed sons of english landlords'.

Taking Ned Kelly

Before Ned was taken from Glenrowan, he was able to meet with his sisters and 'Wild' Wright who had witnessed the whole affray. They all bent down and kissed him, and then he was placed on the floor of a guardvan and delivered by train to Benalla. He was first to be tried in Beechworth Court but it was decided by the government that they, the government and the police, couldn't prosecute a 'fair' trial

ABOVE:
Examination and Remand of Kelly in Melbourne Gaol
Wood engraving, published in *The Australasian Sketcher,*
14 August 1880
Ned was first taken to be tried at Beechworth, but the government, fearful that they would not be able to confidently prosecute their case against Kelly, moved him to Melbourne to face Judge Redmond Barry. There they felt assured of a conviction.
(La Trobe Picture Collection, State Library of Victoria)

in the north-east. Ned was taken to Melbourne by train, and then onto the Melbourne Gaol Hospital where he stayed until he was well enough to stand trial. He eventually stood in the dock at Melbourne Criminal Court on 28 October 1880 charged with the murder of Constable Lonigan. His trial concluded the following day. When Judge Redmond Barry asked if there was anything he wished to say before the sentence of death was passed Ned replied:

> Well it is rather late for me to speak now. I thought of speaking this morning and all day. But there was little use. It's no use blaming anyone now. Nobody knows my case except myself, and I wish I had been allowed to examine the witnesses myself. If I had examined them, I'm confident I could have thrown a different light on the case. It is not that I fear death. I fear it as little as to drink a cup of tea.

As was his usual garrulous style, Ned continued:

> For my own part, I don't care one straw about my life, nor for the result of the trial; and I know very well from the stories I've been told, of how I am spoken of – that the public at large execrate my name . . . let the hand of the law strike me down if it will; but I ask that my story be heard and considered . . .

Judge Redmond Barry was not impressed by Ned's rambling from the dock and remonstrated with the prisoner for his lack of contrition or remorse for his crimes. When he finally pronounced the sentence of death, Ned answered: 'I will see you where I go'.

11 November 1880

Just days before Ned was to be executed he was visited by the gaoler who had to inform him that, as all petitions for a reprieve had been denied, his duty must be done. Ned, who had been indifferent to his fate up until then, became morose and silent.

In his last days, he dictated letters to the Chief Secretary yet again, explaining the reasons for his crimes, never showing remorse, always justifying himself and his actions. He was allowed a visit from his sisters and his mother. Ellen King [Kelly], who was still imprisoned herself, spoke these last words to her beloved son: 'Mind you die like a Kelly, Ned!'

On the fateful day Ned woke at five a.m. and prayed for twenty minutes before he lay down again and slept until eight. The blacksmith went to Ned's cell at nine and removed the irons from his legs.

He was taken from his cell just before ten o'clock on the morning of 11 November. He had to walk to the scaffold past the handcart that would later be used to trundle his body to the morgue. He ascended the steps, and the priest administered the last rites. Taking his last look at the world before the hood was drawn over his head, Ned said: 'Ah well, I suppose it has come to this', then he added his immortal words: 'Such is life!'

RIGHT:
Ned Kelly, photograph taken in Pentridge Gaol
(Courtesy, Ian Jones Collection)

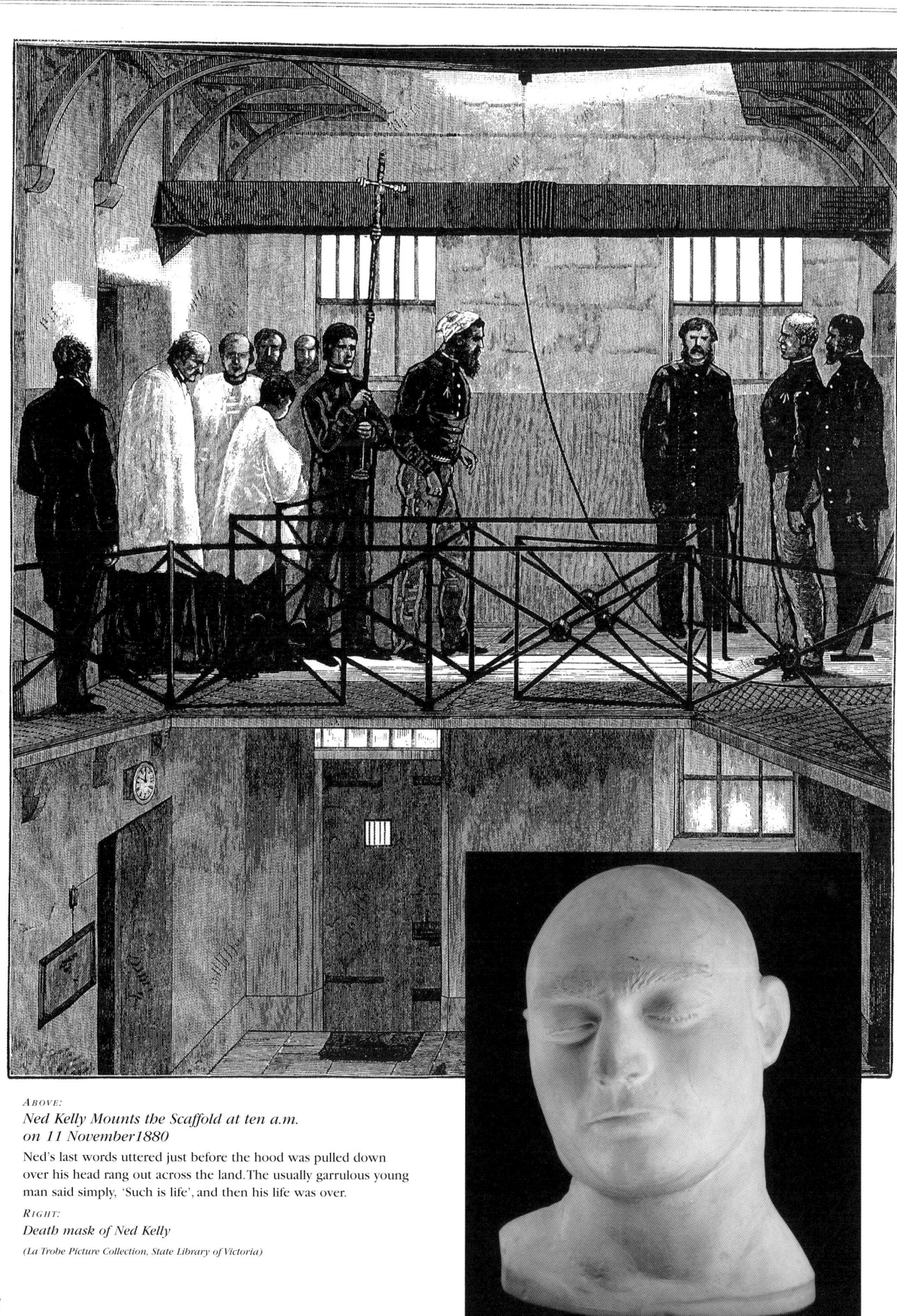

BAIL UP!

Nº 111.—VOL. VIII.   MELBOURNE, SATURDAY, NOVEMBER 20, 1880.   PRICE 6d.

ABOVE:
Ned Kelly Mounts the Scaffold at ten a.m. on 11 November 1880
Ned's last words uttered just before the hood was pulled down over his head rang out across the land. The usually garrulous young man said simply, 'Such is life', and then his life was over.

RIGHT:
Death mask of Ned Kelly
(La Trobe Picture Collection, State Library of Victoria)

Melbourne Gaol

I was present in the Supreme court of the Colony on the twenty seventh of October last when the outlawed prisoner Kelly was sentenced to be hanged – The execution was carried into effect this morning [folloeing] the withdrawal of the Governor[s] proclivities.

The sentence was carried into effect under the Pursuance of this Act for the private execution of criminals.

I [certify] the [signature] of the Medical officer of the gaol who was present as well as one signed by a number of persons who were also present [—] I identify the body of the deceased as that of this Edward Kelly who was sentenced

His age was twenty Eight years
[signed] J. Mastieau
taken and sworn before me, the 11th November 1880 at Melbourne Gaol
[and] signed by the Coroner.

After Ned was taken away, his head was cut off, his hair and beard shaved and a plaster cast taken for 'scientific study'. Ned was interred in a lime-filled pit within the prison walls at the Melbourne Gaol in Spring Street where his headless corpse still lies.

From Ned's mother's incarceration for a crime she did not commit to his own death on the gallows, the Kellys, their friends and sympathisers never forgave the British for the way they hounded the Irish and denied them, and their faith, the equality and freedom they would never cease to demand. The Kellys, like other free-born Irish people who fought the system and also faced the hangman's drop, would never wash away the convict stain.

With Ned's execution, the Crown was, once again, satisfied. And once again the voice of revolution, first heard in 1780 on Castle Hill, then raised again in 1853 at Ballarat, was strangled on the gallows at Melbourne Gaol on 11 November 1880.

Ah, 'such is life!'.

ABOVE RIGHT:
Vignette of Sergeant Steele, the Man Who Took Ned Kelly
Photograph by William Edward Barnes, 3 July 1880
Steele brought Ned down when he put two bullets into his legs. He was about to finish him off until Constable Bracken cried out: 'Shoot him and I shoot you. Take him alive!' As a final gesture Steele booted Ned in the groin – the war against the Kellys was won.
(La Trobe Picture Collection, State Library of Victoria)

Sergeant Arthur Steele

When Sergeant Arthur Steele arrived at Glenrowan on the morning of the siege on 29 June 1880, he was dressed in a tweed sporting outfit looking as though he was out for a day's shooting, and that he surely was. Observers recalled that he looked 'desperate to kill something'.

Steele's first target was a Mrs Reardon and her four children who darted from the Glenrowan Hotel in a moment of cease-fire. Steele opened up with his double-barrelled shotgun and wounded Mrs Reardon's baby and her seventeen-year-old son. They were forced to take cover inside the hotel.

Steele didn't let up until another officer yelled: 'If you fire at that woman again, I'm damned if I don't shoot you!'

The 1881 Royal Commission into police actions during the Kelly affair recommended that Steele be reduced in rank for his failure to follow Kelly into the Warby Ranges in 1878, but this was not done. He shared in the bounty following Ned's demise, receiving a sizeable portion of the reward – £290 – for his part in Ned's capture.

It is ironic that Steele arrested Ned's mother over the Fitzpatrick incident.

Arthur Steele died in Wangaratta in 1914.

BAIL UP!

Ned Kelly's Armour
The heavy steel suits worn by the Kelly gang were fashioned from the mold-boards of a plough by a blacksmith friendly to the gang.

This almost complete suit of Ned's armour has been brought together over many years. The steel plates have been much sought after prizes by collectors and historians alike — at last they are being kept together in the public collection of Victoria's Museum.
(La Trobe Picture Collection, State Library of Victoria)

LEFT:
Ned Kelly, the day before his execution
Ned was hanged in Melbourne Gaol on 11 November 1880, a date that has, over the years, continued to add to its significance in the history of the Australian nation.
(National Library of Australia Collection)

BELOW:
Sir Redmond Barry
Redmond Barry was Irish-born of a Protestant family. He despised poor Catholics and despaired at the short-comings of his own kind. As Kavanagh once accused Cash: 'The English had taken him' — the shamrock discarded for the rose.
(National Library of Australia Collection)

Sir Redmond Barry (1813 – 1880)

Redmond Barry was a powerhouse of a man in the new colony of Victoria. Appointed as Solicitor-General in Governor Charles La Trobe's new administration following the separation of Victoria from New South Wales in 1851, Barry soon established himself as an influential man in the colony.

During his time spent on the diggings, Barry heard the first cases in the Castlemaine Court on 8 December 1851. They included murder, manslaughter, bushranging, burglary, stealing, larceny and assault. Later he heard the case of the bushrangers Goodison and Stallard who were taken to Melbourne for trial after they had stolen five ounces of gold from a digger on the Bendigo creek. Barry gave each of them three years on the roads. He was becoming well versed in the evil ways of desperate men.

Barry heard some of the treason cases against the 'Eureka rebels' and saw a jury of commoners acquit them all. He may well have despaired at the seditious Irish who continued openly to mock and rail against their 'betters'.

Ned Kelly was one 'mick' who wasn't going to get the better of Sir Redmond Barry. As Barry passed the sentence of death on Kelly, the latter said: 'I will see you where I go'. His prophesy was to come true sooner than anyone could have expected. Barry died twelve days later. He was buried in Melbourne General Cemetery on 23 November 1880.

However, his legacy remains to enhance Victoria to this day. He was instrumental in the establishment of The University of Melbourne in 1853, and was appointed president of the Victorian Institute for the Advancement of Science in 1854, and as inaugural president of the Zoological Society in 1858. He was also involved in the establishment of the Melbourne Library and Art Gallery in 1859. He was commander of the Fitzroy Rifles, a company, among others, which had formed to ward off the Russians, or marauding Malay and Chinese pirates, who were ever threatening to invade Victoria's ports.

Barry was furious at the behaviour of another Irishman who had embezzled most of the funds from the newly established Victoria Club which opened in 1856 as a reaction to the growing exclusivity of the Melbourne Club. Barry was furious that the new club had been forced to close its doors, and sentenced Dublin-born James McGuire to eight years hard labour. McGuire was summarily carted away to the Williamstown hulks in irons.

Although Barry remained a single man he did have a long and apparently loving relationship with Mrs Louisa Barrow, who bore him four children.

BAIL UP!

The Jerilderie Letter

When Ned and the gang held up the Bank of New South Wales at Jerilderie on 11 February 1879, he wanted the editor of the local newspaper to typeset, print and publish copies of a 7500-word letter, which he felt explained the reason for his actions. This letter became known as the *Jerilderie Letter*.

Ned never considered that he should accept sole responsibility for his actions, and it is reasonable to suggest that the police did give the Kellys much attention. But it is also reasonable to suggest that the environment into which Ellen Kelly took her young family, among the Quinns and the Lloyds, was the perfect lawless training ground for these boys, who would grow to manhood with a reckless disregard for authority and remain always 'outside the law'.

Joe Byrne had made two copies of Ned's fifty-page letter when they held up Faithful Station some weeks earlier, after having failed to have the letter printed in the papers.

This time Ned was going to succeed in having his letter published. After taking over the Royal Hotel in Jerilderie, Ned went across the street to the home of newspaper editor Samuel Gill. Gill was already hiding in the bush, having written a fiery declamation of the gang only a few weeks earlier. He had no desire to meet with the leader of the gang.

Ned approached Gill's wife who refused to give him up. Once again Ned's plans to get his views before the people of the colony seemed to have been thwarted. The copy of the letter he had sent to Dan Cameron, the local member of Parliament and to Police Superintendent Sadleir earlier, were sent straight on to Premier Berry who said that it was 'clearly written for the purpose of exciting public sympathy for the murderers' and refused to allow its publication. It was one thing to have the papers reporting Ned's actions, which had inadvertently bestowed on Ned a 'Turpinesque' folk-hero status, without actually giving the bandit a voice as well.

Ned insisted that Mr Living, the bank's accountant, take the letter, with an assurance that he would give it to Mr Gill and have it published.

Living managed to get away from the hold-up at the hotel and scurried down to Melbourne by train a day later, just in time to make the morning edition of *The Herald*.

The Herald carried Living's account of the raid, in the nine a.m. edition, but Ned's account remained unpublished. Living handed his copy of the letter to the police, and that was the end of it – until almost fifty years later when it was finally published. Too late to do Ned any good, or was it?

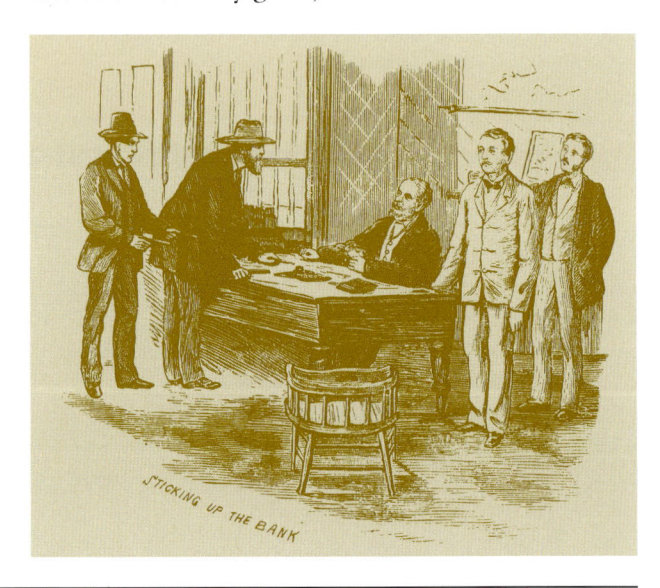

Top:
The Kellys visit to the Police Station, Jerilderie, N.S.W.
Engraving,
published in *Australian Illustrated News*, 21 February 1879
The Kellys held up the Jerildrie Police, locked them in the cells, borrowed their uniforms, and proceeded to the Royal Hotel. They were planning to stick-up the bank next door to the Royal the following day.
(La Trobe Picture Collection, State Library of Victoria)

Above:
The Kellys stick-up the National Bank at Euroa
Engraving,
published in *Australian Illustrated News*, 27 December 1878
Apart from taking £2000 from the bank, Ned was keen for his letter to be published. Unable to locate the local newspaper editor, he handed a copy of his 7500-word essay to Mr Living, the bank's accountant, demanding that Living follow through with his wishes.
(La Trobe Picture Collection, State Library of Victoria)

NED KELLY, THE BUSHRANGER.

The *Jerilderie Letter* was accompanied by a covering note written on letter-paper bearing the address 'Wareena' — Wangaratta. It begins: 'This is the document given to me by Ned Kelly when the Bank at Jerilderie was stuck-up in Feby 1879'.

Page 1 Dear Sir

I wish to acquaint you with some of the occurrences of the present past and future. In or about the spring of 1870 the ground was very soft a hawker named Mr Gould got his waggon bogged between Greta and my mother's house on the eleven mile creek, the ground was that rotten it would bog a duck in places so Mr. Gould had abandon his waggon for fear of loosing his horses in the spewy ground. he was stopping at my Mother's awaiting finer or dryer weather Mr. McCormack and his wife. hawkers also were camped in Greta the mosquitoes were very bad which they generally are in a wet spring and to help them

2 Mr. Johns had a horse called Ruita Cruta although a gelding was as clever as old Wombat or any other Stallion at running horses away and taking them on his beat which was from Greta swamp to the seven mile creek consequently he enticed McCormack's horse away from Greta. Mr. Gould was up early feeding his horses heard a bell and seen McCormack horses for he knew the horse well he sent his boy to take him back to Greta. When McCormack's got the horse they came straight out to Goold and accused him of working the horse; this was false, and Goold was amazed at the idea I could not help laughing to hear Mrs. McCormack

3 accusing him of using the horse after him being so kind as to send his boy to take him from the Ruta Cruta and take him back to them. I pleaded Goulds innocence and Mrs McCormack turned on me and accused me of bringing the horse from Greta to Goolds waggon to pull him out of the bog I did not say much to the woman as my Mother was present but that same day me and my uncle was cutting calves Gould wrapped up a note and a pair of the calves testicles and gave them to me to give them to Mrs McCormack. I did not see her and I gave the parcel to a boy to give to her when she would come instead of giving it

4 to her he gave it to her husband consequently McCormack said he would summons me I told him neither me or Gould used their horse. he said I was a liar & he could welt me or any of my breed I was about 14 years of age but accepted the challenge and dismounting when Mrs McCormack struck my horse in the flank with a bullock's shin it jumped forward and my fist came in collision with McCormack's nose and caused him to loose his equillibrium and fall postrate I tied up my horse to finish the battle but McCormack got up and ran to the Police camp. Constable Hall asked me what the row was about I told him they

---

ABOVE:
Ned Kelly, the Bushranger
Wood engraving, published in *Australian Sketcher*, 31 July 1880
The Kelly story didn't die with Ned on the gallows. Ned's desire was to have his story told, and even in his wildest dreams he could not have foreseen how often the saga of his life, and all the Kellys' lives, would be examined over the following years.
(La Trobe Picture Collection, State Library of Victoria)

Pages 1–6: The incidence of the calf's testicles and Mrs McCormack, and Ned's subsequent three-month detention for the affray with Mr McCormack, are retold here.

BAIL UP!

5 accused me and Gould of using their horse and I hit him and I would do the same to him if he challenged me McCormack pulled me and swore their lies against me I was sentenced to three months for hitting him and three months for the parcel and bound to keep the peace for 12 months. Mrs McCormack gave good substantial evidence as she is well acquainted with that place called Tasmania better known as the Dervon or Vandiemans land and McCormack being a Police man over the convicts and women being scarce released her from that land of bondage and tyranny, and they came to

6 Victoria and are at present residents of Greta and on the 29th of March I was released from prison and came home Wild Wright came to the Eleven Mile to see Mr Gunn stopped all night and lost his mare both him and me looked all day for her and could not get her Wright who was a stranger to me was in a hurry to get back to Mansfield and I gave him another mare and he told me if I found his mare to keep her until he brought mine back I was going to Wangaratta and seen the mare and I caught her and took her with me all the Police and Detective Berrill seen her as Martains girls used to ride her about

7 the town during several days that I stopped at Petre Martains Star Hotel in Wangaratta. She was a chestnut mare white face docked tail very remarkable branded (M) as plain as the hands on a town clock. the property of a Telegraph Master in Mansfield he lost her on the 6th gazetted her on the 12th of March and I was a prisoner in Beechworth Gaol until the 29 of March therefore I could not have Stole the mare. I was riding the mare through Greta Constable Hall came to me and said he wanted me to sign some papers that I did not sign at Beechworth concerning my bail bonds I thought it was the truth he said the papers was at the Barracks and I had no idea he wanted to arrest me or I

8 would have quietly rode away instead of going to the Barracks. I was getting off when Hall caught hold of me and thought to throw me but made a mistake and came on the broad of his back himself in the dust the mare galloped away and instead of me putting my foot on Halls neck and taking his revolver and putting him in the lock up. I tried to catch the mare. Hall got up and snapped three or four caps at me and would have shot me but the colts patent refused. This is well known in Greta Hall never told me he wanted to arrest me until after he tried to shoot me when I heard the caps snapping I stood until Hall came close he had me covered and was shaking with fear and I knew he would pull the

9 trigger before he would be game to put his hand on me so I duped, and jumped at him caught the revolver with one hand and Hall by the collar with the other. I dare not strike him or my sureties would loose the bond money I used to trip him and let him take a mouth ful of dust now and again as he was as helpless as a big guano after leaving a dead bullock or a horse. I kept throwing him in the dust until I got him across the street the very spot where Mrs O'Briens Hotel stands now the cellar was just dug then there was some brush fencing where the post and rail was taking down and on this I threw big cowardly Hall on his belly I straddled him and rooted both spurs onto his thighs he roared like a big calf attacked by dogs and shifted several yards of the fence I got his

10 hands at the back of his neck and trid to make him let the revolver go but he stuck to it like grim death to a dead volunteer he called for assistance to a man named Cohen and Barnett, Lewis, Thompson, Jewitt two blacksmiths who was looking on I dare not strike any of there as I was bound to keep the peace or I could have spread those curs like dung in a paddock they got ropes tied my hands and feet and Hall beat me over the head with his six chambered colts revolver nine stitches were put in some of the cuts by Dr Hastings And when Wild Wright and my mother came they could trace us across the street by the blood in the dust and which spoiled the lustre of

Pages 7–12: Ned explains the situation regarding the stolen horse and 'Wild' Wright's complicity in the matter that sent Ned to gaol for three years, on the evidence of the perjurous Constable Hall and James Murdock [sic].

the paint on the gate-post of the Barracks Hall sent for more Police and Doctor Hastings Next morning I was handcuffed

11 a rope tied from them to my legs and to the seat of the cart and taken to Wangaratta Hall was frightened I would throw him out of the cart so he tied me whilst Constable Arthur laughed at his cowardice for it was he who escorted me and Hall to Wangaratta. I was tried and committed as Hall swore I claimed the mare the Doctor died or he would have proved Hall a perjurer Hall has been tried several times for perjury but got clear as this is no crime in the Police force it is a credit to a Policeman to convict an innocent man but any muff can pot a guilty one Halls character is well known about El Dorado and Snowy Creek and Hall was considerably in debt to Mr L. O.Brien and he was going

12 to leave Greta Mr O.Brien seen no other chance of getting his money so there was a subscription collected for Hall and with the aid of this money he got James Murdock who was recently hung in Wagga Wagga to give false evidence against me but I was acquitted on the charge of horsestealing and on Halls and Murdocks evidence I was found guilty of receiving and got 3 years experience in Beechworth Pentridges dungeons. this is the only charge ever proved against me Therefore I can say I never was convicted of horse or cattle stealing My Brother Dan was never charged with assaulting a woman but he was sentenced to three months without the option of a fine and one month and two pounds fine

13 for damaging property by Mr. Butler P.M. a sentence that there is no law to uphold therefore the Minister of Justice neglected his duty in that case, but there never was such a thing as Justice in the English laws but any amount of injustice to be had. Out of over thirty head of the very best horses the land could produce I could only find one when I got my liberty. Constable Flood stole and sold the most

RIGHT:
Dan Kelly
Photograph by James Bray, Beechworth, c. 1876
(La Trobe Picture Collection, State Library of Victoria)

Dan Kelly (1871–1880)

Daniel Kelly was only ten years old when, emulating his older brother, Ned, he was before the courts for the first time, charged with the 'illegal use of a horse'. He was charged three more times before he was outlawed in 1878, and once this occurred there was no future for him at all.

Dan was before the courts in October 1876 for the theft of a saddle, in March 1877 for the same offence and again in October 1877 for 'wilful damage'. He spent three months in gaol for the last offence.

Dan was only nineteen when he he died. His body was badly burned by the flames of the Glenrowan Hotel on 29 June 1880. The exact cause of his death remains a mystery, as his blackened body was never examined by the coroner. The police were not keen to push his 'heavily armed' family any further, allowing them to take his remains without further interference.

BAIL UP!

of them to the navvies on the railway line one bay cob he stole and sold four different times the line was completed and the men all gone when I came out and Flood was shifted to Oxley. he carried on the same game there all the stray horses that was any time without an owner and not in the Police Gazette Flood used to claim ...

14 He was doing a good trade at Oxley until Mr Brown of the Laceby Station got him shifted as he was always running his horses about. Flood is different to Sergeant Steel, Strachan, Hall and the most of Police a they have got to hire cads and if they fail the Police are quite helpless. But Flood can make a cheque single-handed he is the greatest horsestealer with the exception of myself and George King I know of. I never worked on a farm a horse and saddle was never traced to me after leaving employment since February 1873 I worked as a faller at Mr J. Saunders and R Rules sawmills then for Heach and Dockendorf I never worked for less than two pound ten a week since I left Pentridge

15 and in 1875 or 1876 I was overseer for Saunders and Rule. Bourke's water-holes sawmills in Victoria since then I was on the King River, during my stay there I ran in a wild bull which I gave to Lydicher a farmer he sold him to Carr a Publican and Butcher who killed him for beef, sometime afterwards I was blamed for stealing this bull from James Whitty Boggy Creek I asked Whitty Oxley racecourse why he blamed me for stealing his bull he said he had found his bull and never blamed me but his son-in-law Farrell told him he heard I sold the bull to Carr not long afterwards I heard again I was blamed for stealing a mob of calves from Whitty and Farrell which I knew nothing about. I began to think they wanted

16 me to give them something to talk about. Therefore I started wholesale and retail horse and cattle dealing Whitty and Burns not being satisfied with all the picked land on the Boggy Creek and King River and the run of their stock on the certificate ground free and no one interfering with them paid heavy rent to the banks for all the open ground so as a poor man could keep no stock, and impounded every beast they could get, even off Government roads. If a poor man happened to leave his horse or bit of a poddy calf outside his paddock they would be impounded. I have known over 60 head of horses impounded in one day by Whitty and Burns all belonging to poor farmers they would have to leave their

17 ploughing or harvest or other employment to go to Oxley. When they would get there perhaps not have money enough to release them and have to give a bill of sale or borrow the money which is no easy matter. And along with this sort of work, Farrell the Policeman stole a horse from George King and had him in Whitty and Farrells Paddocks until he left the force. And all this was the cause of me and my stepfather George King taking their horses and selling them to Baumgarten and Kennedy. the pick of them was taken to a good market and the culls were kept in Petersons paddock and their brands altered by me two was sold to Kennedy and the rest to Baumgarten who were strangers to me and I believe honest men.

18 They paid me full value for the horses and could not have known they were stolen. no person had anything to do with the stealing and selling of the horses but me and George King. William Cooke who was convicted for Whittys horses was innocent he was not in my company at Petersons. But it is not the place of the Police to convict guilty men as it is by them they get their living had the right parties been convicted it would have been a bad job for the Police as Berry would have sacked a great many of them only I came to their aid and kept them in their bilits and good employment and got them double pay and yet the ungrateful articles convicted my mother and an infant my brother-in-law and another man

Pages 13–19: Ned canvasses the business of horse-stealing, and dealing. He seems proud of the fact that there was no better thief than his stepfather, the Californian George King, but is always quick to add that they were all forced into it by the crimes of the police.

19 who was innocent and still annoy my brothers and sisters and the ignorant unicorns even threaten to shoot myself But as soon as I am dead they will be heels up in the muroo. there will be no more police required they will be sacked and supplanted by soldiers on low pay in the towns and special constables made of some of the farmers to make up for this double pay and expence. It will pay Government to give those people who are suffering innocence, justice and liberty. if not I will be compelled to show some colonial stratagem which will open the eyes of not only the Victoria Police and inhabitants but also the whole British army and now doubt they will acknowledge their hounds were barking at the

20 wrong stump. And that Fitzpatrick will be the cause of greater slaughter to the Union Jack than Saint Patrick was to the snakes and toads in Ireland. The Queen of England was as guilty as Baumgarten and Kennedy Williamson and Skillion of what they were convicted for When the horses were found on the Murray River I wrote a letter to Mr Swanhill of Lake Rowan to acquaint the Auctioneer and to advertize my horses for sale I brought some of them to that place but did not sell I sold some of them in Benalla Melbourne and other places and left the colony and became a rambling gambler soon after I left there was a warrant for me and the Police searched the place and watched

21 night and day for two or three weeks and when they could not snare me they got a warrant against my brother Dan And on the 15 of April Fitzpatrick came to the Eleven Mile Creek to arrest him he had some conversation with a horse dealer whom he swore was William Skillion this man was not called in Beechworth, besides several other Witnesses, who alone could have proved Fitzpatricks falsehood after leaving this man he went to the house asked was Dan in Dan came out. I hear previous to this Fitzpatrick had some conversation with Williamson on the hill. he asked Dan to come to

Greta with him as he had a warrant for him for stealing

22 Whitty's horses Dan said all right they both went inside Dan was having something to eat his mother asked Fitzpatrick what he wanted Dan for. the trooper said he had a warrant for him Dan then asked him to produce it he said it was only a telegram sent from Chiltren but Sergeant Whelan ordered him to releive Steel at Greta and call and arrest Dan and take him into Wangaratta next morning and get him remanded Dans mother said Dan need not go without a warrant unless he liked and that the trooper had no business on her premises without some Authority besides his own word The trooper pulled out his

23 revolver and said he would blow her brains out if she interfered. in the arrest she told him it was a good job for him Ned was not there or he would ram the revolver down his throat Dan looked out and said Ned is coming now, the trooper being off his guard looked out and when Dan got his attention drawn he dropped the knife and fork which showed he had no murderous intent and slapped heenans hug on him took his revolver and kept him there until Skillion and Ryan came with horses which Dan sold that night. The trooper left and invented some scheme to say that he got shot which any man can see is false, he told Dan to

24 clear out that Sergeant Steel and Detective Brown and Strachan would be there before morning Strachan had been over the Murray trying to get up a case against him and they would convict him if they caught him as the stock society offored an enticement for witnesses to swear anything and the germans over the Murray would swear to the wrong man as well as the right. Next day Williamson and my mother was arrested and Skillion the day after who was not there at all at the time of the row which can be proved by 8 or 9 witnesses And the Police got great credit and praise in the papers for arresting the

Pages 20–24: Ned details the circumstances surrounding the wounding of Constable Fitzpatrick.

BAIL UP!

Steve Hart (1860–1880)

Small as a jockey, this brooding often sullen young man prided himself on his prowess in the saddle. He rarely opened a farm-gate, preferring to jump, and never opened the railway gates when he rode from his father's farm into Wangaratta.

When Ned asked family friend, Steve, to join the gang, Steve is reported to have dropped his tools and said: 'Here's to a short life and a merry one'.

Steve was known to ride about dressed in an unconventional equestrian habit:

> Should they make their appearance, it has been reported that Steve Hart is in the habit of dressing himself in woman's clothes and going through the country in this disguise on horseback. Every person seen riding in the town with a habit or are riding in the bush should be closely scrutinised by speaking to them. It can be easily discovered to which sex they belong.
> – CHIEF COMMISSIONER STANDISH [5]

For Steve dressing as a woman proved to be an excellent disguise, although it was unfortunate for Kate Kelly as she was often blamed for some of Steve's escapades.

Some have read a degree of latent homosexuality into this account of Steve's behaviour. But others suggest that the donning of female apparel was quite common in Ireland as revolutionists, chartists and republicans moved freely about the country disguised as women.

---

mother of 12 children one an infant on her breast and those two quiet

25 hard working innocent men who would not know the difference a revolver and a saucepan handle and kept them six months awaiting trial and then convicted them on the evidence of the meanest article that ever the sun shone on it seems that the jury was well chosen by the Police as there was a discharged Sergeant amongst them which is contrary to law they thought it impossible for a Policeman to swear a lie but I can assure them it is by that means and hiring cads they get promoted I have heard from a trooper that he never knew Fitzpatrick to be one night sober and that he sold his sister to a chinaman but he looks a young strapping rather genteel more fit to be a

26 starcher to a laundress than a Policeman. For to a keen observer he has the wrong appearance or a manly heart the deceit and cowardice is too plain to be seen in the puny cabbage hearted looking face. I heard nothing of this transaction until very close on the trial I being then over 400 miles from Greta when I heard I was outlawed and a hundred pound reward for me for shooting at a trooper in Victoria and a hundred pound for any man that could prove a conviction of horse-stealing against me so I came back to Victoria knew I would get no justice if I gave myself up I enquired after my brother Dan and found him digging on Bullock Creek heard how the Police

27 used to be blowing that they would not ask me to stand they would shoot me first and then cry surrender and how they used to rush into the house upset all the milk dishes break tins of eggs empty the flour out of the bags on to the ground and even the meat out of the cask and destroy all the provisions and shove the girls in front of them into the rooms like dogs so as if anyone was there they would shoot the girls first but they knew well I was not there or I would have scattered their blood and brains like rain I would manure the Eleven mile with their bloat-

LEFT:
Studio portrait of Steve Hart
Photograph by William Barnes, Beechworth, c. 1876
(La Trobe Picture Collection, State Library of Victoria)

ed carcasses and yet remember there is not one drop of murderous blood in my Veins

28 Superintendent Smith used to say to my sisters, see all the men I have out today I will have as many more tomorrow and we will blow him into pieces as small as paper that is in our guns Detective Ward and Constable Hayes took out their revolvers and threatened to shoot the girls and children in Mrs Skillions absence the greatest ruffians and murderers no matter how deprived would not be guilty of such a cowardly action, and this sort of cruelty and disgraceful and cowardly conduct to my brothers and sisters who had no protection coupled with the conviction of my mother and those men certainly made my blood boil as I dont think there is a man born could have

29 the patience to suffer it as long as I did or ever allow his blood to get cold while such insults as these were unavenged and yet in every paper that is printed I am called the blackest and coldest blooded murderer ever on record But if I hear any more of it I will not exactly show them what cold blooded murder is but wholesale and retail slaughter something different to shooting three troopers in self defence and robbing a bank. I would have been rather hot-blooded to throw down my rifle and let them shoot me and my innocent brother, they were not satisfied with frightening my sisters night and day and destroying their provisions and lagging my mother and infant

30 and those innocent men but should follow me and my brother into the wilds where he had been quietly digging neither molesting or inter-fering with anyone he was making good wages as the creek is very rich within half a mile from where I shot Kennedy. I was not there long and on the 25 of October I came on Police tracks between Table top and the bogs. I crossed them and returning in the evening I came on a different lot of tracks making for the shingle hut I went to our camp and told my brother and his two mates me and my brother went and found their camp at the shingle hut about a mile from my brothers house saw they carried long

31 firearms and we knew our doom was sealed if we could not beat those before the others would come As I knew the other party of Police would soon join them and if they came on us at our camp they would shoot us down like dogs at our work as we had only two guns. we thought it best to try and bail those up take their fire-arms and ammunition and horses and we could stand a chance with the rest We approached the spring as close as we could get to the camp as the intervening space being clear ground and no battery We saw two men at the logs they got up and one took a double barreled fowling-piece and fetched a horse down and hobbled him at the tent

32 we thought there were more men in the tent asleep those being on sentry we could have shot those two men without speaking but not wishing to take their lives we waited McIntyre laid the gun against a stump and Lonigan sat on the log I advanced, my brother Dan keepin McIntyre covered which he took to be constable Flood and had he not obeyed my orders, or attempted to reach for the gun or draw his revolver he would have been shot dead but when I called on them to throw up their hands McIntyre obeyed and Lonigan ran some six or seven yards to a battery of logs insted of dropping behind the one he was sitting on, he had just got to the logs and put

33 his head up to take aim when I shot him that instant or he would have shot me as I took him to be Strachan the man who said he would not ask me to stand he would shoot me first like a dog. But it happened to be Lonigan the man who in company with Sergeant Whelan Fitzpatrick and King the Boot maker and constable O.Day that tried to put a pair of hand-cuffs on me in Benalla but could not and had to allow McInnis the miller to put them on, previous to

---

Pages 25–28: Ned is angered by the actions of Fitzpatrick, and is spurred on to revenge for fear of what the police had bragged they would do to him if they could only catch up with him. He is particularly enraged at the treatment of his female friends and family.

Pages 29–44: The shooting at Stringey Bark Creek and the deaths of the three policemen Kennedy, Lonigan and Scanlan are chronicled.

BAIL UP!

Fitzpatrick swearing he was shot, I was fined two pounds for hitting Fitzpatrick and two pounds for not allowing five curs like Sergeant Whelan O.Day Fitzpatrick King and Lonigan who caught me by the privates

34 and would have sent me to Kingdom come only I was not ready and he is the man that blowed before he left Violet Town if Ned Kelly was to be shot he was the man would shoot him and no doubt he would shoot me even if I threw up my arms and laid down as he knew four of them could not arrest me single-handed not to talk of the rest of my mates, also either me or him would have to die, this he knew well therefore he had a right to keep out of my road, Fitzpatrick is the only one I hit out of the five in Benalla this shows my feeling towards him as he said we were good friends & even swore it but he was the biggest enemy I had in the country with the exception

35 of Lonigan and he can be thankful I was not there when he took a revolver and threatened to shoot my mother in her own house it is not fire three shots and miss him at a yard and a half I dont think I would use a revolver to shoot a man like him when I was within a yard and a half of him or attempt to fire into a house where my mother brothers and sisters was. and according to Fitzpatricks statement all around him a man that is such a bad shot as to miss a man three times at a yard and a half would never attempt to fire into a house among a house full of women and children while I had a pairs of arms and bunch of fives on the end of them

36 hat never failed to peg out anything they came in contact with and Fitzpatrick knew the weight of one of them only too well, as it run against him once in Benalla, and cost me two pound odd as he is very subject to fainting. As soon as I shot Lonigan he

---

ABOVE:
The Bushranging Tragedy: Scenes and Incidents
Wood engraving,
published in *The Australasian Sketcher*, 23 November 1878
This comprehensive illustration details the murder of the three policemen at Stringey Bark Creek.
Anticlockwise from upper left: Bushranger's hut in the Glenmore Ranges — Packing the bodies of Constables Scanlan and Lonigan — The funeral of Sergeant Kennedy — Mansfield from Longwood Road — The Wombat Ranges, Mount Battery in the foreground — The spot where Kennedy's body was found — Finding the bodies of Scanlan and Lonigan, Arrival of black trackers at Benalla — Scene of the murder, the police camp in the Ranges *(centre picture)*.
(La Trobe Picture Collection, State Library of Victoria)

jumped up and staggered some distance from the logs with his hands raised and then fell he surrendered but too late I asked McIntyre who was in the tent he replied no one. I advanced and took possession of their two revolvers and fowling-piece which I loaded with bullets instead of shot. I asked McIntyre where his mates was he said they had gone down the creek, and he did not expect them that night he asked me was I

37 going to shoot him and his mates. I told him no. I would shoot no man if he gave up his arms and leave the force he said the police all knew Fitzpatrick had wronged us. and he intended to leave the force, as he had bad health, and his life was insured, he told me he intended going home and that Kennedy and Scanlan were out looking for our camp and also about the other Police he told me the N.S.W Police had shot a man for shooting Sergeant Walling I told him if they did, they had shot the wrong man And I expect your gang came to do the same with me he said no they did not come to shoot me they came to apprehend me I asked him what they carried spenceir rifles and breech loading fowling pieces and so much ammunition for as the Police was

38 only supposed to carry one revolver and 6 cartridges in the revolver but they had eighteen rounds of revolver cartridges each three dozen for the fowling piece and twenty one spenceir-rifle cartridges and God knows how many they had away with the rifle this looked as if they meant not only to shoot me only to riddle me but I dont know either Kennedy Scanlan or him and had nothing against them, he said he would get them to give up their arms if I would not shoot them as I could not blame them, they had to do their duty I said I did not blame them for doing honest duty but I could not suffer them blowing me to pieces in my own native land and they knew Fitzpatrick wronged

39 us and why not make it public and convict him but no they would rather riddle poor unfortunate creoles. but they will rue the day ever Fitzpatrick got among them, Our two mates came over when they heard the shot fired but went back again for fear the Police might come to our camp

ABOVE:
The Bushranging Tragedy: Scenes and Incidents
Wood engraving,
published in *The Australasian Sketcher*, 21 December 1878
Troopers starting out in pursuit of the Kellys
(La Trobe Picture Collection, State Library of Victoria)

BAIL UP!

Opposite:
Kelly's Cave, Mansfield
Engraving, published in *Picturesque Atlas of Australasia*,
(ed. Andrew Garran), 1888
(Private Collection)

---

while we were all away and manure bullock flat with us on our arrival. I stopped at the logs and Dan went back to the spring for fear the tropers would come in that way but I soon heard them coming up the creek. I told McIntyre to tell them to give up their arms, he spoke to Kennedy who was some distance in front of Scanlan he reached for his revolver and jumped off, on the off

40 side of his horse and got behind a tree when I called on them to throw up their arms and Scanlan who carried the rifle slewed his horse around to gallop away but the horse would not go and as quick as thought fired at me with the rifle without unslinging it and was in the act of firing again when I had to shoot him and he fell from his horse. I could have shot them without speaking but their lives was no good to me. McIntyre jumped on Kennedys horse and I allowed him to go as I did not like to shoot him after he surrendered or I would have shot him as he was between me and Kennedy therefore I could not shoot Kennedy without shooting him first. Kennedy kept firing from

41 behind the tree my brother Dan advanced and Kennedy ran I followed him he stopped behind another tree and fired again. I shot him in the arm pit and he dropped his revolver and ran I fired again with the gun as he slewed around to surrender I did not know he had dropped his revolver. the bullet passed through the right side of his chest & he could not live or I would have let him go had they been my own brother I could not help shooting there or else let them shoot me which they would have done had their bullets been directed as they intended them. But as for handcuffing Kennedy to a tree or cutting his ear off or brutally treating any of them, is a falsehood, if Kennedys ear was cut off it was not done by me and none

42 of my mates was near him after he was shot I put his cloak over him and left him as well as I could and were they my own brothers I could not have been more sorry for them this cannot be called wilful murder for I was compelled to shoot them, or lie down and let them shoot me it would not be wilful murder if they packed our remains in, shattered into a mass of animated gore to Mansfield, they would have got great praise and credit as well as promotion but I am reconed a horrid brute because I had not been cowardly enough to lie down for them under such trying circumstances and insults to my people certainly their wives and children are to be pitied but they must remember those men came into the bush with the intention

43 of scattering pieces of me and my brother all over the bush and yet they know and acknowledge I have been wronged and my mother and four or five men lagged innocent and is my brothers and sisters and my mother not to be pitied also who has no alternative only to put up with the brutal and cowardly conduct of *a parcel of big ugly fat-necked wombat headed big bellied magpie legged narrow hipped splaw-footed sons of Irish Bailiffs or english landlords which is better known as Officers of Justice or Victorian Police who some calls honest gentlemen but I would like to know what business an honest man would have in the Police as it is an old saying It takes a rogue to catch a rogue* and a

44 man that knows nothing about roguery would never enter the force an take an oath to arrest brother sister father or mother if required and to have a case and conviction if possible Any man knows it is possible to swear a lie and if a policeman looses a conviction for the sake of swearing a lie he has broke his oath therefore he is a perjurer either ways. A Policeman is a disgrace to his country, not alone to the mother that suckled him, in the first place he is a rogue in his heart but too cowardly to follow it up without having the force to disguise it. next he is traitor to his country ancestors and religion as they were all catholics before the Saxons and Cranmore yoke held sway since then they were perse

---

Pages 41–42: On these pages the death of Sergeant Kennedy is chronicled. Ned always maintained that his shooting of Kennedy was a mercy killing; Kennedy was so badly wounded that to leave him to slowly die was inhuman. Ned also believed that if you kill an enemy it wasn't murder, it was self-defence.

Page 43: While Ned may not have been the Shakespeare of his day, in many instances he has become as quotable as the bard. His comment on the attributes of the Victoria Police has remained one of the more 'quotable quotes' from the colonial era [Author's emphasis].

45 cuted massacreed thrown into martrydom and tortured beyond the ideas of the present generation What would people say if they saw a strapping big lump of an Irishman shepherding sheep for fifteen bob a week or tailing turkeys in Tallarook ranges for a smile from Julia or even begging his tucker, they would say he ought to be ashamed of himself and tar-and-feather him But he would be a king to a policeman who for a lazy loafing cowardly bilit left the ash corner deserted the shamrock, the emblem of true wit and beauty to serve under a flag and nation that has destroyed massacreed and murdered their fore-fathers by the greatest of torture as rolling them down hill in spiked barrels

46 pulling their toe and finger nails and on the wheel. and every torture imaginable more was transported to Van Diemand's Land to pine their young lives away in starvation and misery among tyrants worse than the promised hell itself all of true blood bone and beauty, that was not murdered on their own soil, or had fled to America or other countries to bloom again another day, were doomed to Port Mcquarie Toweringabbie norfolk island and Emu plains and in those places of tyrany and condemnation many a blooming Irishman rather than subdue to the Saxon yoke Were flogged to death and bravely died in servile chains but true to the shamrock and a credit to Paddys land* What would people say if I became a policeman and took

47 an oath to arrest my brothers and sisters & relations and convict them by fair or foul means after the conviction of my mother and the persecutions and insults offered to myself and people Would they say I was a decent gentleman, and yet a police-man is

---

Pages 45–47: Ned revisits the tragedy of the hundreds of Irish lives that were sacrificed to English greed.
   How Ned saw the tragedy of the Irish reinforced his desire to excuse his behaviour in revolutionary terms. He began to see himself as a just warrior fighting for the life-blood of his homeland, against the hated oppressor — history shows that he may just have been right.

BAIL UP!

still in worse and guilty of meaner actions than that The Queen must surely be proud of such herioc men as the Police and Irish soldiers as It takes eight or eleven of the biggest mud crushers in Melbourne to take one poor little half starved larrakin to a watch house. I have seen as many as eleven, big & ugly enough to lift Mount Macedon out of a crab hole more like the species of a baboon or Guerilla than a man.

48 actually come into a court house and swear they could not arrest one eight stone larrakin and them armed with battens and neddies without some civilians assistance and some of them going to the hospital from the affects of hits from the fists of the larrakin and the Magistrate would send the poor little Larrakin into a dungeon for being a better man than such a parcel of armed curs. What would England do if America declared war and hoisted a green flag as its all Irishmen that has got command of her armies forts and batteries even her very life guards and beef tasters are Irish would they not slew around and fight her with their own arms for the sake of the colour they dare not wear

49 for years. and to reinstate it and rise old Erins isle once more, from the pressure and tyrannism of the English yoke, which has kept it in poverty and starvation, and caused them to wear the enemys coats. What else can England expect. Is there not big fat-necked Unicorns enough paid to torment and drive me to do thing which I dont wish to do, without the public assisting them I have never intereferred with any person unless they deserved it, and yet there are civilians who take firearms against me, for what reason I do not know, unless they want me to turn on them and exterminate them without medicine. I shall be compelled to make an example of some of them if they cannot find no other employment

50 If I had robbed and plundered ravished and murdered everything I met young and old rich and poor. the public could not do any more than take firearms and Assisting the police as they have done, but by the light that shines pegged on an ant-bed with their bellies opened their fat taken out rendered and poured down their throat boiling hot will be fool to what pleasure I will give some of them and any person aiding or harbouring or assisting the Police in any way whatever or employing any person whom they know to be a detective or cad or those who would be so deprived as to take blood money will be outlawed and declared unfit to be allowed human buriel their property

51 either consumed or confiscated and them theirs and all belonging to them exterminated off the face of the earth, the enemy I cannot catch myself I shall give a payable reward for, I would like

---

ABOVE:
The Bushranging Tragedy: Scenes and Incidents
Wood engraving,
published in *The Australasian Sketcher*, 21 December 1878
Troopers attempting to capture bushrangers
(La Trobe Picture Collection, State Library of Victoria)

Pages 48–49: This section is Ned's call to the republic, or something like that.

to know who put that article that reminds me of a poodle dog half clipped in the lion fashion, called Brooke E. Smith Superintendent of Police he knows as much about commanding Police as Captain Standish does about mustering mosquitoes and boiling them down for their fat on the back blocks of the Lachlan for he has a head like a turnip a stiff neck as big as his shoulders narrow hipped and pointed towards the feet like a vine stake and if there is any one to be called a murderer

52 regarding Kennedy, Scanlan and Lonigan it is that misplaced poodle he gets as much pay as a dozen good troopers, if there is any good in them, and what does he do for it he cannot look behind him without turning his whole frame it takes three or four police to keep sentry while he sleeps in Wangaratta, for fear of body snatchers do they think he is a superior animal to the men that has to guard him if so why not send the men that gets big pay and reconed superior to the common police after me and you shall soon save the country of high salaries to men that is fit for nothing else but getting better men than him self shot and sending orphan children to the industrial school

53 to make prostitutes and cads of them for the Detectives and other evil disposed persons Send the high paid and men that received big salaries for years in a gang by themselves after me, As it makes no difference to them but it will give them a chance of showing whether they are worth more pay than a common trooper or not and I think the Public will soon find they are only in the road of good men and obtaining money under false pretences, I do not call McIntyre a coward for I reckon he is as game a man as wears the jacket as he had the presence of mind to know his position, directly as he was spoken to, and only foolishness to disobey, it was cowardice that made Lonigan and the others fight it is only

54 foolhardiness to disobey an outlaw as any Police-man or other man who do not throw up their arms directly as I call on them knows the consequence which is a speedy dispatch to Kingdom Come, I wish those men who joined the stock protection society to withdraw their money and give it and as much more to the widows and orphans and poor of Greta district wher I spent and will again spend many a happy day fearless free and bold as it only aids the police to procure false witnesses and go whacks with men to steal horses and lag innocent men it would suit them far better to subscribe a sum and give it to the poor of their district and there is no fear of anyone stealing their property for no man

55 could steal their horses without the knowledge of the poor if any man was mean enough to steal their property the poor would rise out to a man and find them if they were on the face of the earth it will always pay a rich man to be liberal with the poor and make as little enemies as he can as he shall find if the poor is on his side he shall loose nothing by it, If they depend in the police they shall be drove to destruction, As they can not and will not protect them if duffing and bushranging were abolished the police would have to cadge for their living I speak from experience as I have sold horses and cattle innumerable and yet eight head of the culls is all ever was found I never was interfered with whilst I kept up this successful

56 trade. I give fair warning to all those who has reason to fear me to sell out and give £10 out of every hundred towards the widow and orphan fund and do not attempt to reside in Victoria but as short a time as possible after reading this notice, neglect this and abide by the consequences, which shall be worse than the rust in the wheat in Victoria or the druth of a dry season to the grasshoppers in New South Wales I do not wish to give the order full force without giving timely warning. but I am a widows son outlawed and my orders must be obeyed.

– First published in the *Melbourne Herald*, 1930

Pages 50–56: Ned continues to rail against the police. He has little time for the officers who commanded the men killed at Stringey Bark Creek, and, in conclusion returns again to the accusations against him for horse-stealing; accusations that he always, vehemently, rejected.

Ned, in turn, continues to accuse the police of the same misdeeds. There is no doubt that there is some truth in his accusations, and in theirs, but what good did it do any of them — in the end?

BAIL UP!

Left.
Prison photograph of Harry Power
Harry Power spent many years in Pentridge, both before and after he made his name as a bushranger.
(Public Records Office, Victoria Collection)

Harry Power, the Man Who Taught Ned Kelly

'Old Harry' Power was one of the last of the old 'T'other-siders', having been transported to Van Diemen's Land in 1842 for stealing a pair of shoes.

Born in Waterford, Ireland, in 1819, Power had a long career as a practised criminal before he ever took to bushranging. His long list of criminal deeds is quite extraordinary, and it is surprising that he was able to survive until the ripe old age of 79.

He escaped from Pentridge by hiding in the rubbish dump where he was working, pushing a handcart to carry refuse to the pit. Power slipped inside the cart just as it was about to be up-ended and he fell into the pit, lying hidden beneath a pile of garbage. When Power's absence at the evening muster was noticed, he was long gone.

Power took to the roads, but first he needed a change of clothes, so he simply stole some from the first farmhouse he came upon. He needed a weapon, but had a lot of difficulty obtaining one so, for a while, he was an un-armed bandit. He did grab hold of an old shearing blade and fastened it to a long pole. Brandishing this lance, he proceeded about the business of bushranging. Eventually, he held up an old traveller who had the requisite weapon, and after relieving the poor chap of his revolver, and his money, of course, Power was well on his way.

He raided farms, highways and byways, and once he had taken some horses, he could travel miles in one day, raiding and returning to one of the many hideaways he had in the hills around Beechworth.

Young Ned Kelly was arrested on one occasion when all he was doing was holding Power's horse.

On another occasion, Power held up some carriers on the Seymour Road. When one refused to hand over his money, Power had to give him a smart lecture and complained that, if he let him get away without taking his purse others may refuse to hand theirs over, and where would he be then, his business would be ruined as rumours would quickly get about that he was afraid to shoot.

Power told the carrier to go away and think about this, and after five minutes if the man hadn't change his mind he would have to shoot him. Power went behind a tree to let the carrier think it over. After five

'T'other-siders'

'The Convict blood is in the population nothing will efface it. This colony is a fearful place for crime ...,' wrote Andrew Scott 'Captain Moonlite' to his father. Although Scott was not a transportee, he soon felt the tap of the long arm of the law, and learned the ways of the 'T'other-siders'.

Convicts from Tasmania referred to themselves as being from the other side — 'T'other-siders' — and even affected a manner of address, and tonsorial-style that were recognisable one to the other. Vandemonians would fashion a lock of hair into a curl in the centre of the forehead, and would greet each other with the password 'Diamond cut Diamond' or 'D. cut D.' for short.

minutes, the carrier handed over his purse and that was the end of that.

Power always worked alone, apart from the times when he had young Ned to hold his horse for him, as he believed that having to deal with partners was what brought most bushrangers undone. Too many eyes and too many mouths to spill the beans, and he was the only one who knew where he had his hide-away — or so he thought.

Police had always suspected that Power used the trails known 'only' to 'Bogong Jack' when he left the north-east and crossed the mountains to Omeo. They were also afraid that Power had shown the Kellys the same tracks and that they too had escaped over the mountains after the murders at Stringey Bark Creek.

A police party working from information from an unnamed person were led to Power's hideaway.

The police tested their informant. Power had taken a gold watch from squatter Robert MacBean J.P. of Kilfera near Benalla, and was offering to sell it back to him for £15. As the police reward posted for Power was £50, the police informant was told that he would receive the entire amount if he led them to the bushranger's hideaway. They started out from Kilfera with £15 marked by MacBean, heading into the hills to retrieve the watch and the robber.

The ground was wet and the police party were unheard as they eventually crept up to Power's gun-yah in the hillside opposite Quinn's farm. One of the black trackers spied a wisp of smoke among the trees and the police party rushed silently up the mountain track. The bushranger was asleep inside his low, blanket-covered hut; his revolver lay at his side and his loaded shotgun was suspended from the ridge-pole when Superintendent Nicolson leapt upon him, pinning him to the floor.

The others ran to the hut and grabbed Power by his ankles and, with one almighty heave, pulled him into the open where he was handcuffed. He was taken to Beechworth, then on to Pentridge, where he began his fifteen-year sentence for highway robbery.

OPPOSITE:
Power in his Prison Cell, Pentridge
The once mountain-roving old rogue was brought to heel in the confines of Pentridge Gaol.
(La Trobe Picture Collection, State Library of Victoria)

The Bushranger, Jack Power

On the eighth day of August
In the year of sixty-nine
On a lovely spring morning
The weather being fine
When a bolter from Pentridge,
Jack Power by name,
An aspirant for the gallows,
To Beechworth he came.

Well armed, well mounted,
The traps for his foes,
To a scrub for concealment
The highwayman goes
From Beechworth to the Buckland
And on the highway
Run Cobb & Co's coaches
By night and by day.

Early one morning
The outlaw approached
Towards Bowman's Forest
and bail'd up the Coach
And he bail'd up two draymen
A new saddle stole
And a horse, a coachwheeler —
It's true, by my soul!

He met with a trooper
Near the small town of Yea —
'Good morning,
Hand here that revolver
Or, if you refuse
You must fight or deliver
Pray, which do you choose?'

The Trooper surrender'd
His horse and his arms
Then hastened to Yea Town
To give the alarm
'Farewell,' shouts the rover,
'This revolver's my shield
To the traps or the gallows
I never will yield.'

We may sing of young Gilbert,
Dan Morgan, Ben Hall,
But the bold reckless robber
Surpasses them all,
The pluck that is in him
Is beyond all belief —
A daring highwayman,
A professional thief!

— WRITTEN BY ISAAC HALL,
PUBLISHED IN THE ARGUS, *20 AUGUST 1950*

BAIL UP!

GREAT BOURKE STREET, MELBOURNE

Superintendent Hare's report suggests that someone known only as L——* was responsible for guiding the police to Power's hideaway. Power always believed it was young Kelly. However, he managed to survive his young apprentice by more than a decade. Power was released after fourteen years, but by this time he had no desire to go back to the bush-life.

Power took a job as a guide aboard the old *Success* where he had once been imprisoned. A party of showmen had taken it over and toured the ship as an historic attraction. Power left the ship in Sydney, where it had docked for a refit before they were to head off for London, and he went to Victoria on account of his health. He travelled along the Murray River until misadventure befell him. On 11 October 1891, his lifeless body was dragged from the river near Tyntynder Station, ten miles from the port.

Identification was difficult as Power had been in the water for more than a week. His face was partially eaten away by crayfish, but there were enough people in the district who had seen the old man in the past weeks previous to confirm that the drowned man was indeed Harry Power.

In 1891, the year of Power's death, a report appeared in a Wangaratta newspaper that recalled a man who had declared himself to be 'a retired bushranger' and was on his way to search for a bag of gold he had hidden beneath a gumtree on the banks of the King River many years before. The bag was supposed to contain more than 200 sovereigns, the results of the robbery of Robert McBean in his earlier bushranging days. It is not known if he ever found the bag. When Power was fished out of the Murray he had only 12s 2d tied up in the corner of a handkerchief found in his pocket.

The *Success* sank in Sydney, and the wax figures that formed the 'historical' display of torture and imprisonment in the colonies were so severely damaged that the trip to London was delayed.

Harry Power, the only surviving real-life character from that period of horror, was, unfortunately, no longer available for display.

---

* Local knowledge suggests that it was Jack Lloyd who led the police to Power. He was married to one of the Quinn girls, who were related to the Kellys, and had been in Pentridge with him. Power trusted a man with a pedigree such as that.

Lloyd died in a fall from his horse a few years later. Local knowledge also suggests that Lloyd did not fall at all. Whatever, he was dead just the same.

ABOVE:
Great Bourke Street, Melbourne
Hand-coloured engraving by W. Ralston,
from *News Letter of Australasia*, c. 1860
A pair of likely lads eye off the girls in 'Marvellous Melbourne'.
A poster on the wall offers a reward for the capture of the bushranger POWER.
(Private Collection)

— 1860—1880 THE WAR AGAINST THE KELLYS —

Capture of the Bushranger "Power"

ABOVE:
Capture of Power, the Bushranger
Wood engraving by Samuel Calvert,
published in *Illustrated Australian News*, 18 June 1870
Power was captured in his low gunyah up on the hills opposite Quinn's farm, 'Glenmore'. Quinn had a peacock that could be heard for miles when any stranger entered the valley.

Unfortunately for Power, the bird had taken cover from the heavy rain, which had been falling all day, and fallen asleep. After he was taken Power seemed not to be perplexed but asked the police who had belayed him so successfully if they would care for 'a cup of tay'.
(National Library of Australia Collection)

BAIL UP!

The Last of Their Kind

Governors Hack Their Way into the History Books

The Outlaws:

New South Wales has at last got rid of the Breelong Outlaws. Jimmy Governor on October 28, was captured by a cluster of civilians who discovered the camp of the outlaw, and crept close to it, under cover of darkness. When they challenged the fugitive, he leaped to his feet, and ran like a deer, but was pursued, wounded and captured. Three days later in more daring fashion Joe Governor was shot dead . . . this closes the most remarkable chapter of crime in Australian history.
– REVIEW OF REVIEWS, 20 NOVEMBER 1900

Even after the public vilification of the notorious Kellys, the public taste for horror was to be whet once more by the hideous crimes committed by the group of Aborigines led by Jimmy and Joe Governor. Joe Governor was a half-caste Aboriginal, educated and well adapted to white society. He had worked as a tracker for the police and was a renowned horse-breaker. Both brothers were integrated natives, and Jimmy, at the age of twenty-three, had courted and wed a sixteen-year-old white girl, Ethel Page.

The women of the Breelong were disgusted by this mixed marriage and held Jimmy and his bride in deep contempt. The couple shifted out to a hut when Jimmy took a fencing job on the West Breelong property of pastoralist John Mawbey.

One day when Ethel came into Breelong for supplies, Mrs Mawbey and school teacher Helen Kurz abused her for marrying a black man and sent her away empty-handed.

Jimmy complained to Mawbey about this insult, and although the pastoralist assured Jimmy that he and Ethel would have their supplies, the proud native man was still not satisfied.

Upset and brooding over the insult to his bride, Jimmy and his mate, the half-blind full-blood Jacky Underwood, decided to pay Mawbey a visit. They arrived one evening armed with an axe and a rifle – just in case. Mrs Mawbey opened the door and the men saw the other cause of their insult, Helen Kurz, standing alongside her. Jimmy asked for an apology, but, in those days, whites rarely, if ever, apologised to a black man, and they were not going to start with Jimmy Governor. Instead he was ordered off the property, then Helen Kurz added further insult to injury when she shouted: 'You black rubbish! You should be shot for marrying a white woman!'

Enraged by this remark both Governor and Underwood attacked. There were the two women at the door and eight children inside when Jimmy and Jacky burst in, swinging and hacking as they went. They brought Mrs Mawbey down, and Helen Kurz was struck a fell blow. Grace and Percy Mawbey had made a run for it, but they were brought low too. Young Percy's head was almost severed by the savage blows. Elsie Clark, a friend sleeping over, lay dead, too.

The attackers ran off into the night. When Mawbey was alerted by

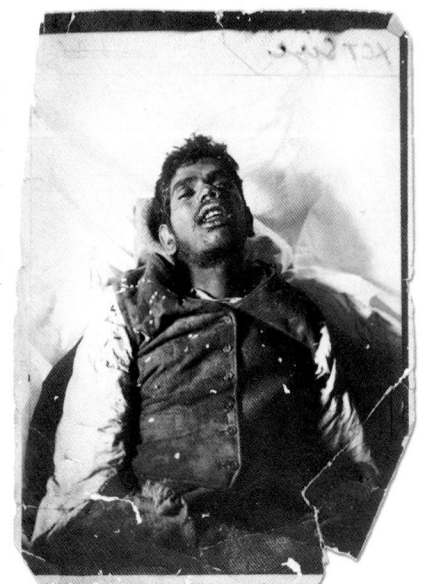

TOP:
Jimmy Governor
Nearly fifty slugs were removed from Jimmy's back and legs after he was taken into custody, but he was still able to walk to the gallows to be hanged at Darlinghurst on 18 January 1901.
(Private Collection)

LEFT:
Post Mortem Photo of Joe Governor
From *Review of Reviews*, 20/11/1900
Red-headed half-caste Joe Governor was shot by farmer John Wilkinson in October 1900.
(State Library of New South Wales Collection)

eight-year-old Bert, who had managed to escape the slaughter, he rushed into the house to find a bloody scene.

The people of Breelong rose as one to revenge the brutal murders. Not since the days of Musquito and the Oyster Bay tribes' attack on the settlers of Van Diemen's Land had the white community been so afeared of their black neighbours.

More than 200 police and 2000 civilians joined in the wide search for the desperate threesome (Joe Governor had also joined them on the run). But, unfortunately, for Kiernan Fitzpatrick, Alex McKay, Elizabeth O'Brien, and her baby who were attacked by the three men as they continued their rampage, they couldn't catch them up quickly enough. Before they were captured, the trio managed to commit a further eighty crimes, from murder to robbery under arms, and it is believed that Jimmy also raped a fifteen-year-old girl. A reward of £1000 was placed upon their heads as their pursuers began to close in on Jimmy and the boys.

After nearly four months the trio's run was brought to an end. Jacky Underwood was the first to be captured and he was sent to prison to await his fate. Jimmy was peppered with buckshot as he lay sleeping on 27 October 1900, having survived a terrible wound when a bullet ripped apart his mouth, smashing five teeth away, in a shoot-out two weeks earlier. Again Joe managed to evade capture.

On 30 October, a man named John Wilkinson came upon a campfire in the bush. He crept forward until he recognised Joe. He signalled for his brother to join him. Although they had only one gun between them, the pair stepped out, surprising the outlaw and called on him to surrender. Joe made a dash for his rifle, but Wilkinson fired first. He missed, and fired again, but he missed once more. Taking careful aim he fired yet again, and Joe Governor was killed.

The New South Wales police have had a difficult task in the pursuit of such criminals in a district so savage and wild. It is, for them, a somewhat cruel incident that the capture of the outlaws is due entirely to the daring and enterprise of half-a-dozen citizens
– *REVIEW OF REVIEWS*, 20 NOVEMBER 1900

Jacky Underwood was hanged on 14 January 1901. Before Jacky was led to the gallows, he asked of the warder whether he would be in heaven in time for dinner. Jimmy was hanged four days later. Jimmy went to the gallows sullen and irritable. He was unconsolable and in denial of his fate.

ABOVE:
The Hunt for the Governor Gang of Bushrangers
A posse of more than two-hundred police, Aboriginal trackers and 2000 volunteers searched for four months across a vast area for the gang. The gang evaded capture by walking along fences and railway lines, tying rabbit skins to their feet and driving sheep to cover their tracks.
(State Library of New South Wales Collection)

Above:
Convicts Embarking for Botany Bay
Pen and wash drawing by Thomas Rowlandson, c. 1800
(Rex Nan Kivell Collection NK228, National Library of Australia)

Convicts of the First Fleet

Above:
Black-eyed Sue and Sweet Poll of Plymouth take leave of their lovers who are going to Botany Bay
Hand-coloured engraving, published by Rbt. Sayer & Co, 1792
(Rex Nan Kivell Collection NK6972. National Library of Australia)

The First Fleet sailed from Portsmouth on 13 May 1878.

Captain Arthur Phillip R.N. made landfall in New South Wales on 26 January 1788, with 717 convicts, 191 marines and nineteen officers on board. There were a few whose names featured later in the lists of bushrangers, bolters and bandits among this motley crew.

Some of the felons listed below never stepped onto Australia's shores as forty-two had died en route. However, forty babies were also born en route, almost restoring the balance.

Convicts transported to the new colony

Name	Where sentenced	Term
A		
ABEL, Robert	London	7
ABELL, Mary, alias Tilley	Worcester	7
ABRAMS, Henry	–	–
ABRAHAMS, Esther	London	7
ACRES, Thomas	Exeter	7
ADAMS, John	London	7
ADAMS, Mary	London	7
AGLEY, Richard	Winchester	7
ALLEN, Charles	London	7
ALLEN, Jamasun, alias Boddington	London	7
ALLEN, John	Hertford	7
ALLEN, Mary,	London	–
ALLEN, Mary, alias Conner	London	7
ALLEN, Susannah	London	7
ALLEN, William	Ormskirk	7
ANDERSON, Elizabeth	London	7
ANDERSON, Fanny	Winchester	7
ANDERSON, John	Exeter	7
ANDERSON, John	London	7
ARCHER, John	London	7
ARSCOTT, John	Bodmin	7
ATKINSON, George,	London	7
AULT, Sarah	London	7
AYNERS, John, alias Agnew	London	7
AYRES, John	London	7
B		
BAILS, Robert	Reading	Life
BAKER, Martha	London	7
BAKER, Thomas	Exeter	7
BALDING, James, alias William	London	7
BALDWIN, Ruth, alias Bowyer	London	7
BALL, John	Exeter	7
BANNISTER, George	London	7
BARFERD, John	London	7
BARLAND, George	London	7
BARNES, Stephen	York	7
BARNETT, Henry, alias Barnard, alias Burton	Warwick	7
BARRER, Elizabeth	–	–
BARRET, Daniel		
BARRETT, Thomas	Exeter	Life
BARRY, John	Bristol	7
BARSBY, George	Winchester	Life
BARSBY, Samuel	Exeter	7
BARTLETT, James	Winchester	7
BATLEY, Caten	Exeter	7
BASON, Elizabeth, wife of William Bason	New Sarum	7
BAYLEY, James	New Sarum	7
BAZLEY, John	Exeter	7
BEARDSLEY, Ann	Derby	5
BECKFORD, Elizabeth	London	7
BELL, William	London	7
BELLAMY, Thomas	Worcester	7
BELLET, Jacob	London	7
BENEAR, Samuel	London	7
BEST, John	–	–
BINGHAM, John, alias Boughan	–	–
BINGHAM, Elizabeth alias Mooring	London	–
BISHOP, Joseph	–	–
BIRD, Elizabeth, alias Winifred	Maidstone	7
BIRD, Samuel	Croydon	7
BLACKHALL, William	Abingdon	7
BLUNT, William	London	7
BLAKE, Francis	London	7
BLATHERHORN, William	Exeter	Life
BLOEDWORTH, James	Kingston	7
BLANCHETT, Susannah	Kingston	7
BOND, Peter	London	7
BOGGIS, William		–
BOND, William	Exeter	7
BOND, Mary, wife of John Bond	Wells	7
BOULTON, Rebecca	Lincoln	7
BOYLE, John	London	7
BONNER, Jane	London	7
BOLTON, Mary	Shrewsbury	7
BRADBURY, William	London	7
BRADFORD, John	Exeter	7
BRADLEY, James	London	7
BRAND, Curtis		–
BRAND, Lucy, alias Wood	London	7
BRANHAM, Mary	London	7
BRANNEGAN, James	Exeter	7
BREWER, William	Exeter	7
BRICE, William	Bristol	7
BRID, James	Croydon	7
BRINDLEY, John	Warwick	7
BROUGH, William	Stafford	7
BROWN, James	Hertford	7
BROWN, Richard	Reading	7
BROWN, Thomas	Exeter	7
BROWN, Thomas	London	7
BROWN, William	Exeter	7
BROWN, William	Southwark	7
BRUCE, Elizabeth	London	7
BRUCE, Robert	Exeter	7

183

BAIL UP!

BRYANT, John	*Exeter*	7
BRYANT, Michael		–
BRYANT, Thomas	*Maidstone*	7
BRYANT, William	*Launceston*	7
BUCKLEY, Joseph	*Dorchester*	7
BUFLEY, John		–
BUNN, Margaret	*London*	7
BURDO, Sarah	*London*	7
BURKITT, Mary	*London*	7
BURLEIGH, James	*London*	7
BURN, Patrick		–
BURN, Peter	*London*	7
BURN, Simon		–
BURNE, James,	*London*	7
BURRIDGE, Samuel	*Dorchester*	7
BUTLER, William,	*London*	7

C

CABLE, Henry		–
CAMPBELL, James alias George	*London*	7
CAMPBELL, James	*Guildford*	7
CARNEY, John	*Exeter*	7
CARTY, Francis	*Bodmin*	7
CAREY, Ann	*Taunton*	7
CARROLL, Mary wife of James Carroll	*London*	7
CARTER, Richard, alias Michael Cartwright	*Shrewsbury*	7
CARVER, Joseph,	*Maidstone*	7
CASTLE, James	*London*	7
CESAR, John	*Maidstone*	7
CHAAF, William	*Exeter*	7
CHADDICK, Thomas	*London*	7
CHANIN, Edward	*Exeter*	7
CHIELDS, William	–	–
CHINERY, Samuel	*Exeter*	7
CHURCH, William	*Dorchester*	7
CLARK, Elizabeth	–	–
CLARK, John, alias Hosier	*London*	7
CLARK, William	*London*	7
CLARKE, John	*Exeter*	7
CLOUGH, Richard	*Durham*	7
CLEAR, George	–	–
CLEAVER, Mary	*Bristol*	7
CLEMENTS, Thomas	*London*	7
COFFIN, John	*Exeter*	7
COLE, Elizabeth	*Exeter*	7
COLE, Elizabeth	*London*	7
COLE, William	*London*	7
OLLEY, Elizabeth	*London*	14
COLLIER, Richard	*Kingstone*	7
COLLING, Joseph	*London*	7
COLMAN, Ishmael	*Dorchester*	7
COLPITTS, Ann	*Durham*	7
CON, James	*Exeter*	Life
CONELLY, Cornelius	*Exeter*	7
CONNOLLY, William	*Bodmin*	7
CONNELLY, William	*Bristol*	7
COOKE, Charlotte	*London*	7
COOMBES, Ann wife of Samuel Coombes	*Taunton*	7
COOPER, Mary	*Worcester*	7
COPP, James	*Exeter*	7
CORMICK, Edward	*Hertford*	7
CORDEN, James	*Warwick*	7

COX, John Matthew	*London*	7
CREAMER, John	*Exeter*	7
CREEK, Jane	*London*	7
CROPPER, John	*London*	7
CROSS, John	*New Sarum*	7
CROSS, William	*Coventry*	7
CUCKOW, William		–
CUDLIP, Jacob, alias Norris	*Bodmin*	7
CULLEN, James Bryen	*London*	7
CULLYHORN, John,	*Exeter*	7
CUNNINGHAM, Edward	*London*	7
CUSS, John, alias Hunsboy	*New Sarum*	7

D

DANIELLS, Daniel,	*London*	7
DALEY, Ann, wife of Gore Daley, alias Ann Warburton *Nether Knutsford*		7
DALEY, James	*London*	7
DALTON, Elizabeth	*London*	7
DARNELL, Margaret	*London*	7
DAVIS, Aaron	*Bristol*	7
DAVIS, Ann	*London*	7
DAVIS, Frances	*Chelmsford*	14
DAVIS, James	*London*	7
DAVIS, Richard	–	–
DAVIS, Samuel	*Glocester*	7
DAVIS, William	*Brecon*	Life
DAVIS, William	–	–
DAVIES, Edward	*Stafford*	7
DAVIES, Mary	*Shrewsbury*	7
DAVIES, Sarah	*Worcester*	7
DAVIDSON, John	*London*	7
DAVIDSON, Rebecca wife of Robert Davidson	*London*	7
DAWSON, Margaret	*London*	7
DAY, Richard	*Reading*	7
DAY, Samuel	*Glocester*	14
DELANY, Patrick	–	–
DENISON, Barnaby	*Bristol*	7
DENNISON, Michael	*Poole*	7
DEYER, Leonard	*Southwark*	7
DICKENSON, Mary	*Southwark*	7
DICKSON, Thomas, alias Ralph Raw	*Durham*	7
DISCALL, Timothy	*Bodmin*	7
DIXON, Mary	*London*	7
DOUGLAS, William	*Lincoln*	7
DOWLAND, Ferdinand	*London*	7
DODDING, James, alias Doring	–	–
DRING, William *Kingston upon Hull*		7
DUDGENS, Elizabeth	–	–
DUNDASS, Jane,	*London*	7
DUNNAGE, Joseph	*London*	Life
DUTTON, Ann	*London*	7
DYKES, Mary,	*London*	7

E

EAGLETON, William, alias Bones	*Kingston*	7
EARLE, William	*New Sarum*	7
EATON, Mary, alias Shephard	–	–
EARLY, Rachel	*Reading*	7

EATON, Martha	–	–
ECCLES, Thomas	*Guildford*	Life
EDMUNDS, William	*Monmouth*	7
EDWARDS, William	–	–
EGGLESTON, George	*Maidstone*	7
ELAM, Deborah	*Chester*	7
ELLAM, Peter	*Ormskirk*	7
ELLIOT, Joseph	*Croydon*	7
ELLIOT, William	*Croydon*	7
ENGLISH, Nicholas	*London*	7
EVANS, Elizabeth	*London*	7
EVANS, Williams	*Shrewsbury*	7
EVERETT, John	*Hertford*	7
EVERINGHAM, Matthew	*London*	7

F

FARLEY, William	*Bristol*	7
FARMER, Ann	*London*	–
FARRELL, Phillip	*London*	7
FENTUM, Benjamin	*London*	7
FERGUSON, John	*Exeter*	7
FIELD, Jane,	*London*	–
FIELD, William,	–	–
FILLESEY, Thomas	*Bristol*	7
FINLOW, John, alias Hervey	–	–
FITZGERALD, Elizabeth	*London*	7
FITZGERALD, Jane, alias Phillips	*London*	7
FLARTY, Phebe	*London*	7
FLYN, Edward	–	–
FORBES, Ann	*Kingston*	7
FORRESTER, Robert	*London*	7
FOWLES, Ann	*London*	7
FOWKES, Francis	*London*	7
FOWNES, Margaret	*Shrewsbury*	7
FOYLE, William	*New Sarum*	7
FRANCIS, William	*London*	7
FRANCISCO, George	*London*	7
FRASER, Ellen	*Manchester*	7
FRASER, William	*Manchester*	7
FREEMAN, James	*Hertford*	7
FREEMAN, Robert	*London*	7
FRY, George	–	7
FRYER, Catherine, alias Prior	–	–
FULLER, John	*Manchester*	7

G

GABEL, Mary	*Southwark*	7
GARDNER, Francis	*London*	7
GARLAND, Francis	*Exeter*	7
GARTH, Edward	*London*	7
GARTH, Susannah, alias Grath	–	–
GASCOYGNE, Olive	*Worcester*	7
GEARING, Thomas	*Oxford*	Life
GEORGE, Anne	*London*	7
GESS, George	*Gloucester*	7
GLENTON, Thomas	*Northallerton*	7
GLOSTER, William	*London*	7
GORDON, Daniel	*Winchester*	7
GOODWIN, Edward	*London*	7
GOODWIN, Andrew	*London*	7
GOULD, John,	*Exeter*	7
GRACE, James	–	–
GRANGER, Charles	*Plymouth*	7
GRAY, Charles	*Southwark*	7

Name	Place	Term
GREEN, Ann	London	7
GREEN, Hannah	-	-
GREEN, John	Reading	7
GREEN, Mary	London	7
GREENWELL, Nicholas	London	7
GREENWOOD, Mary	London	7
GRIFFITHS, Samuel, alias Briscow, alias Butcher	Gloucester	7
GRIFFITHS, Thomas	London	7
GROVES, Mary	Lincoln	7
GUNTER, William	Bristol	7

H

Name	Place	Term
HADON, John	Exeter	7
HAINES, Joseph	Gloucester	7
HALL, Elizabeth	Newcastle	7
HALL, Margaret	-	-
HALL, John	Exeter	7
HALL, Joseph	Exeter	Life
HALL, Samuel	London	7
HALL, Sarah	London	7
HAMILTON, Maria	London	7
HAMLIN, William	Exeter	7
HANDLAND, Dorothy, alias Gray	London	7
HANDFORD, John	Winchester	7
HANDY, Cooper	-	-
HARBINE, Joseph	London	7
HARPER, Joshua	London	7
HARRIFON, Joseph	-	-
HARRIS, John	London	Life
HARRIS, William	Maidstone	7
HARRISON, Joseph	London	7
HARRISON, Mary	Lincoln	7
HARRISON, Mary	London	7
HART, Catherine	London	7
HART, Frances	-	-
HART, John	London	7
HART, John	Stafford	7
HARTLEY, John	Oxford	7
HARWOOD, Ester, alias Howard	London	7
HATCH, John	Reading	7
HATCHER, John	Winchester	7
HATFIELD, William	Maidstone	7
HATHAWAY, Henry	Gloucester	7
HATTOM, Joseph	-	-
HAWELL, Thomas	Stafford	7
HAWKES, Richard	Reading	7
HAYES, Dennis	London	7
HAYES, John	Guildford	7
HA[-]ES, William	-	-
HAYNES, William	-	-
HAYTON, George, alias Clayton	London	7
HAYWARD, Elizabeth	London	7
HEADING, James	Chelmsford	Life
HEADINGTON, Thomas	Abingdon	7
HENRY, Catherine	London	7
HERBERT, Jane, alias Rose, alias Jenny Russell	London	7
HERBERT, John	Exeter	7
HERBERT, John	London	7
HERVEY, Elizabeth	-	-

Name	Place	Term
HILL, John	London	7
HILL, John	Maidstone	Life
HILL, Mary	London	7
HILL, Thomas	London	7
HILL, Thomas	-	7
HINDLE, Ottiwell	Preston	7
HINDLEY, William, alias Platt	Ormskirk	7
HILT, William	Exeter	Life
HIPSLEY, Eliabeth	London	7
HOGG, William	London	14
HOLLISTER, Job	Bristol	7
HOLLOWAY, James	London	7
HOLMES, William	London	7
HOLLAND, William	Exeter	7
HOLMES, Susannah	-	-
HOLLOGIN, Elizabeth	London	7
HORTOP, James	Exeter	7
HOWARD, John	London	7
HOWARD, Thomas	London	7
HUBBARD, William	-	-
HUDSON, John	-	-
HUFFNELL, Susannah	Worcester	7
HUGHES, Frances Ann	Lancaster	7
HUGHES, Hugh	Southwark	7
HUGHES, John	Maidstone	7
HUGHES, Thomas	-	-
HUMPHREY, Edward	London	7
HUMPHREYS, Henry	Exeter	7
HUMPHRIES, Mary	-	-
HURLEY, Jeremiah	Exeter	7
HUSBAND, William	London	7
HUSSEY, James	-	-
HYLIDS, Thomas	Guildford	7

I

Name	Place	Term
INETT, Ann	Worcester	7
INGRAM, Benjamin	London	7
IRVINE, John, alias Aderson, alias Law	Lincoln	7

J

Name	Place	Term
JACKSON, Hannah	Bristol	7
JACKSON, Jane, alias Esther Roberts	London	7
JACKSON, Mary	London	7
JACKSON, William	Durham	7
JACOBS, David	London	7
JACOBS, John	London	7
JAGET, Joseph	Exeter	7
JAMESON, James	-	-
JEFFERIES, John	Maidstone	7
JEFFRIES, Robert	Devizes	7
JENKINS, Robert, alias Brown	Maidstone	7
JENKINS, William	Exeter	7
JEPP, John	London	7
JOHNS, Stephen	Launceston	7
JONES, Edward	London	7
JONES, Francis	Winchester	7
JONES, John	Exeter	14
JONES, Margaret	Launceston	14
JONES, Richard	Shewsbury	7
JONES, Thomas	Bristol	14
JONES, Thomas	Warwick	7
JONES, William	Shewsbury	7

Name	Place	Term
JOHNSON, Catherine	London	7
JOHNSON, Charles	Manchester	7
JOHNSON, Edward	Dorcester	7
JOHNSON, Mary	London	7
JOHNSON, William	Kingston	7
JOSEPHS, Thomas	London	7

K

Name	Place	Term
KELLAN, John, alias Keeling	London	Life
KELLY, Thomas	Pontefract	7
KENNEDY, Martha	Kingston	7
KIDNEY, Thomas	Bristol	7
KILBY, William	Reading	7
KILPACK, David	London	Life
KIMBERLEY, Edward	Coventry	7
KING, John	London	7
KNOWLAND, Andrew	-	-
KNOWLER, John	Maidstone	7

L

Name	Place	Term
LAMBETH, John	Bristol	7
LANE, Richard	Winchester	7
LANE, William	Chelmsford	7
LANKEY, David	London	7
LANGLEY, Jane	London	7
LARA, Flora	London	-
LARNE, James	Exeter	7
LAVELL, Henry	-	-
LAWRELL, John	Bodmin	7
LAWRENCE, Mary	London	7
LAYCOCK, Caroline	London	-
LEARY, Jeremiah	Bristol	14
LEARY, John	Winchester	7
LEE, Elizabeth	London	7
LEGG, George	Dorchester	7
LEGROVE, Stephen	-	-
LEMON, Isaac	Chelmsford	7
LEONARD, Elizabeth	London	7
LEVY, Amelia	Southwark	7
LEVY, Joseph	London	7
LEWIS, Sophia	London	7
LIFT, George	London	Life
LIGHTFOOT, Samuel	Exeter	7
LIMEBURNER, John	New Sarum	7
LIMPUS, Thomas	Exeter	Life
LOCK, Elizabeth	Gloucester	7
LOCKLEY, John	London	7
LONG, Joseph	Gloucester	14
LONG, Mary	London	Life
LONGSTREET, Joseph	Marlborough	7
LOVE, Mary	Maidstone	7
LUCAS, Nathaniel	London	7
LYDE, John	-	-
LYNCH, Ann	Bristol	14
LYNCH, Humphry	New Sarum	7

M

Name	Place	Term
M'DONALD, Alexander	London	7
M'DONNAUGH, James	Maidstone	7
M'LAUGHLIN, Charles	Durham	7
M'LEAN, Edward	Maidstone	7
M'LEAN, Francis	Guildford	7
M'LEAN, Thomas	Guildford	7

McCABE, Eleanor	London	7
McCORMACK, Mary	Liverpool	7
McCORMICK, Sarah	Manchester	7
McDEED, Richard	–	–
McGRAH, Redman	–	–
McNAMAR, William	–	–
MACINTIRE, John	Durham	7
MACKRIE, James	–	–
MANSFIELD, John	Chelmsford	7
MARINER, William	Oxford	7
MARNEY, William	London	7
MARRIOTT, Jane	London	7
MARROTT, John	Gloucester	7
MARSHALL, Joseph	London	14
MARSHALL, Mary	London	7
MARTIN, Abraham	New Sarum	7
MARTIN, Ann	Southwark	–
MARTIN, John	London	7
MARTIN, Stephen	Bristol	7
MARTIN, Thomas	Exeter	7
MARTYN, James	Exeter	7
MASON, Betty	Gloucester	14
MASON, Susannah, alias Gibbs	London	–
MATHER, Ann	London	7
MATHER, Mather	London	7
MATON, Thomas	Maidstone	7
MAY, Richard	New Sarum	7
MEECH, Jane, wife of William Meech	Exeter	7
MESSIAH, Jacob	–	–
MEYNELL, John, alias William Radford	Nottingham	7
MIDDLETON, Richard	London	7
MIDGLEY, Samuel	Lancaster	7
MILLS, Matthew	–	–
MILTON, Charles	Maidstone	7
MITCHCRAFT, Mary	Kingston	7
MITCHELL, Mary	Kingston	7
MITCHELL, Nathaniel	Dorchester	7
MOBBS, Samuel	London	7
MOLLANDS, John	Launceston	7
MOOD, Charles	–	7
MOORE, William	London	7
MOORIN, John	London	7
MORGAN, Richard	Gloucester	7
MORGAN, Robert	London	7
MORGAN, William	London	7
MORLEY, John	London	7
MORLEY, Joseph	–	–
MORRIS, Peter	Bristol	7
MORRISBY, John	London	7
MORTIMORE, John	Exeter	7
MORTON, Mary	London	7
MOULD, William	Guildford	7
MOWBRAY, John	Lincoln	7
MOYLE, Edward	Launceston	7
MULLENS, Hannah	London	Life
MULLIS, Stephen	Exeter	7
MULLOCK, Jesse	New Sarum	7
MUNRO, Lydia	Kingston	14
MUNROE, John, alias Nurse	London	7
MURPHY, James	–	7
MURPHY, William	Liverpool	–

N
NEAL, James	Bristol	7
NEAL, John	London	7
NEEDHAM, Elizabeth	London	7
NETTLETON, Robert	Kingston upon Hull	7
NEWLAND, John	London	7
NICHOLLS, John	London	7
NORTON, Phebe	London	7
NUNN, Robert	London	7

O
O'CRAFT, John	Exeter	7
OGDEN, James	Manchester	7
OKEY, William	Gloucester	7
OLDFIELD, Isabella	Manchester	7
OLDFIELD, Thomas	Manchester	7
OPLEY, Peter	Maidstone	7
ORFORD, Thomas	London	7
OSBORNE, Elizabeth, alias Jones	London	7
OSBORNE, Thomas	London	7
OWEN, John	London	7
OWEN, Joseph	Shewsbury	14
OWLES, John	Croydon	7

P
PALMER, John Henry	London	7
PANE, William	Nottingham	7
PARFLEY, Ann	London	7
PARISH, William	London	7
PARKER, Elizabeth	Gloucester	7
PARKER, John	London	7
PARKER, Mary	London	7
PARKINSON, Jane, alias Partington, alias Ann Marsden	Manchester	7
PARR, William	Liverpool	7
PARRIS, Peter	Exeter	7
PARRY, Edward	Stafford	7
PARRY, Sarah	London	Life
PARTRIDGE, Richard	London	Life
PARTRIDGE, Sarah, alias Roberts	London	7
PEAULET, James	London	7
PECK, Joshua	Exeter	7
PEET, Charles	London	Life
PENNY, John	–	7
PERCIVAL, Richard	London	7
PERKINS, Edward	Plymouth	7
PERROT, Edward Bearcroft	Bristol	7
PETHERICK, John	Plymouth	7
PETRIE, John	London	7
PETTITT, John	London	7
PEYTON, Samuel	London	7
PHILLIMORE, William	London	7
PHILLIPS, Mary	Taunton	7
PHILLIPS, Richard	London	7
PHYFIELD, Roger, alias Twyfield	Shrewsbury	7
PHYN, Mary	London	7
PIGOTT, Samuel	Exeter	7
PINDER, Mary	Lincoln	7
PIPKIN, Elizabeth	London	7
PILES, Mary	London	7
PONTIE, John	London	Life
POOLE, Jane	Wells	7
POPE, David	Southwark	7
POWELL, Ann	London	7
POWER, John	London	7
POWER, William	–	–
POWLEY, Elizabeth	–	–
PRICE, James	Gloucester	7
PRICE, John	Southwark	7
PRIOR, Thomas	Reading	7
PRITCHARD, Thomas	–	–
PUGH, Edward	Gloucester	7

R
RAMFEY, John	Kingston	7
RANDALL, John	Manchester	7
READ, Ann	London	Life
READ, William	Croydon	7
REARDON, Bartholomew	Winchester	7
REPEAT, Charles	Warwick	7
REYMOND, George	London	7
RICE, John	Exeter	7
RICHARD, David	London	7
RICHARD, James	East Grinstead	7
RICHARD, James	Launceston	7
RICHARDS, John, alias Williams	Winchester	7
RICHARDSON, Hardwicke	London	7
RICHARDSON, James	Maidstone	7
RICHARDSON, John	London	7
RICHARDSON, Samuel	London	7
RICHARDSON, William	London	7
RICKSON, William	Chelmsford	7
RISBY, Edward	Gloucester	7
RISDALE, Thomas, alias Crowder	Bristol	Life
ROACH, Henry	Exeter	7
ROBERTS, John	Liverpool	7
ROBERTS, William	Bodmin	7
ROBINS, John, alias Major	Exeter	7
ROBINSON, George	Lincoln	7
ROBINSON, George	London	7
ROBINSON, Thomas	Kingston upon Hull	7
ROBINSON, William	Exeter	7
ROGERS, Daniel	Croydon	7
ROGERS, Isaac	Gloucester	14
ROLT, Mary	London	7
ROMAIN, John	London	7
ROPE, Anthony	Chelmsford	7
ROSSON, Isabella	London	7
ROUS, Walton, alias Batley	–	–
ROWE, John	Launceston	7
ROWE, William	Launceston	7
RUCE, James	Bodmin	7
RUGLASS, John	London	Life
RUSSEL, John	London	7
RUSSLER, John	London	Life
RUTH, Robert	Exeter	7
RYAN, John	–	–

S
SALTMARSH, William	Kingston	7
SAMPSON, Peter	London	7
SANDERSON, Thomas	Lincoln	7

SANDLIN, Ann, alias Lynes, alias Pattens	*London*	7
SANDS, William	*Lincoln*	7
SCATTERGOOD, Robert	*Stafford*	7
SCOTT, Elizabeth	*London*	7
SELSHIRE, Samuel	*London*	7
SEYMOUR, John	*Sherborne*	7
SHARPE, George	*Durham*	7
SHAW, Joseph	*Stafford*	7
SHEARMAN, William	*Reading*	7
SHEPHERD, Robert	*Durham*	7
SHIERS, James	*London*	Life
SHORE, John	–	–
SHORE, William	*Lancaster*	7
SIDEWAY, Robert	–	–
SILVERTHORN, John	*New Sarum*	7
SLATER, Sarah	*London*	7
SMALL, John	*Exeter*	7
SMART, Daniel	*Gloucester*	7
SMART, Richard	*Gloucester*	7
SMITH, Ann, wife of John Smith	*Winchester*	7
SMITH, Ann	*London*	7
SMITH, Ann	*London*	7
SMITH, Catherine	*London*	7
SMITH, Catherine	*London*	7
SMITH, Edward	*Exeter*	7
SMITH, James	*London*	7
SMITH, John	*Exeter*	7
SMITH, John	*Guildford*	7
SMITH, Edward	*London*	7
SMITH, Hannah	*Winchester*	7
SMITH, Mary	*London*	7
SMITH, Thomas	*Lancaster*	7
SMITH, Thomas, alias Haynes	*London*	7
SMITH, William	*Bodmin*	1
SMITH, William	*Dorchester*	7
SMITH, William	*Liverpool*	7
SMITH, William	*London*	7
SNALEHAM, William	*London*	7
SPARKS, Henry	–	–
SPENCE, Mary	*Wigan*	5
SPENCER, Daniel	*Dorchester*	14
SPENCER, John, alias Pearce		
SPRIGMORE, Charlotte	*London*	7
SPRINGHAM, Mary	*London*	7
SQUIRES, James	*Kingston*	7
STANLEY, William	*New Sarum*	7
STANTON, Thomas, alias Ebden	*Launceston*	7
STEPHENS, John Morris	*Dorchester*	7
STEWART, Margaret	*Exeter*	7
STOGDELL, John	*London*	14
STOKEE, John	*Durham*	7
STONE, Charles	*London*	7
STONE, Henry	*London*	7
STONE, Martin	*Warwick*	7
STOW, James	*Lincoln*	7
STRECH, Thomas	*Shrewsbury*	7
STRONG, James	*Dorchester*	7
STUART, James	*London*	7
SUMMERS, John	*Gloucester*	7

T

TAYLOR, Henry	–	–
TAYLOR, Joshua	*Manchester*	7
TAYLOR, Sarah	*Kingston*	7
TENANT, Thomas Hilton, alias Phillip Divine	*Chelmsford*	7
TEAGUE, Cornelius	*Bodmin*	7
TENCHALL, James, alias Tenninghill	–	–
THACKERY, Elizabeth	*Manchester*	7
THOMAS, Elizabeth	*Wigan*	7
THOMAS, James	*London*	7
THOMAS, James	*London*	7
THOMAS, John	*London*	7
THOMPSON, James	*London*	7
THOMPSON, William	*Durham*	7
THOMPSON, William	*London*	7
THORNTON, Ann	*London*	7
THOUDY, James	–	–
TILL, Thomas	*London*	7
TILLEY, Thomas	*Stafford*	7
TODD, Nicholas	*London*	7
TRACE, John	*Exeter*	7
TROTTER, Joseph	*Maidstone*	7
TRIPPETT, Susannah	*London*	7
TUCKER, Moses	*Plymouth*	7
TUNMINS, Thomas	*Warwick*	7
TURNER, John	–	–
TURNER, John	–	–
TURNER, Mary	*Worcester*	7
TURNER, Ralph	*Manchester*	7
TURNER, Thomas		
TUSO, Joseph	*London*	Life
TWYNEHAM, William	*Reading*	7
TWYFIELD, Ann, since said to be married to William Dawley, a convict,	*Shrewsbury*	7
TYRRELL, William	*Winchester*	7

U

UNDERWOOD, James	*New Sarum*	14
USHER, John	*Maidstone*	7

V

VANDELL, Edward	*East Grinstead*	7
VICKERY, William	*Exeter*	7
VINCENT, Henry	*London*	7

W

WADDICOMB, Richard	*Exeter*	7
WADE, Mary, alias Cacklane	*London*	14
WAGER, Benjamin	*London*	7
WAINWRIGHT, Ellen, alias Esther Eccles	*Preston*	7
WALBOURNE, James	*London*	7
WALKER, John	*London*	7
WALL, William	*Oxford*	7
WALSH, William	*London*	7
WARD, Ann	*London*	7
WARD, John	*Lowth*	7
WARE, Charlotte	–	–
WATERHOUSE, William	*Kingston*	7
WATKINS, Mary	–	–
WATSAN, John	*Maidstone*	7
WATSON, Thomas	*Exeter*	7
WELCH, James	*Maidstone*	7
WELCH, John	*Durham*	7
WELCH, John	*London*	Life
WELSH, John	*London*	7
WEST, Benjamin	*London*	7
WESTLALE, Edward	*Exeter*	7
WESTWOOD, John	*London*	7
WHEELER, Samuel	*Croydon*	7
WHITAKER, George	*Maidstone*	7
WHITE, James	*Maidstone*	7
WHITING, William	*Gloucester*	7
WHITTON, Edward	*Maidstone*	Life
WICKHAM, Mary	*New Sarum*	14
WILDING, John, alias Warren	*Bury*	7
WILCOCKS, Richard	*Exeter*	7
WILCOCKS, Samuel	*Dorcester*	7
WILSON, Charles	*London*	Life
WILSON, Peter	*Manchester*	7
WILTON, William	*Bristol*	7
WILLIAMS, Charles	*London*	7
WILLIAMS, Daniel	*Preston*	7
WILLIAMS, Frances	*Mold*	7
WILLIAMS, James	*London*	7
WILLIAMS, John	*Exeter*	7
WILLIAMS, John, alias Black Jack	*Maidstone*	7
WILLIAMS, John, alias Floyd	*Bodmin*	7
WILLIAMS, Mary	*London*	7
WILLIAMS, Peter, alias Flaggett, alias Creamer	*Exeter*	7
WILLIAMS, Robert	*Launceston*	7
WISEHAMMER, John	*Bristol*	7
WOOD, George	*London*	7
WOOD, Mark	–	–
WOODCOCK, Francis	*Shrewsbury*	7
WOODCOCK, Peter	*London*	7
WOODHAM, Samuel	*London*	Life
WOOLCOT, John	*Exeter*	Life
WORSDELL, William	*Launceston*	7
WRIGHT, Ann	*London*	7
WRIGHT, Benjamin	*London*	7
WRIGHT, James	*Maidstone*	7
WRIGHT, Joseph	*London*	7
WRIGHT, Thomas	*Reading*	7
WRIGHT, William	*London*	7

Y

YARDSLEY, Thomas	*Shrewsbury*	7
YATES, Nancy	*York*	7
YOUNG, John	*London*	7
YOUNG, Simon	*London*	7
YOUNGSON, Elizabeth	*Lancaster*	7
YOUNGSON, George	*Lancaster*	7

Notes

Bound for Botany Bay
1. M. C. I. Levy, *Governor George Arthur*, Georgian House, Melbourne, 1953, p. 150.
2. ibid., p. 166.
3. Quoted in R. Hughes, *The Fatal Shore*, Collins Harvill, London, 1987, p. 202.
4. Letter written by Mary Reiby, National Library of Australia Collection.
5. id.

The Bolters
1. W. Thornley, *Van Diemen Desperadoes, the Pursuit of Bushrangers Gypsey and Musquito and Other Tales from an Early Tasmanian Diary*, ed. J. S. Mills, Angus & Robertson Publishers, Sydney, 1975, pp. 79–80.
2. ibid., p. 84.
3. ibid. p. 92.
4. Levy, op. cit., p. 108.
5. *Records of the Castlemaine Pioneers*, Rigby, Melbourne, 1972, p. 143.

Port Arthur and Norfolk Island.
The Last of The Convict Outlaws
1. J. D. Emberg and B.T. Emberg, *The Uncensored Story of Martin Cash (Australian Bushranger) as Told to James Lester Burke*, compiled and edited by J. D. Emberg and B. T. Emberg, Regal Publicatons, Launceston, 1991, p. 233
2. *Chronicle of Australia*, ed. J. Ross, Viking Books, Penguin, Ringwood, 2000, p. 311.
3. ibid., p. 388.

Robbery Under Arms!
1. Lord Robert Cecil, *Gold Field's Diary, 1852*, Melbourne University Press, Carlton, 1935, p. 29.
2. W. Craig, *My Adventures on the Australian Goldfields*, Cassell & Co., London, 1853, p. 28.
3. ibid., p. 29.
4. S. Korzelinski, *Memoirs of Gold-Digging in Australia*, trans. and ed. by S. Robe, University of Queensland Press, St Lucia, 1979.
5. *Records of the Castlemaine Pioneers*, op. cit., p.57.
6. J. Chandler, *Forty Years in the Wilderness*, ed. by M. Cannon, Loch Haven Books, Arthur's Seat, 1990, p. 71.
7. ibid., p. 136.
8. ibid., p. 172.
9. *Records of the Castlemaine Pioneers*, op. cit., p.46.
10. ibid., p.229.
11. J. Sherer, *The Gold-Finder in Australia*, Penguin, Ringwood, (first published 1853) 1973, p. 227.
12. ibid., p. 228.
13. Craig, op. cit., p. 321.
14. Craig, loc. cit.
15. E. Harding, *Bogong Jack, The Gentleman Bushranger*, Yandoo Publishing Company, South Melbourne, 1967, p. 27.
16. ibid., p. 30.
17. ibid., p. 76.

Flash Coves & Currency
1. C.White, *History of Australian Bushranging, Vols 1 & 2*, Lloyd O'Neill Pty. Ltd., Windsor, 1979, p. 246.
2. T. Barker, *Armidale: A Cathedral City of Education and the Arts*, Cassell Australia Ltd, North Ryde, 1980, p. 14.
3. C.White, op. cit., p. 187.
4. R. Boldrewood, *Robbery Under Arms*, with an introduction by Dr Thomas Wood, Oxford University Press, London, 1951, p. 1.

The War Against the Kellys
1. E. Kelly, *Jerilderie Letter*, p. 20.
2. ibid., p. 43.
3. id.
4. F. Hare, *The Last of the Bushrangers: An Account of the Capture of the Kelly Gang*, The Henneberry Company, Chicago, 1894.
5. id.

Bibliography

AUSTIN, K.A. *The Lights of Cobb & Co.* Rigby Limited, James Place, Adelaide, 1967.

Australians From Everywhere, Rogues, Misfits and Adventurers Who Formed a New Society. Bay Books, Sydney and London, 1980.

BARKER, Tony. *Armidale: A Cathedral City of Education and the Arts.* Cassell Australia Ltd, North Ryde, 1980.

BOLDREWOOD, Rolf. *Robbery Under Arms,* with an Introduction by Dr Thomas Wood. Oxford University Press, London, 1951.

BOXALL, George. *Australian Bushrangers: An Illustrated History.* Curry O'Neil, Melbourne, 1975.

BRADSHAW, Jack. *Highway Robbery Under Arms: Sticking-up of the Quirindi Bank; and Full account of Thunderbolt,* Sydney, c. 1920.

CANNON, Michael. *Melbourne After the Gold Rush.* Loch Haven Books, Arthur's Seat, 1993.

CECIL, Lord Robert. *Gold Field's Diary, 1852.* Melbourne University Press, Carlton, 1935.

CHANDLER, John. *Forty Years in the Wilderness.* Ed. Michael Cannon. Loch Haven Books, Arthur's Seat, 1990.

CLACY, Mrs Charles. *A Lady's Visit to the Gold Diggings of Australia in 1852–1855: Written on the Spot by Mrs Charles Clacy.* Landsdowne Press, Melbourne, 1963; first published 1853.

CRAIG, William. *My Adventures on the Australian Goldfields.* Cassell & Co., London, 1853.

EMBERG, J. D. AND EMBERG, B. T. (ed. and trans.). *The Uncensored Story of Martin Cash (Australian Bushranger) as Told to James Lester Burke.* Regal Publicatons, Launceston, 1991.

HARDING, Eric. *Bogong Jack, the Gentleman Bushranger.* Yandoo Publishing Company, South Melbourne, 1967.

HARE, Francis. *The Last of the Bushrangers: An Account of the Capture of the Kelly Gang.* The Henneberry Company, Chicago, 1894.

HOCKING, Geoff. *To The Diggings.* Lothian Books, Port Melbourne, 2000.

HUGHES, Robert. *The Fatal Shore.* Collins Harvill, London, 1987.

JONES, Hugh (ed.). *The Bible Of The Bush: 125 Years of The Weekly Times.* Hamlyn, Reed Books Australia, Port Melbourne, 1994.

KORZELINSKI, Seweryn. *Memoirs of Gold-Digging in Australia.* Trans. and ed. by Stanley Robe. University of Queensland Press, St Lucia, 1979.

LEVY, M.C.I. *Governor George Arthur.* Georgian House, Melbourne, 1953.

MORRIS, E. E. (ed.). *Australia's First Century, 1788–1888.* Cassell's Picturesque Australasia, Cassell & Company, Ltd, Melbourne, 1889.

NIXON, Allan M. *Stand & Deliver! 100 Australian Bushrangers 1789–1901.* Lothian Books, Port Melbourne, 1991.

O'SHAUGHNESSY, Peter, INSON, Graeme and WARD, Russel. *The Restless Years, Being Some Impressions of the Origin of the Australian.* The Jacaranda Press Pty Ltd, Milton, 1968.

PRIOR, Tom, WANNAN, Bill AND NUNN, H. *A Pictorial History of Bushrangers.* Paul Hamlyn, London, New York, Sydney, Toronto. First published by Landsdowne Press, Melbourne, 1966.

Records of the Castlemaine Pioneers. Rigby, Melbourne, 1972.

ROSS, John (ed.). *Chronicle of Australia.* Viking Books, Penguin, Ringwood, 2000.

SHERER, John. *The Gold-Finder in Australia.* Penguin, Ringwood, 1973; first published 1853.

THORNLEY, William. *Van Diemen Desperadoes, the Pursuit of Bushrangers Gypsey and Musquito and Other Tales from an Early Tasmanian Diary.* Ed. by J. S. Mills. Angus & Robertson Publishers, Sydney, 1975.

WHITE, Charles. *History of Australian Bushranging Vols 1 & 2.* Lloyd O'Neill Pty Ltd, Windsor, 1979.

Acknowledgements

I would like to thank the generous assistance of the following libraries and museum collections: Armidale Folk Museum, Art Gallery of New South Wales, Forbes Folk Museum, La Trobe Library, State Library of Victoria, Mitchell Library, State Library of New South Wales, National Library of Australia, Queen Victoria Museum, Launceston, State Library of Tasmania.

There are also a number of people who lent works from their own libraries and personal collection. In particular I would like to thank Graeme Bennett, now of Darwin, whose collection of *Picturesque Atlas of Australia* has proved to be of invaluable assistance for several years, and across several projects; Felix Cappy and Doug Mills of Castlemaine, Victoria whose pistols appear on page 1; Ian Jones for permission to reproduce two photographs of Ned Kelly and Anna Gregory of Hobart who went out and photographed Martin Cash's grave.

While every attempt has been made to find the owners of all images reproduced in this book, there are always some who remain unknown. No attempt has been made to avoid the author's or publisher's responsibility to the copyright holder, and they apologize for any omissions that may have occurred.

Index

Abercrombie district, NSW 91
Aborigines 13, 16, 33
  Black Jack 32, 35
  Black Mary 33, 35
  Black Tom 32, 35
  black trackers 146
  Governor, Jimmy 180-181
  Governor, Joe 180-181
  Musquito 31, 35
  Oyster Bay tribe 35, 181
  Underwood, Jacky 180, 181
  Yellilong 127, 128
Aitken's Gap 74, 84
Alma goldfield 68
Anti-Transportation League 62
  flag *62*
Apis Creek, Queensland 93
Armstrong, William 88, 89
Arthur, Governor George 12, 28, 29, 30, 39, 42, 44
Ashton, Julian 151
Atkins, William 81
Bacchus Marsh, Vic 123
Ballarat 67, 82, 124
  Reform League 85
Bakery Hill, Ballarat 82
Bank of New South Wales, Jerilderie 143, 162
Bank of Victoria, Ballarat 82, 83, 84
Barker's Creek 97, 100
Barry, Judge Redmond 97, 137, 157, 161
Batavia 27

Bathurst, NSW 78, 106, 108
Bathurst Free Press 89, 92
Batman, John 42, 45
Bawfree, Mr and Mrs 74
Baylie, John 84
Bayliss, Magistrate 97
Beechworth, Vic 88, 136, 145, 146, 150, 154, 156
Benalla, Victoria 156
Bendigo 67
Bennett, Graham 124
Bennett, Mary 56
Berry, Premier 162
Beveridge, Victoria 135
Bigge, J.T. 20, 21
Billy-Can Mutiny, The 60-62
Binalong 108, 115
Black Forest 69
Black Jack 32, 35
Black Springs 114
Black Tom 32, 35
Blanche's Inn 128
Bligh, Governor William 18, 19
'Blue Cap' 131
Bodenham, Thomas 40
'Bogong Jack' 86-89
Boldrewood, Rolf 131, 132
Bolton, John 82, 83, 84
bounty migrants 135
Bourke, Michael (Mickey) 96, 105, *106*
Bow, Charles 84
Bow, John 93

Bowen, Constable 126
boy convicts 75
Bracken, Constable 147, 148
Brady, Matthew 42-45
Brady's Lookout 45
Braidwood 120
Breelong, NSW 180, 181
Brown, James 39, 40
Brown(e), Thomas A. [see Boldrewood]
Brunn, Ludwig 123
Bryan, William 28
Bryant, Mary 27
Bryant, William 27
Bugg, Mary-Ann 128
Bullarook Forest 76
Bulletin, The 126
Buninyong 84
Burns, John 43
Bushrangers Act, The 53
Byrne, Joseph 150, *151*

Caesar, John, 'Black' 24
Cameron, Dan, MP 162
Campbell, Alexander 50
'canaries' 10, *23*
Canowindra 105
Cash, Martin 48-56, 60, 61, 89
Cash, Martin Junior 56
Castle Hill Riot 14-15, 18
Castlemaine 65, 68, 97, 100
Cecil, Lord Robert 66
Chamberlain, George 88, 89
Charters, Dan 93

China
  escape to 13, 20, 28, 33
Chinese 88, 94, 96, 98
Chisholm, Caroline 17, 63
Clark, Elsie 180
Clarke, John 120-121
Clarke, Marcus 63
Clarke, Thomas 120-121
Clifford, Bessie 48, 54, 55
Cobb & Co. 78, 92
Cockatoo Island 91, 113, 114, 127
Collins, Lieutenant-Governor David 20
Comerford, George 65
Condell, Sergeant 92, 93, 112
Connelly, Mick 111
Connolly, Patrick 43
Convicts of the First Fleet 7-22, 27, 183-187
Cox, Thomas 41
Cox's River Crossing 18
Craig, William 67, 68, 75, 76, 77
Crawford, James 43
Crowley, Catherine 21
Cummins, Larry 118, 119
Cunningham, Phillip 15
Curnow, Mr 147
'currency' 21

Dalton, Alexander 40
Dalton, James 55
Darcy, Charles 93
Dargin, Billy 112
Darlinghurst 91, 121
  gaol 121
Davey, Lieutenant-Governor T. 30
Dignum, Joseph 65
Donohoe, Jack 57-60
  song lyrics 59
Donovan, John 84
Douglas, 'Black' 68-69
Downes, John 43
Drew, William 33
Dubbo 116
Duggan, Robert 14
Duncan, James 71
Dunn, John 96, 104, 110, 111, 114, 115, 116

Eaglehawk Neck, Tasmania 50, 51
Egerton, Mt 84, 123
Eleven Mile Creek 135
emancipists 21-22
escorts 79, 92
Eugowra gold escort 92-95, 103
Eureka gang 84
Eureka Stockade 84-85
Euroa, Victoria 143, 162
exclusives 21-22

Faithful Creek Station 143
Felon's Act, The 110, 113, 114, 141-142, 145
Finegan, John 84
First Fleet 7, 8, 19, 24, 183-187
Fitzpatrick, Constable 136, 137
Fitzpatrick, Kiernan 181
Flanigan, John 72, 74
flogging 17, *19*, *26*, 48
Fogg 91, 93
Foley, John 118, 119
Forbes, NSW 78, 92, 103
  The Streets of Forbes, song lyrics 110
Fordyce, Alexander 93
Forest Creek, Victoria 85, 113
Fourth of July rebellion 52

Fox, Stephen 71
Francis, George 81
Franklin, Governor John 54

Galvin, Paddy 16
Gardiner, Frank 'Darkie' 91, 93, 94, 96, 103, 104, 107, 114
Garrett, Henry 82, 83
Geelong, Victoria 76, 82, 83, 84
Gellibrand Quarry 48, *49*, 74, 76, 89
Georgetown, Tasmania 42
Gilbert, Johnnie 93, 94, 103, 105, 111, 113, 114, 115, 116
Gill, Samuel 162
Glenorchy, Tasmania 56
Glenrowan 145
  Glenrowan Hotel 146, 147, 152, 154
  Glenrowan Station 152, 154
Goimbla Station 107
gold discovery 64
gold escorts 78
gold rush 66-70
Goonoo Goonoo Gap 127
Governor, Jimmy 180-181
Governor, Joe 180-181
Gray, leader, '*Nelson*' robbery 81, 82
Green, Cornelius 88, 89
Greenhill, Bob 39, 40
Greta 153
Griffiths, John 43
'Gypsey' 30-37

Haydock, Mary 22
Hall, Ben 93, 96, 102-113, 143
  pistol 110
Hare, Francis, Police Superintendent 141, 144, 148, 178
Hart, Steve 168
Haviland, Constable 93
Heathcote, Victoria 79
Hepburn, Captain John 65
Herald, The 162
Hobart Town Gazette 30, 31, 42
Hobson's Bay 74, 81
Holt, General Joseph 15, 16
Hopkins, 'Looney' 31, 38
Hosie, Trooper 91
Howe, Michael 31, 32, 33
hulks 76
Hunter, Governor John 14, 24

James, John 71
Jeffery, Thomas 'Mark' 41-42, 45
Jerilderie 143, *162*
Jerilderie Letter, The 136, 140, 141, 144
  transcription 162-175
Johnston, Major George 14, 18, 19
Johnstone, Henry 84
Jones, George 50, 52, 53, 54, 55

Kavanagh, Lawrence 50, 52, 53, 54, 55, 56, 60, 61
Keightley, Mr 106
Kelly gang 133-160
  Barry, Redmond 138, 161
  Byrne, Joseph *138*, 139, 144, 145, 147, 149, *150-151*, 154
  Curnow, Mr 147
  Kelly, Edward, 'Ned' 58, 133-160, 161, 162-175, 176
    armour 152, *160*
    death mask *158*

hanging 157, *158*
shooting 152-156
trial 157, 158
Fitzpatrick, Constable 136, 137
Glenrowan Hotel, The
  burning *152*, 154
  seige 146, 147, *148*, 149
Glenrowan Station 152
Hart, Steve *138*, 139, 147, *168*
Kelly, Dan 136, 138, 144, 145, 146, 149, 154, 156, *165*
Kelly, John, 'Red' 135
Kelly, Kate 136, *138*, 144
Kennedy, Michael, Sergeant 137-140
King, George 136
Lonigan, Thomas, Constable *137*-140, 157
McIntyre, Thomas, Constable *139*, 140
Quinn, Ellen 135, 157
Scanlan, Michael, Constable 137-40
Sherritt, Aaron *144*, 145
Skillion, Mrs 154, 155
Steele, Arthur, Sergeant 150, 152, *159*
stopping the train 147
Stringey Bark Creek 137, 138, 145
wake 155
Kentucky Creek 128
Kiandra goldfield 93
King, Governor Phillip Gidley 15, 20
King River 178
Kooyoora, Mt 77
Korzelinski, Seweryn 68
Kurz, Helen 180

La Trobe, Governor Charles 66
Lacy, George 43
Lalor, Peter 85
Lambing Flat, NSW 93, 96
Leversha, Henry 68
Liardet, Mr 70
Liddell, John 55
Liverpool, NSW 20
Living, Mr 162
Lloyd, Jack 153, 178
London Chartered Bank, The 123
Lonigan, Constable Thomas *137*-140, 157
Loveless, George 26
Lowry, Fred 118-119
Lord Rodney Hotel, Tasmania 56

Macarthur, John 18
MacBean, Robert 177
Macquarie Harbour, Tasmania 12, *38*, 39, 41, 43, 54
Macquarie, Governor Lachlan 38
McCabe, James 43
McCallum, Frank 75-77, 81
McCarthy, Reverend Father 106
McCormack, Jeremiah 136
McCoy 51
McIvor diggings 79-81
McIvor Escort 79-81
McKay, Alex 181
McPherson, Mrs 100
Madden, William 76
Manns, Harry 93
Maria Island 12
Marriott, Henry 82, 83, 84
Marsden, Reverend Samuel 38, 57
Maryborough, Victoria 68
Mathers, John 39, 40
Mawbey, John, Grace and Percy 180
Melbourne Gaol 124, 159

INDEX

Melville, 'Captain' [see McCallum, Frank]
Melville, George 81
Melville's Caves 77
Middleton, Sgt 91
Mitchell, Thomas 58
'Moonlite', Captain [see Scott, Andrew]
Morgan, Daniel 'Mad Dan' 97-101
Morgan, James 71
Mt Alexander Road 74
Mudgee Mail, The 118, 119
Muggleston, John 57
Muir, Thomas 8
Mulhall, Constable 128
murderer's mound 61
Murrurundi 102
Musquito 30-37

Namoi River 128
National Bank, Euroa 143, *162*
Nesbitt, James *124*
New Norfolk, Tasmania 52
Newcastle Penal Settlement 16
Nicolson, Police Superintendent 177
Norfolk Island 12, 16, 48, 52, 56, 60-61
   'Billy-Can' Mutiny 60-61
NSW Corps 14, 19

O'Brien, Elizabeth 181
O'Meally, John 103, 105, *107*, 114
O'Reilly, John Boyle 63
Omeo, Victoria 88
Orange, NSW 92
Ovens Valley, Victoria 97
Oyster Bay tribe 35, 37, 181

Page, Ethel 180
Paine, Thomas 8
Parkes, Henry 94
Parramatta 16, 18
   lunatic asylum 124
Paterson, Lieutenant-Colonel William 14
Paxton, Sir James 86
Payne, John 86-89
Pearce, Alexander 39-41
Peechelba Station 99
Penny, Sydney 88
Pentridge 97, 124, 176, 177
Phillip, Governor Arthur 7, 8, 9
Piesley, John 91-92
Poo, Sam 88
Port Arthur, Tasmania 9, 28-29, *46-63*
Port Jackson, NSW 9
Port Phillip, Victoria 72, 89
Pottinger, Sir Frederick 102, 103, 104, *113*
Power, Harry 88, 135, 138, *176-179*
Price, John 48, 50, 52, 61, 74, 77, 89
prisons 12
prison hulks *6*, 76
Pugh, 'Big Bill' 33

Queen Anne flag 9
Queenborough, Norfolk Island 55
Quinn, Ellen 135, 157
Quinn, Thomas 82, 83, 84
Quinn's farm 177

Radford, Henry 132
Reardon, Mrs 148, *159*
Reiby, Mary 22
Reiby, Thomas 22
Review of Reviews, The 180
Rider, Charles 43

Roberts, Tom 94
Roberts, William 75, 76, 77
Robinson, Sir Hercules, Governor of NSW 143
Rocky River 128
Rogan, Thomas 124
Rose Hill 13
Round Hill Station 99
Royal Hotel, Jerilderie 143, 144, 162
Ryan, Jeremiah 43, 99

Sadlier, Police Superintendent 162
Sandridge 70
Scanlan, Michael, Constable 137-40
Scott, Andrew 123-126
Sherer, John 72
Sherritt, Aaron 144, 145
shipping
   Ann and Amelia 57
   Charlotte 27
   Ferguson 52
   Harvies 41
   Hougoumont 63
   HMS *Calcutta* 14
   Indefatigable 33
   Julianna 42
   Madagascar 81, 82
   Marquis of Hartley 48
   Minerva 31
   Nelson 70-71, 81, 82
   Parramatta 18
   St Vincent 63
   Success 76, 89, 179
   Supply 9
Shirley, George 37
Shirley, Georgina 37
Skillion, Mrs 154, 155
Smith, Joseph 17, 18
Smyth, Father 85
Sorell, Governor 33
Southern Cross 85
St Kilda Road 72-74
Standish, Chief Commissioner 136
Starlight, Captain 131-132
Steele, Arthur, Sergeant 152, *159*
Stephensen, Senior Sergeant 118, 119
'sterling' 21
Sturt, Charles 57
Sydney Harbour 9

Tench, Watkin 27
Thompson, John 43
Thornley, William 32, 35, 36
Thunderbolt, Captain [see Ward, Frederick]
Tolpuddle Martyrs 24
'T' other-siders 84, 176, 177
transportation 62-63
Travers, Mathew 40
Tumbarumba, NSW 98
Tyntynder Station 178

Underwood, Jacky 180, 181
Underwood, William, 'Darky' 57

Van Diemen's Land 30, 31, 33, 42, 48, 50, 51, 66, 75, 176
vandemonians 66, 71, 75
Vane, John 105, *106*
Vincent, Isaac 98
Vaux, James Hardy 12

Wagga Wagga, NSW 97, 124

Walker, Constable 128, 129
Walker, Isaac 43
Walmsley, Jack 57
Wangaratta, Victoria 99
Wantabadgery Station 124
Warby Ranges 141
Ward, Frederick *127-129*
Waring, Anthony 74
Warwick, Queensland 127
Watts, George 33
Wearne, Thomas 75, 76
Webb, Inspector 83
Webber, Bill 57
Weddin Mountains, NSW 107
Weekes, Anton 144
Weekly Times, The 145
Wentworth, D'Arcy 21
Wentworth, William 21, 22
Wernicke, Augustus *125*
West, Major 57
Westlick, Richard 33
Westwood, 'Jacky Jacky' 52, 60, 61
Wheogo 103, 104
Whitfield 99
Whitehead, John 30, 31
Wild Colonial Boy, The 58-59
   song lyrics 59
Wilkinson, John 181
Williams, Thomas 72, 74
Williams, Thomas 124
Wilson, George 81
Windeyer, Justice 126
Windsor, NSW 20, 57, 127
Wombat Ranges 139
Wood's Point diggings, Victoria 88
Woolloomooloo Hill 20
Woolpack Inn, Van Diemen's Land 52
Woolshed Creek 145
Worrall, Thomas 33
Wright, Isaiah 'Wild' 135, 156
Wright, Judith 127
Wyndham, Mr 127

Yackandandah, Victoria 97
Yellow Long [see Aborigines, Yellilong]

Following Page:
Theatre Poster
Theatre Royal, Hobart Tasmania, c. 1908
(State Library of Tasmania Collection)

BAIL UP!

THEATRE ROYAL.

Lessee .... ALLAN HAMILTON

A HAPPY NEW YEAR!
WEDNESDAY, JAN. 1ST, 1908.
SECOND WEEK,

AND NIGHTLY INCREASING SUCCESS OF
THE REPRESENTATIVE ACTRESS OF THE COMMONWEALTH

LILIAN MEYERS
AND HER POPULAR COTERIE OF PLAYERS.
UNDER THE DIRECTION OF FRED. R. PAVEY.

Still Another Startling Novelty.
WEDNESDAY, JANUARY 1st, 1908,
and Thursday, January 2nd,

First Production in Hobart of an Entirely New and Original Sensational Australian Drama, entitled

THE KELLYS,
Founded on Incidents and Episodes connected with the Lives of the Notorious Kelly Gang.

CAST OF CHARACTERS

[cast list]

MARY STONE   AND   LILIAN MEYERS

SCENARIO.
ACT I.—THE HOME OF THE KELLYS, VICTORIA.
ACT II.—SCENE 1.—POLICE STATION, EUROA. SCENE 2.—KELLY'S RETREAT, WOMBAT RANGES. SCENE 3.—A ROAD NEAR JERILDERIE, N.S.W.
SCENE 4.—THE COMMERCIAL BANK, JERILDERIE.
ACT III.—THE GOLD DIGGINGS, FISH RIVER.
ACT IV.—SCENE 1.—INTERIOR JONES HOTEL, GLENROWAN. SCENE 2.—THE BUSH NEAR GLENROWAN. SCENE 3.—THE BURNING HOTEL AND
CAPTURE OF THE KELLYS.

INCIDENTAL TO THE PLAY
AN EXCITING WOOD-CHOP CONTEST. SHEEP-SHEARING COMPETITION, where Live Sheep will be Shorn in the presence of the Audience.
THE STICKING-UP OF THE MAIL COACH.

NEW SCENERY!   NOVEL EFFECTS!   SENSATIONAL MECHANICAL CHANGES!

FRIDAY, JANUARY 3rd,
BY REQUEST OF THOUSANDS,

THE SORROWS OF SATAN
SATURDAY AFTERNOON & NIGHT,
January 4th,

UNCLE TOM'S CABIN
With all the Original Songs, Dances, Juvenile Plantation Pastimes, etc.
MAGNIFICENT SCENERY AND EFFECTS.
CHILDREN: SIXPENCE TO ALL PARTS AT THE MATINEE.

POPULAR PRICES: 3s., 2s., and 1s.

NO EARLY DOORS.   NO BOOKING FEE.   PLAN AT WALCH'S. DAY SALES AT CRAIGIE'S.

MUSICAL DIRECTORS .... MADAME GRAY
STAGE MANAGER .... MR. GEO. L. HORSMAN
SCENIC ARTIST .... MR. GIL LAKE

FRED. W. DUVAL, Business Manager.

192